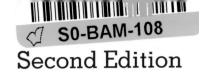

Second Edition

Introduction to Macrosociology

James W. Russell

Eastern Connecticut
State University

Prentice Hall
Upper Saddle River, NJ 07458

32347793

Library of Congress Cataloging-in-Publication Data

Russell, James W., (date)
  Introduction to macrosociology / James W. Russell. —2nd ed.
    p.   cm.
  Includes bibliographical references and index.
  ISBN 0-13-228230-5
    1. Macrosociology.   I. Title.
HM51.R885   1996
301'.01—dc20   95-8748
                                                   CIP

Acquisitions Editor: Nancy Roberts
Editorial/production supervision, interior design,
  and electronic page makeup: Mary Araneo
Editorial assistant: Pat Naturale
Buyer: Mary Ann Gloriande
Cover designer: Bruce Kenselaar

Printed in the United States of America

10 9 8 7 6 5 4 3 2 1

ISBN   0-13-228230-5

PRENTICE-HALL INTERNATIONAL (UK) LIMITED, *London*
PRENTICE-HALL OF AUSTRALIA PTY. LIMITED, *Sydney*
PRENTICE-HALL CANADA INC., *Toronto*
PRENTICE-HALL HISPANOAMERICANA, S.A., *Mexico*
PRENTICE-HALL OF INDIA PRIVATE LIMITED, *New Delhi*
PRENTICE-HALL OF JAPAN, INC., *Tokyo*
SIMON & SCHUSTER ASIA PTE. LTD., *Singapore*
EDITORA PRENTICE-HALL DO BRASIL, LTDA., *Rio de Janeiro*

for my daughters,
Julia, Magdalena, and Armida,
with love

Contents

Preface   xi

About the Author   xiv

Chapter One
Sociology   1

    The Promise, 1
    History, 3
    Specialized Concepts, 5
    Social and Individual Explanations, 6
    Relation to Other Disciplines, 9
    Occupations and Uses, 10
    Summary, 10
    Key Terms and Concepts, 11

Chapter Two
Individuals and Societies   12

    Human Beings, 12
    Human Beings as Social Beings, 14
    Components of Social Interaction, 15
        Roles, Institutions, and The Self, 17
        Structure, Society, and Culture, 24
    Summary, 26

Key Terms and Concepts, 28
Endnotes, 29

Chapter Three
Classifying Societies 30
Technological Eras, 30
Socioeconomic Structures, 35
Summary, 37
Key Terms and Concepts, 38
Endnotes, 38

Chapter Four
Past Societies 39
Communal Societies, 39
    Formation of Surplus Products, 44
Village Communities and State Societies, 46
Slave Societies, 48
Feudal Societies, 52
Summary, 55
Key Terms and Concepts, 56
Endnotes, 56

Chapter Five
Contemporary Societies and the World Economy 57
Origins and Spread of Capitalist Development, 1500-, 57
The Socialist Challenge, 1917-1989, 61
The World Economy After 1989, 66
    Theories and Classifications, 66
    Developed Societies, 72
    Economies in Transition, 78
    Asian Socialist Societies, 81
    Developing Societies, 81
    New Problems, 88
Summary, 90
Key Terms and Concepts, 91
Endnotes, 92

Chapter Six
Classical Sociological Theory 94
Marxian Theory, 95
    The Dialectics of History, 95
    Value Theory and Exploitation, 96
    Alienation and Labor, 97

Class Conflict and Revolution, 98
Leninist Theory, 99
Marx and Modern Sociology, 105
Emile Durkheim, 105
Positivism and Functionalism, 106
The Division of Labor in Society, 106
Suicide, 111
Durkheim and Modern Sociology, 113
Max Weber, 115
Comparative Research, 115
The Protestant Ethic and the Spirit of Capitalism, 116
Rationalization, 118
Bureaucracies, 120
Weber, Modern Sociology, and Postmodernism, 121
Summary, 122
Key Terms and Concepts, 123
Endnotes, 123

Chapter Seven
Power, Politics, and the State   126

Power Structures, 127
The State, 130
Legitimations of Power, 135
Traditional, 136
Legal-Rational, 136
Charismatic, 136
Democracy, 137
Political Stability, 139
Politics and Ideology, 141
Fascism, 142
Conservatism, 143
Liberalism, 143
Socialism, 144
Communism, 144
The Future of Political Ideology, 145
Summary, 146
Key Terms and Concepts, 147
Endnotes, 147

Chapter Eight
Class, Race, and Gender   148

Economic and Social Classes, 150
Developed Societies, 152
Developing Societies, 155

Postwar Socialist Societies, 158
Distributions of Wealth and Income, 159
Race and Ethnicity, 162
Class and Race in North America, 163
Gender, 168
Summary, 173
Key Terms and Concepts, 174
Endnotes, 174

Chapter Nine

Organizations 176

Organizational Functioning, 177
Types of Organizations, 178
Small Businesses, 179
Cooperatives, 180
Bureaucracies, 180
Membership Associations, 185
Mixed Types, 186
Summary, 187
Key Terms and Concepts, 188

Chapter Ten

The Family 189

Family, Economy, and Society, 189
Family Social Problems, 191
Poverty, 191
Divorce and Family Reorganization, 192
Alcoholism, 196
Domestic Violence, 197
Child Care, 198
Health Care, 199
Family Social Policy and Legislation, 201
Summary, 203
Key Terms and Concepts, 203

Chapter Eleven

Population 204

Malthus and Overpopulation Theories, 204
Contemporary World Population Conditions, 208
Population Control and Development, 211
National Population Policies, 213
Migration and Urbanization, 214

Summary, 216
Key Terms and Concepts, 218
Endnotes, 218

Chapter Twelve
Social Research   220

Defining Research Problems, 221
Review of the Literature, 221
Research Designs, 222
    Sources of Existing Data, 223
    Interviews and Surveys, 223
    Case Studies, 225
    Experiments, 226
Analysis of Results, 227
Ethics and Social Research, 228
    Research for Whom? 228
    Rights of Research Subjects, 229
Summary, 230
Key Terms and Concepts, 231
Endnotes, 231

Glossary   232

Appendix   249

Bibliography   253

Photo Credits   262

Index   263

Preface

The classic nineteenth- and early twentieth-century founders of sociology began their quest for objective social knowledge by addressing the large, macro-level questions—where did their societies come from, what were their characters, where were they going? Put more exactly, they sought out the origins of Western capitalism, analyzed its major economic, political, and social institutions, and tried to predict future developments. Sociology's original intellectual mission was thus to objectively analyze societies and social life. Its promise was that by doing so it could help people make collective sense of the social conditions within which they lived.

As we approach the third millennium, understanding the large questions of social life has become even more important. Societies have grown more complex. People have become caught up in ever more intricate and extensive sets of economic, political, and social relationships which transcend national boundaries. New problems of social life have grown up alongside of old, unresolved ones. Despite spectacular technological advances in this century, social contradictions abound. Astronauts travel in space but fear to walk crime-ridden streets. Stretch limousines crawl uneasily down New York City's crowded streets past growing legions of homeless people.

The following text was written to introduce sociology in a way that maintains the classic, macro-level focuses of its founders—to provide conceptual tools for addressing the large questions of social life, such as, for example, making intelligent sense of changes sweeping Eastern

Europe and parts of the Third World or the outbreak of wars in different regions of the world. The text therefore incorporates a comparative approach in which types of past and present societies and their major economic, political, and social features are examined.

The macrosociological orientation of the text is not meant though to be an exclusive focus that denies or neglects the important classical contributions that have come from more social psychologically oriented microsociological concerns. Conceptualization of the relationship between individuals and societies—between psychology and sociology—is a necessary foundation for all social knowledge and research. The text therefore of necessity includes discussions of microsociological, as well as macrosociological, issues and concepts.

The logic of presentation of the text is to begin in Chapter One with an introductory description of sociology as a field of study. From there the text progressively builds up the conceptual apparatus of macrosociology. Chapter Two, Individuals and Societies, describes the basic terminology that sociologists use to conceptualize and analyze social life in all types of societies. Chapters Three through Five contain descriptions, analyses, and discussions of different types of past and contemporary societies. Chapters Six through Eleven are devoted to discussions of major sociological units of analysis: power, the state, class, race, gender, organizations, the family, and population. The text ends with a final chapter on techniques of social research. I recommend that Chapters One through Five be read first and in order since they contain themes that build. Chapters Six through Twelve can then be read in any order.

In my experience the best way to learn a new discipline is to study its basic concepts. For that reason basic sociological as well as other social science concepts are progressively introduced, discussed, and defined throughout the text. Each chapter concludes with a list of its key concepts, and following the final chapter there is a complete glossary.

This text in many ways is the long-term product of my attempts to teach sociology in a manner that encourages historical, critical, and international thinking about contemporary social concerns. As such, it has developed out of the practice of teaching and learning from students at universities in San Francisco, along the U.S.-Mexico border, in the Pacific Northwest, New England, and Mexico City. Those students were the sounding boards and constructive critics for much of the modes of expression and explanation that follow. From a distance, I therefore express my gratitude. Intellectual debts—some recent and some long-standing—are also owed to a number of individuals who I have had the good fortune to encounter along the way. These include Hans H. Gerth, Maurice Zeitlin, Harvey Goldberg, James O'Connor, James P. O'Brien,

Carolyn Howe, Jerry Lembcke, Martin Hart-Landsberg, Alexander Taylor, Angela Morales, Sevin Koont, and John Mraz. Nancy Roberts, Mary Araneo, and Henry Pels at Prentice Hall provided encouragement and skilled and very helpful editorial assistance. The manuscript also benefited significantly from the suggestions of Prentice Hall's reviewers: Robert K. Miller, Jr., of the University of North Carolina, Wilmington; and Saul Feinman of the University of Wyoming, for which I am grateful. All of the above are of course absolved of responsibility for any errors of fact, style, or just plain thinking that may remain.

NOTE TO THE SECOND EDITION

Those familiar with the first edition will find slight shifts in the concepts employed in Chapters Two and Three. The most important is that communal, state, slave, feudal, capitalist, and socialist societies are now referred to as different socioeconomic, rather than economic, varieties. The new concept has the advantage of accenting the interdependency of social relations and economic structures in world history. I have also substantially revised the chapter on contemporary societies and the world economy to take into account the many changes that have occurred since 1992; added a new chapter on power, politics, and the state; significantly enlarged the chapter on class, race, and gender; and made a number of other, more minor, revisions and additions.

About
The Author

Educated at the University of Wisconsin, James W. Russell has taught at universities in the United States and Mexico. He is currently professor of sociology at Eastern Connecticut State University and was formerly visiting Fulbright professor at the Universidad Nacional Autónoma de México in Mexico City (1990-1992). His other books include *After the Fifth Sun: Class and Race in North America* and *Modes of Production in World History*.

Chapter One

Sociology

Sociology is most commonly defined as the scientific study of societies and social life in general. The fundamental premise of sociological explanations is that most of human conduct occurs and is shaped within group and social contexts. It follows that the social properties as such of societies need to be understood and studied because they are important determining factors of human conduct.

THE PROMISE

The promise of sociology is that it will help us to understand better our societies and social life within them. Through such social awareness and understanding, it is hoped, humans will then be able to resolve social problems as they develop and design social programs and legislation to both prevent future social problems from occurring and enhance the social quality of life.

All societies in history have had their own particular types of social problems. The ancient Romans faced periodic slave revolts. More recently, deteriorating rural economic conditions in large parts of nineteenth-century Europe undermined the quality of traditional social life and propelled generations of European peasants to seek better lives in the United States. Moving into East Coast and Midwestern cities, these immigrants found new living conditions that were rife with crime, poverty, alienation, and other social problems. More than a century

1

later the theme of deteriorating rural economic conditions has shifted to the Third World countries of Africa, Asia, and Latin America, where generation after generation of peasants are being uprooted from the land and moving into either burgeoning Third World cities, such as Lagos, Bombay, Sao Paolo, and Mexico City, or across international boundaries in search of greater prosperity in First World countries.

But despite their greater prosperity, the First World countries are beset with a series of social problems. Today, people in the relatively prosperous United States, for example, look with considerable anxiety at cities where drug trafficking and gangs appear to have turned peaceful streets into dangerous ones, a theme that Hollywood has capitalized on in such social-science horror visions of the near future of U.S. cities as *Blade Runner*. In that film, the elites, with more and more high technology including genetic engineering at their disposal, live and work within high-security tower buildings far above streets which have been left to teem with poverty, blight, crime, gangs, and chaos in general.

The vision of social hell projected in *Blade Runner* was based on the assumption that social consequences of economic policies begun in the early 1980s in many of the leading First World countries would continue on into the future. Most notably, the conservative Reagan administration in the United States and the Thatcher government in Great Britain had initiated policies which favored private sector businesses and the upper classes at the expense of public sector social programs and the working and lower classes. Social inequality thus began to grow greatly during the 1980s. In a parallel sense, the sense that is captured in *Blade Runner*, the upper strata retreated into private spaces—such as residential areas, malls, and private schools—which were well guarded by private security forces, while public spaces open to all social classes—such as parks, public schools, and streets—were starved of revenues, were allowed to deteriorate, and became dangerous.

Ironically, the vision of social hell projected in *Blade Runner*, where large parts of cities are out of control, was the opposite of George Orwell's *1984*, which disturbed an earlier generation. Orwell projected the social future in terms of a society being totally controlled, with every citizen being under constant surveillance by panoptic eyes.

The promise of sociology is that through study, the origins, characteristics, and consequences of these social problems can be determined and that the future need not be one of *Blade Runner* or *1984* societies. With such knowledge it will then be possible to become both socially aware and able to find solutions. Social awareness is the first step toward finding solutions. For many, though, social awareness is limited to their immediate circles of interaction—family and immediate associates—with outside social conditions and issues appearing as alien, remote, scary, or even personally irrelevant.

During the nineteenth century many people in the United States escaped the problems of the East Coast cities by moving west, attracted by free or cheap land for farming. Today, many people escape the problems of inner cities by moving out to suburbs or into increasingly fortified fortresses within them—the *Blade Runner* solution. Rather than understand the problems that make their cities unliveable, much less find solutions to them, they choose to put as much distance as possible between themselves and the problems. For them, the solution to bad public schools is either other public schools or private schools.

In part, therefore, sociology is engaged in developing social awareness. But that is not all. It also attempts to develop solutions to some of society's most pressing social problems. Its promise is that the social knowledge that it develops will inform policy decisions or, at the very least, contribute to public debates over how to resolve existing problems and create better societies for the future.

HISTORY

The word *sociology*—a hybrid of the Latin *socia,* or "society," with the Greek *logos,* or "knowledge"—first appeared in 1837 in a writing by the conservative French philosopher Auguste Comte (1798–1857). Comte advocated that sociology be established as a new field of inquiry to counteract the value-laden claims of, on the one hand, socialist ideologists who criticized the social conditions found in Europe's nineteenth-century industrial capitalist societies, and on the other, religious writers who evaluated societies on the basis of theological and moral concerns. Comte believed that it was possible to develop a specifically *scientific* approach to the acquisition of social knowledge that would not be based on political, moral, or other types of values. This could be achieved, he believed, if social knowledge was acquired through the same value-free methods and techniques of research that were practiced in the physical and organic sciences such as biology, chemistry, and botany. He thus prescribed that the scientific methods developed in the physical and organic sciences be directly transferred to the social sciences where they would presumably yield objective, value-free social knowledge. Nevertheless, Comte's motives for establishing this scientific sociology were as much political as methodological. He used the term *positivism* to describe his approach to sociology because with it he sought to improve, rather than criticize or subvert, the structures of existing societies. Socialists and other revolutionaries, in Comte's view, were negativists who sought to destroy the existing structures. Despite these originally conservative origins, the concept of positivism is today more identified with Comte's methodological principle that sociologists follow the same general scientific approach to research as practiced in the physical and organic sciences.

Ironically, the types of socialist writers of whom Comte was most critical were also concerned with developing a scientific understanding of society. Karl Marx (1818-1883) and Frederick Engels (1820-1895) devoted an entire section of "The Communist Manifesto" to criticizing socialist writings which were based on religious and moral rather than scientifically founded criteria. But Marx and Engels never called themselves sociologists, in part because of the conservative connotations of the term in Comte's hands. They saw themselves rather as founders of *scientific* socialism, by which they meant socialist change based upon the discoverable laws of history. Unlike Comte, they believed that there were unresolvable problems deep within the structures of capitalist societies, such as class inequality, alienation, and crisis-prone economies, whose ultimate solutions could only be attained through socialist restructuring. According to their dialectical methodology and reasoning, there is a logic to world historical change in which rising new types of societies supplant declining old types. In this respect, they believed that capitalism would eventually decline and be replaced by a new socialist type of society.

In many ways Comte, the conservative and positivist, and Marx, the revolutionary and dialectical thinker, established the poles of Western sociology. They shared a common desire that the study of society be scientific. But they differed profoundly though over how to develop a scientific study of society and the political implications of that endeavor.

Sociology, whichever its guise, Comtean or Marxian, emerged as mid-nineteenth-century Europe was undergoing rapid economic, political, and social transformations. The Industrial Revolution, roughly between 1780 and 1820, altered the physical and social landscapes of European countries by accelerating the growth of factory life and cities. Country peasants became urban workers. The slow pace and certainty of rural life gave way to the seeming chaos, long workdays, and uncertainties of urban life for increasing proportions of the population. At the same time, political revolutions swept across Western and Central Europe, continuing the trend set off by the 1789 French Revolution. Old autocratic governments ruled by royalties and aristocracies were increasingly swept away to be replaced by republican forms of government which rising business classes could influence and control more easily. In the face of the rapidity and dizzying scale of these changes, as well as the life-altering nature of their consequences for millions of people, the realization grew that the understanding of society in and of itself was problematic. If in the past rural-based agricultural society, where the pace of social change was very slow, one could with fair confidence predict the foreseeable future because it would not be that different than the present, in the new conditions in which Europeans found themselves, certainties about the likely shape of things to come evaporated. Social knowledge could no longer be assumed. It had to be produced.

By the second half of the century the term *sociology* was in wide circulation. To some extent it was simply a catchall and convenient label for general writings about societies which did not seem to fit neatly into the existing and already defined categories of political economy, history, or philosophy. But it was also becoming a recognized and respectable academic discipline. By 1900, universities in France, England, and the United States had established departments of sociology which awarded degrees.

Throughout the twentieth century sociology expanded further, primarily as a result of two developments. First, as governments increased spending on education, welfare, and other social programs, they enlisted the aid of sociologists. Second, universities in the United States—the country which has the greatest number of sociologists—expanded sociology departments in the aftermath of perceived social crises. In the 1920s, as mass migrations from Europe and the south caused rapid growths of northern and eastern cities to the point that elites feared that they would become ungovernable, universities expanded sociology programs. Sociologists from that era turned out a number of now classic studies of urban lower classes, ethnic minorities, and patterns of urban development. In the middle and late 1960s, when riots broke out in large numbers of black ghettos, universities likewise expanded their sociology programs both because students sought such courses and because they thought that increased social knowledge could help to avoid future riots.

Today sociology is a recognized academic discipline in most parts of the world. As the discipline has developed and expanded, it has generated its own specialized fields, including demography, stratification, organizational research, family research, Third World development, the sociology of knowledge, criminology, and gerontology.

SPECIALIZED CONCEPTS

In addition to having evolved an internal specialized division of labor (demography, stratification, etc.), sociologists have generated a large number of specialized concepts (such as social classes, roles, and norms) which they use to classify and explain the social properties of societies and social life.

Sociological work shares in common with all human work a basic method or approach. All laborers use tools to transform raw materials into products. Carpenters, for example, use saws and other tools to transform wood into cabinets. Sociologists use their own types of physical and intellectual tools to transform raw data or observations about the social world into knowledge. Their physical tools include word-processors, filing cabinets, computers, and calculators. Their intellectual tools are explanatory concepts that are used to order and make sense of the data. The product of sociological work is presumed to be knowledge which can take forms that range from simple self-clarification to books, articles, speeches, and social programs.

Concepts are the most important element of this sociological labor process. They are our fundamental intellectual tools for making sense of the social world. Facts rarely speak for themselves. They must be interpreted with the use of concepts, which are intellectual abstractions used to categorize and illuminate the essential meanings of real-world occurrences. Human language is built from concepts which symbolically represent objects of human experience. *Water*, for example, is a word that is a concept or symbol which represents not this or that particular body of water, but rather what all bodies of water share in common. The meaning of the word *water* thus is an abstract concept constructed from the common properties of all particular examples of water. Sociologists have their own particular concepts which they use to name and analyze aspects of social experience. Such concepts include social class, power, roles, and norms. As with any trade, in order to learn it, one must become familiar with its tools.

The conceptual tools of sociology, however, are not as straightforward as one might wish. The concept of social class, for example, has a variety of general connotations to people. Sociologists, on the other hand, have technical meanings in mind when they use the concept—meanings rather than meaning because sociologists do not always agree on the meanings of a number of such key concepts as social class. It follows that in order to be introduced to sociology it is necessary to become familiar with the meanings of its key concepts. This is true even if there is disagreement among sociologists about which meanings are the most adequate. It is after all not unusual for workers to disagree over which tools are the most appropriate.

SOCIAL AND INDIVIDUAL EXPLANATIONS

Sociologists approach a number of society's problems from a perspective that is often different than that dictated by individual experience or common sense. For many social problems—such as alcoholism, unemployment, and crime—there is a tendency to assume that the individual alcoholic, unemployed person, or criminal is the source of the problem. In other words, perhaps because we live in a highly individualistic society, we tend to assume individual causation of social problems. Most sociologists acknowledge the obvious, that there are individual factors involved in social problems. It would be difficult to treat the problem of a particular alcoholic without at least partially focusing on that person's particular characteristics. But sociologists are more interested in investigating the less obvious social dimensions of such problems. In addition to describing the social consequences of the problem—alcohol consumption impairs driving ability and can lead to accidents, and alcoholism is a source of stress in many families which affects spouses and children—sociologists attempt to explain either why different groups have different rates of particular problems such as alcoholism or how the structure of society itself may be responsible for part of the problem. To exemplify these less obvious sociological explanations, we will briefly look at two social problems—suicide and unemployment—and compare individual to sociological explanations.

Suicide, it is often said, is more of a tragedy for families and friends than for the victim. The families and friends must continue to live with the tragedy for the rest of their lives. They quite reasonably attempt to explain the suicide by looking to the person and her or his problems to try to determine what caused her or his despondency. This manner of explanation is logical, and it goes a long way toward explaining the causes of the suicide, but it does not go all of the way.

Emile Durkheim (1855–1917), a turn of the century French sociologist, made the first systematic study of the social factors involved in suicide. Durkheim (1897) was struck by the fact that different countries had different rates of suicide and within them groups had different rates. Hence, Durkheim reasoned that if different groups had different rates, then nonindividual social factors had to be involved in the causation of suicide.

His most famous finding was that Catholics had significantly lower rates of suicide than Protestants. He concluded that the cause of this difference lay not in the religious belief differences between Catholicism and Protestantism—in fact, both religions equally condemned suicide as a personal option—but rather in the different structures of the religious communities. The Catholic community, according to Durkheim, was much more structurally integrated than the Protestant community. Individual Catholics embraced and internalized a highly developed set of religious beliefs that left little leeway for free thinking. The Protestant churches, on the other hand, had a looser ideological hold on their members. It followed, according to Durkheim's interpretation, that when a Catholic suffered deep despondency, such suicidal impulses as he or she might feel were held in check by the internalized moral authority of the church. But when a Protestant suffered deep despondency her or his church's moral authority was less binding.

Unemployment is another problem which people tend to explain in individual terms, seeing it as being primarily caused by personal defects such as lack of motivation to work, lack of adequate skills or education, or being fired for poor performance. Those factors may indeed explain why some people rather than others lose jobs or are not hired in the first place. But they do not explain why in market societies there always seem to be more people looking for jobs than available places, which gives employers the leverage of power to pick and choose among applicants and to dismiss those that do not work out. Sociological explanations thus place greater emphasis on understanding the role that unemployment plays in the functioning of the whole economic and social system than on determining what individuals need to do to make themselves employable or to hold on to their jobs. The existences of labor surpluses—an economic euphemism for people out of work—have been a nearly constant feature of market societies since their origins in the sixteenth century. Hence, unemployment must be an unavoidable side effect of the structuring of market societies. Seen that way, social explanations of unemployment hinge on determining the function or role that it plays in the overall economic organization of market societies. For that, there is a lot of evidence that indicates that the existence of unemployed populations is beneficial to employers. Competition for jobs allows employers to offer low wages, knowing that there is someone desperate enough to accept them. Fear of unemployment keeps workers working hard at the job. The existences of labor reserves in the country give owners the flexibility to move or open surpluses. Sociologists are also interested in tracing the social and physical consequences of unemployment. As unemployment increases, so too do a number of social problems, such as family stress and strife, alcohol abuse, and even suicide. It follows that unemployment negatively affects both mental and physical health. Thus, Brenner (1976), in a pioneering and influential study, found that increases in unemployment rates are associated with increases in mortality rates in the United States and England; and Stefansson (1991) found that the long-term unemployed in Sweden had a 37 percent higher death rate than the employed population.

Personal problems therefore rarely are completely personal. There is a social component in the causes and consequences of virtually all personal problems. It is the job of sociologists to ferret out those social components and, where possible, propose policy alternatives for alleviating them. It is the job of all of those who wish to understand sociology to employ what C. Wright Mills (1961) called a sociological imagination to trace the linkages between personal troubles and public issues.

RELATION TO OTHER DISCIPLINES

The very nature of its subject matter—society and social life in general—guarantees that the field of sociology will often overlap with and sometimes be difficult to distinguish from other academic fields. There is thus no hard and fast line which separates sociology from other social science disciplines, such as political science, economics, or anthropology. The concerns and types of research pursued by sociologists also often overlap with those of disciplines in the humanities, such as philosophy, history, and literature. Many sociologists hold that the existence of these overlapping concerns and approaches is good because they believe that sociology must proceed on the basis of combining broad understandings drawn from such fields as philosophy, history, economics, political science, and literature with the results being its own specialized researches.

The two fields that sociology is most closely related to are anthropology and social work. For that reason, in many small colleges and universities those three fields are often combined into single departments. Anthropologists share with sociologists the goals of understanding how the cultures and social institutions of total societies function. But while sociologists have tended to concentrate on studying contemporary industrial-based societies, anthropologists have been primarily concerned with studying the cultures of preliterate and preindustrial societies, focusing on contemporary native peoples or those of the recent past in Africa, Asia, the Americas, Australia, and the Pacific Islands. The traditional boundaries between sociology and anthropology, however, are often overstepped. A number of anthropologists now apply their methods for studying the cultures of preindustrial and preliterate peoples to studying subcultures in industrially based societies; and macro and historical sociologists, concerned with developing an understanding of the varieties of prehistorical and historical societies, venture into areas that have traditionally been the terrain of anthropology.

Sociology is often confused with social work, largely because both fields focus on society and its problems. The difference between the two is that sociology seeks a general understanding of the functioning of all aspects of society, while social workers specialize in understanding and treating the human casualties of concrete social problems, such as poverty, substance abuse, and domestic violence. Clearly there are overlaps between the two areas; in some respects social work is an applied form of sociology. But in other respects social work includes its own specialized techniques for working with clients.

With respect to other social science fields, the focuses are also related but distinguishable. Economists focus on how goods are produced, exchanged, and distributed in contemporary societies. Many economists and others believe that the nature of an economic system is the most powerful determinant of other institutional features of societies. Hence, economic understandings are often considered basic to sociological understanding. Political scientists focus on the workings of governments—how laws are made, elections won, budgets proposed, and so forth. For sociologists, the state or government is a basic institution of nearly all societies. Its character, like that of the economy, is a powerful determinant of other societal features. For that reason alone, knowledge derived from political science studies is useful to sociologists.

OCCUPATIONS AND USES

By far the largest occupation of people who call themselves sociologists in the United States is as university teachers. In a far distant second place are some government and private corporation researchers. Many times those numbers though graduate with sociology degrees, and many times more still pass through university sociology courses. This pyramid of numbers from those who pass through courses to those who major and on to the much smaller numbers who become full professionals in the field may appear unusual, but it is common in all of the humanities and social sciences fields. Few history majors, for example, ultimately become historians. Sociology thus, like other liberal arts fields, prepares students for a wide variety of occupations and careers apart from those directly associated with teaching or research in the field.

Through sociology courses, students gain the skills that are necessary for all occupational positions which require abilities to think logically and creatively and to communicate well in written form. In addition, sociology programs expose students to contemporary social issues and problems, a preparation which is useful for legal, political, media, and social work careers.

The question of whether to major—or take more courses—in sociology reduces to the question of interest. There are no real differences in employment prospects or money worths of different humanities and social sciences degrees. All are of roughly equal value for entering those professional and managerial job markets and career ladders which require general rather than particular skills.

SUMMARY

Sociology is a discipline with nineteenth-century origins which scientifically studies societies and social life in general. Sociologists share the view that most of individual behavior both occurs within and is influenced by social contexts. Hence, they investigate the social properties of societies in order to determine how these influence human conduct.

Sociology emerged as a separate academic discipline as Europe was undergoing significant economic, political, and social changes. These changes produced a perceived need for greater social knowledge. Sociology as a discipline has also grown in the twentieth century in the aftermaths of significant social changes and crises.

Today sociology is a recognized discipline in most parts of the world. It has its own specialized fields such as demography, stratification, organizational research, and family research, and it has evolved its own specialized concepts (such as social class, norms, and roles) which are used to classify and explain the social properties of societies.

Sociologists seek out and attempt to explain the specifically social dimensions of societies and their problems. Sociologists investigate how social causes are involved in such problems suffered by individuals as suicide, unemployment, and alienation.

Given the very general focuses of its subject matter—societies and social life—sociology overlaps with other social science and humanities disciplines. There is thus no hard and fast line that separates sociology from political science, history, economics, anthropology, or even philosophy. Because of the very nature of its subject matter, sociology in many ways must embrace an interdisciplinary approach.

Most sociologists work within universities, but most people who major or take courses in sociology go on to other types of occupations. Hence, sociology offers a general preparation for a wide variety of fields such as law, business, government, education, politics, media, and social work.

Key Terms and Concepts
(in order of presentation)

Sociology   Anthropology
Positivism   Social Work
Concept

Chapter Two

Individuals and Societies

If concepts are the basic intellectual tools of sociology, as presented in the previous chapter, and if the focus of sociology is on understanding human societies and social life in general, then it follows that clarity on the conceptual meaning of human beings is in order as a first step toward understanding the nexus between individuals and their social conditions of existence. While it may at first glance seem obvious what the meaning of human beings is, more reflection indicates that the concept has been the subject of rigorous debate in the life sciences, philosophy, and psychology. There is not even agreement on when human life begins—whether at conception, birth, or some point in between. In general, how one conceptually defines humans influences how one understands the workings of societies and social life.

Once the concept of the human being has been explored, we will then be in position to analyze and explore the relationship between humans and their social conditions of existence. In particular, we will be in position to conceptually describe the basic components of social interaction, entering into what has become the classic language of sociology.

HUMAN BEINGS

From an evolutionary and biological point of view, human beings are members of the subspecies *homo sapiens sapiens* that emerged from a long line of antecedents about 100,000 years ago. In defining their concept of the human being, biologists have tended to concentrate on those human features that are species-distinguishing: First, humans walk in a upright gait, as opposed to on all fours. The upright gait has social importance because it frees the hands for tool use, which in turn has allowed humans to technologically advance. Second, the structure of the hand allows for dexterity, that is, free movement of the fingers and thumb. This has given humans the capacity to grasp tools. Third, and most important, the human brain has a capacity, centered in the cerebrum, for creative thought that no other species either has or has to the same degree—hence, *sapiens*, from Latin, means "capable of knowing." This human thinking capacity has enormous social importance. Humans are capable of learning, reducing that knowledge to symbols and concepts, and passing it on to future generations, such that human history is, at least in technological terms, developmental. The histories of other species are cyclical, composed of a series of birth, life, and death cycles whose only development is unwilled evolutionary physiological change. Fourth, humans are capable of articulate speech, the social importance of which is self-evident, since it allows them to communicate in more complex manners than other species. Finally, twentieth-century biology has identified the species' uniqueness of the human genetic structure. That too has social importance, as gene splicing and other new technologies allow humans to treat one of their own species' conditions as variable.

Of these defining characteristics, it has been the capacity for creative thought that has most consumed traditional philosophical discussions of the conceptual meaning of human life. If *homo sapiens sapiens* is the biological term, human *being* is the philosophical term, with the concept of "being" being the subject of intense scrutiny in classical philosophy. Being, philosophically, means existing. Human existence though means a thinking or conscious existence. In this respect, philosophy and psychology were originally merged, since both focused on the human thinking capacity.

At the center of all attempts to define the conceptual meaning of human beings thus has been an emphasis on the species' unique thinking capacity. Humans are uniquely capable of thinking abstractly and creatively. They think abstractly when they use symbols, concepts, and language in general to name and group into categories objects that they perceive. Other species only see the objects concretely. A dog, for example, is familiar with his owner but unaware of the meaning of "owner." Because humans can think abstractly, they can labor creatively. Creativity is the two-step process by which humans first imagine something, an abstract possibility, and then second, proceed to concretize it. An engineer first thinks out the possibility of a dam and then proceeds to oversee its construction. A student first thinks about what he or she is going to write and then puts it down on paper. Other species labor, but they do not labor creatively. Beavers build dams, but only because the knowledge is instinctually encoded within them. They do not learn to build dams, nor do they improve dam building designs over generations.

HUMAN BEINGS AS SOCIAL BEINGS

George Herbert Mead (1863–1931), one of the classic theorists of twentieth-century sociology, indicated that the capacity for abstract thought made a unique form of intersubjective social life possible. In Mead's view, much of human social communication occurs as a two-step creative process similar to that of creative labor. The communicator mentally evaluates and rehearses a message according to its imagined effect on the other and then delivers it. A student who misses an exam may mentally run through a menu of possible excuses, imagining the possible reactions of the professor, before approaching her or him. Job hunters strategize how they will talk to prospective employers. Much of communication requires no such actual rehearsal, but that is so only because what was once established creatively has become routinized. Other species communicate through gestures, as when a dog snarls, but they are incapable of refining their message after abstractly taking the role of the other. *Human being* thus implies social being in the sense that humans have a capacity for a unique form of intersocialability.

Human beings are social beings in another sense too. Because of their unique ability to communicate, they can be greatly affected by other members of their species. A child learns and develops her or his personality through the medium of language, which is itself a product of social interaction. Words are, after all, labels for socially agreed-upon meanings. Hence, one's innermost thoughts are always couched within socially produced forms, that is, words. A dog may be subject to the negative actions of another dog but not to another dog's negative thoughts.

Beyond agreement that humans share these capacities, there is considerable disagreement over whether the species has other immutable qualities. Much of this revolves around the concept of instincts, that is, unchangeable in-born behavioral predispositions. On one side of the conflict are those who argue that nonhuman animals have instincts but humans do not. Their behavior is learned. On the other side are those who argue that there are instinctual bases to human and social conduct.

Undoubtedly, the most provocative and influential argument for human conduct being instinctually based is associated with Sigmund Freud (1856–1939). He argued that there was a contradiction between the needs of societies to maintain order and the needs of individuals for instinctual fulfillment. According to Freud (1930, 1933), each individual is driven by a contradictory bundle of instincts. One set—called eros or life—produces a need to have loving relations with others and self-preservation. The other set—thanatos or death—produces the need for aggression against others and self-destruction. Each instinct, if allowed to go to its logical conclusion, would be socially destructive. Hence societies must have structures which reign in human instincts. Those structures allow societies to survive and enable a modicum of order, but by inevitably frustrating instinctual fulfillment, they also ensure continuation of psychological frustration and misery. Freud thus pessimistically concluded that human misery could never be fully ended.

Herbert Marcuse (1955), though, in the most important and sustained critique of Freud's social conclusions, cast doubt on the existence of an immutable death instinct, while accepting as valid the existence of a life instinct. According to Marcuse, the way that societies are structured can curtail the expression and fulfillment of the life instinct, but they need not do that inevitably. Contrary to Freud, Marcuse concluded that it was historically possible for humans to construct societies that met both the needs of social order and psychological fulfillment. Still others argue, as mentioned, that there are no instincts at all, that all behavior is learned, and that whatever psychological fulfillment might be, it will be what humans make of it. In other words, the good society in which individual and social needs harmonize remains a possibility, neither precluded nor advanced by innate human qualities, instinctual or otherwise.

However one might conceptualize the meaning of human existence, it is clear that humans have the unique species capacity to create their social conditions of existence, for better or worse. They can create concentration camps, genocide, and harsh dictatorships as well as love, solidarity, and freedom. But it is also clear that while humans have the capacity to create those social conditions abstractly, they are not free at any time to create any social conditions. Pre-existing social conditions, the products of previous generations, constrain what it is possible to socially create. One may abstractly believe in the superiority of free love, but tradition, custom, and institutions concretely weigh against it. Humans thus create their social conditions of existence but within limits established by previous generations. For the analysis of whichever case—newly created or inherited forms of social interaction—early twentieth-century sociologists constructed a set of concepts, to which we now turn.

COMPONENTS OF SOCIAL INTERACTION

We can begin by defining as "social" any interpersonal situation or setting in which a person orients her or his actions to one or more others. The interaction may be initiated by the person or the others. Others

FIGURE 2-1 The Components of Social Interaction

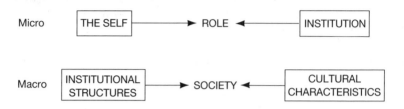

may be physically present, as when a conversation takes place, but they need not be for social conduct to take place, as when a person dresses to impress or please others. Social life thus has both objective and subjective dimensions. The term *objective* denotes the observable actions of people when they interact with others as family members, labor force participants, citizens, and so on. The term *subjective* denotes how people think and feel about themselves and others, and what they do. Clearly objective and subjective are interrelated. Objective circumstances affect feelings. Death of a close family member results in grief. Emotional states of being affect interactions with others. An emotionally distraught driver is a potentially dangerous driver. Quite clearly most of what people do is objectively or subjectively socially influenced and oriented and therefore falls within social interaction patterns.

Sociologists have tended to analyze these social interaction patterns from two different angles. The first, the microsociology tradition, concentrates on the linkage between the individual and her or his social existence and experience. The second, the macrosociology tradition, concentrates on whole societies and how they function. Common to both traditions is the premise that individuals are the products of both their social relationships that they have been a part of as they have grown and matured within societies and their unique characteristics. If it were possible via a time machine to have the same baby grow up both in the contemporary United States and in ancient Rome, the resulting adults would have distinctly different personalities, since they would have matured and formed their personalities within different social relationships. Key to understanding the individual sociologically thus is the specification of the social relationships that have influenced her or his development.

Within the microsociological tradition, the key concept for analyzing social interaction has been the role. Humans play roles within the contexts of family, work, religion, and other institutions. What their roles are and how they play them are both affected by and influence how they view their own being, that is, their concepts of self. In the macrosociological tradition, the key concept of analyzing social interaction has been the society itself. Different societies are analyzable according to their different configurations of institutional structures and cultural characteristics. The common analytical concept that links the micro and macro orientations is thus the institution which both orients individual social behavior and serves as an internal societal structure. Also common to both traditions is the premise that individuals are products of both the social relationships that they have been a part of in their lives and their own unique characteristics.

Roles, Institutions, and the Self

From a microsociological perspective, social life occurs and is experienced in settings ranging from chance street encounters involving two people to ongoing societal interactions involving millions. Face-to-face social interaction takes place in families, classrooms, stores, workplaces, and on streets, among other settings. More indirect interaction takes place in larger social settings, as when legislatures approve new laws that affect their citizens. In the analysis of patterns of social interaction we thus first must specify the settings within which they occur and that are of interest.

Once the setting of the interaction has been determined, the next step is to identify the social positions, or what some sociologists call the statuses, of the people involved. In a chance street encounter, there may be no distinguishable social positions—each person is an equal. There is social interaction among people occupying, at least for the moment, the indistinguishable social position of being a person-on-the-street. But street encounters also occur between people who occupy immediately distinguishable social positions, as between blacks and whites where racial discrimination exists, or between state troopers and stopped motorists. Obviously in these encounters, the differences of social position affect the quality of the interaction. In most settings—including families, workplaces, classrooms, and whole societies—social positions are immediately distinguishable. Such differences are horizontal when they involve interaction among people who are equal in terms of power, wealth, prestige, or any other similar hierarchically based criteria, but whose positions are distinguishable, as when teachers of different subjects meet for curricula planning. Differences are vertical when they involve interaction among people who occupy positions that carry unequal amounts of power, wealth, prestige, or some other relevant resource, as between employers and employees or rich and poor. Types of social interaction thus range on a continuum between those in which the participants occupy relatively equal social positions and those in which they do not.

Once the settings where the interaction takes place and the positions of the participants have been specified, we are then ready to identify roles and role behavior. Attached to each position in the setting is a socially defined behavioral expectation, that is, role. People in particular positions are supposed to act in predictable ways. When we go to class we expect the professor to teach, not to start juggling, unless of course it is a course in juggling.

Social life does indeed, as Shakespeare keenly observed, resemble a play in which we all learn to perform parts or roles. We learn to do what is expected of us as children in families. We learn how to be and perform as students. Later we become workers of one type or another, adult citizens, community leaders, and family creators. The analogy between a play and social life is so compelling that sociologists took their concept of the role directly from the theater. The theatrical concept of the role was a perfect metaphor for the patterned ways in which humans socially orient their conduct to meet the expectations of others. As different plays are structured around different roles, different types of social situations have different roles. The role metaphor indicates that people both intentionally orient their conduct to the expectations of others and that to some extent, their performances are just that—performances—for there is a being behind the role who may or may not be comfortable with the roles which he or she is playing or how the performance is going.

People occupy different social positions and play different roles in different contexts—in the family, at work, as citizens, as members of voluntary groups—as they move between settings. The more complex the society, the more each person must play a multitude of different roles in daily life. He or she, so to speak, moves from scene to scene or perhaps play to play, first awakening and interacting with family members, then leaving for work and interacting with people on the street, arriving at work and interacting with co-workers and those above or below in power, going out to lunch with friends, and so forth. The more modern the society, the more the individual belongs to multiple groups. He or she becomes, in the words of the classic theorist Georg Simmel (1922, p. 150) "determined sociologically in the sense that the groups 'intersect' in his person by virtue of his affiliation with them."

In each frame or setting of interaction the person performs a role that is expected of the situation. As newspaper buyer, he or she flashes the paper to the clerk so that the clerk will know which paper is being bought, then advances the money, and perhaps mutters a perfunctory thank you when change is returned. Such routine role playing as that of a customer in a store is so automatic and usually depersonalized that we literally think nothing of it.

Some sociologists and social theorists though worry that the routinization of much human interaction in modern societies has produced mass alienation, making it increasingly difficult to recognize the human behind the role. The newspaper vendor might as well be a coin depositing machine. Many restaurant customers cannot remember who their waiters or waitresses are when it comes time to request the bill. In earlier, less complex societies there were fewer roles that each person played in daily life. For peasants, probably the most populated social position in world history, human interaction was closely circumscribed both geographically and in terms of people encountered. Peasants lived and rarely traveled out of the area where they tilled land. Their household was the unit from which they worked. They left the house and went directly to the fields. They did not, as in contemporary urban societies, leave home in the morning to go to another social setting from or within which to work. Aside from household members, the most social interaction that peasants had was with other peasants who either lived or worked close by. They most likely on occasion had dealings with religious and political authorities, but in general these contacts were not numerous or complicated. Peasant human interaction thus involved far fewer people than that of contemporary urban dwellers. Whether it was therefore qualitatively fuller or less fragmentary than that typical in modern urban-based societies is open to interpretation.

The more stable the social situation, the more people take their roles for granted. But periods also occur when given role expectations cannot be taken for granted. For most of medieval feudalism, peasants assumed that they were born into their roles and that God had ordained it to be that way. But there were also times in which peasants revolted against the whole system of feudal roles. For much of the twentieth century, men and women in the United States assumed that in normal families the man earned a paycheck and the woman stayed home taking care of the house and children. But within the last generation those role expectations no longer match the reality of most families where both adults now have to work outside of the household in order to make ends meet.

Roles clearly incorporate rules for how they are to be played. The origins of those rules are norms, which are the values which specify how roles should be played. Professional norms, among others, govern how a professor should relate to students. He or she should concentrate on the pertinent subject matter, not wander off into irrelevant areas. Similarly, ethical norms dictate that the professor should treat students fairly and with respect. Other norms govern how students are supposed to act. Norms are a subset of the general values which exist within a society. They represent the application of societal values to the shoulds and oughts of role conduct.

Each role thus carries with it a set of norms of how it is to be played. Each family has its spoken and unspoken rules. Each work organization has rules. And there are rules governing how to buy a newspaper. Such rules vary from informal to highly formalized. Norms can be imposed by the powerful on the powerless, as in a prison—or family—or they can be developed through general agreement, as in a small club.

The norms governing roles vary in how clearly defined they are. For many roles it is absolutely clear what you are supposed to do. You pay money to the clerk in order to take possession of the newspaper. But for other roles the rules or norms may be ill defined, ambiguous, or nonexistent. When parents disagree, children may find contradictory sets of norms in the household. During periods of rioting, ordinary norms governing citizen behavior evaporate.

Sanctions are social forms of approval and disapproval for role performances. These range from mild gestures and comments to outright rewards and punishments. The student who disrupts a class by talking indiscreetly to a neighbor may be glared at by the teacher, asked to stop, or in extremes, thrown out. The suburban homeowner who does not keep the lawn mowed may directly experience from subtle gestures or at least imagine the disapproval of neighbors. The Roman citizen who did not pay his taxes or debts ended up in prison. The insubordinate slave faced the whip. The conduct expected from the role of being a citizen is ultimately enforced by laws. Legal sanctions range from warnings and fines to capital punishment.

Sociologists use the concept of *socialization* to refer to the processes by which people learn the norms and roles necessary for functioning within groups and societies. Socialization begins at birth. The newborn comes into the world as an unsocialized being who must continually learn and adopt values, norms, and forms of behavior if he or she is to perform as a member of society. Socialization continues throughout life as individuals learn to interact within new social environments, such as neighborhoods, workplaces, or, for that matter, delinquent gangs.

In sum, objective observable social life takes place in a variety of different settings. Within each of those settings people occupy different social positions, for which they perform roles, that is, engage in socially expected behavior patterns. Norms are the values which govern the rules incorporated in the conduct of particular roles. Sanctions are forms of social rewards and punishments which are used to uphold the rules of role conduct.

Institutions are ongoing configurations of social positions, roles, values, and norms—patterns of social behavior—which exist to meet particular needs within societies. The most basic material needs of any society, around which economic and kinship institutions form, are production of food, shelter, and clothing necessary for survival and reproduction of the species itself. Most societies have also developed political and religious institutions. Secondary, often subsidiary, institutions develop around other social needs such as health, education, recreation, sports, courtship, and science.[1]

Economic institutions, such as farms, workshops, and multinational corporations, are concerned with the production and distribution of goods and services. They vary according to the complexity of their internal role differentiations. Hunting groups in early societies, for example, had simple role divisions of labor with each member performing similar tasks. In contrast, contemporary industrial corporations contain highly differentiated role structures. There are vertical power and authority role differences from the top levels of management to the shop floor; and there are horizontal differences of specialization—such as in engineering, production, sales, and advertising. In general, the earlier the society, the less the role differentiation and the simpler the division of labor within institutions. The more modern the society, the greater the role differentiation and the more complex the division of labor.

Kinship refers to networks of people interrelated on the basis of common ancestry or marriage. Each family is thus a kinship institution within which members play different roles as wives, husbands, mothers, fathers, children, grandparents, or other relatives. Roles vary in terms of work expected, power, and authority accorded. Cross-cultural and historical studies indicate that there have been a variety of different types of kinship institutions.

Political institutions include political parties, government bureaucracies, and military organizations which are involved in the struggle for and administration of territorial power. The government—the *state* in a more classical language—is the arena within or against which political institutions function. The state itself is an institution which attempts to pattern the ways in which its subsidiary administrative, military, and other institutions perform roles. Whole institutions in that sense can perform roles within encompassing institutions. Constitutions are the most formalized expressions of intended patterns of role interrelationships within states, their subsidiary institutions, and the institutions over which they have power. As with all other institutional areas, there are a variety of historical types of political institutions.

Religious institutions are based on belief systems about ultimate meanings of life that are practiced within churches, synagogues, mosques, temples, and other settings. Religious institutions vary according to the nature of their role configurations and differences. The respective powers and degrees of authority accorded to leaders and members vary. In some, the spiritual leader is assumed to be omniscient; in others, as merely a facilitator.

Subjective social life refers to how people internalize and react to their experiences with objective social life. Its most important analytical concepts are the self and character structure, or personality.

By the term *self* sociologists mean a person's concept of her or his own being, life, or inner identity. Sociologists have long noted that the sense of self is greatly influenced by interactions with others. Charles

Horton Cooley (1864–1929) introduced the wonderfully evocative and metaphorical concept of "the looking glass self." Through use of that expression, Cooley (1902) conveyed that how a person is received by others greatly influences how he or she perceives his or her own self. A shunned person will feel insecure if he or she desires the approval of those who are doing the shunning.

George Herbert Mead developed the most influential sociological concept of the self. Building on the work of the psychologist William James, Mead (1934) conceptualized the self as having two parts: the *me* and the *I*. The me is the self as object, as formed by internalization of the attitudes of others. The I is the self as subject, developed by the individual's own impulses and response to the attitudes of others. The me is the socialized self, the I the unsocialized self. Hence, one's sense of self is formed from both without and within, from both internalization of others' attitudes and purely internally generated beliefs and reactions to outside attitudes.[2]

Self-esteem is a direct consequence of the perception of self. Whether one feels comfortable with or unhappy about who one is is importantly shaped by outside social factors. Sociologists are hence concerned with investigating the social correlates and distributions of self-esteem in societies.

Social positions and roles affect perceptions of self and self-esteem in a variety of ways. They usually, but not always, carry with them different levels of prestige or status.[3] There are low-, high-, and in-between status positions and roles in society. The status of janitor is relatively low, that of a professional is relatively high. A person who occupies a role that enjoys considerable status may feel high self-esteem and satisfaction. A member of an oppressed minority who is forced by racism and discrimination into low-status roles may feel low self-esteem and, in extremes, personal dislike.

There is thus a relationship between the status attached to a person's role and her or his self-esteem, but it is not necessarily in all circumstances direct. It is probable that roles with high status tend to enhance self-esteem. Respect and recognition for what a person does enhance his or her self-image. But it is not always the case. A high-status position can be occupied, but the role may be performed or may be perceived to be performed badly. In that case the benefits of status can evaporate quickly, as when a high public official is judged to be incompetent.

People who perform low-status roles may draw compensatory existential or spiritual meanings for their lives from elsewhere. A lower-class worker can see himself as first and foremost a good father. An oppressed peasant can have faith that there is a better world awaiting to compensate for the misery and low social status in this one.

In between role and self lies the character structure of an individual. As in theater, a character represents a unique personality. To play a character in theater or film requires more than the playing of standard roles. It requires mastering and evoking what is unique about how a particular person performs in her or his social roles. Character structures in real life similarly are determined by the unique ways in which people integrate innate physiological and organic capacities, psychological dispositions, and the social roles that they perform (for the most insightful sociological discussion of character structure, see Gerth and Mills, 1953).

One becomes a person (from the Latin *persona*, meaning "mask") in society by playing a variety of roles. Roles make the person, but they do not completely define the individual. How people react to the roles they play, as well as the reactions of others, determines their concept of who they really are and the development of their unique character structures. A person can be proud and satisfied with the roles that he or she plays or ashamed or dissatisfied. Others also react to how well they believe one is playing her or his appointed roles. How good a mother are you in the eyes of others? How responsible a worker? How much do these judgments affect your sense of being? If the person is playing the role badly enough and the persons reacting have power enough, sanctions come into play. The state can take children away from negligent mothers; workers can be fired. A clumsy actor in a theater elicits yawns and perhaps boos from the audience. An inept social actor may receive ostracism. In the end, each unique character or personality emerges from the interplay of a wide variety of internal and external forces.

At the same time, there can be a disjuncture between public and private personalities. Who one appears to be in a position or role may be quite different from who one really is. "What do you do?" is a useful question for beginning to learn about someone. But if by it you only mean, "What is your job?" you will not learn all there is to be learned about that person. Behind the role at work is always a human being who has beliefs, values, hopes, dreams, and experiences. There are quite extraordinary people who occupy quite ordinary positions. Many different kinds of people can share similar positions and roles. What is behind the role can also be disappointing. No man is a king to his butler.

In contemporary Western societies there is a public fascination with the lives of those who occupy highly visible celebrity roles. Gossip magazines and tabloids endlessly and mercilessly pore over their lives to tell the public "who they really are"—the more scandalous, the better. As has become clear from recent presidential elections in the United States, candidates for the role of the highest office are not only expected to be able to do that job well—to perform that position's role—but also to lead a flawless private life. For the celebrity the boundaries of public and private life are increasingly fuzzy. Public religious personalities have found that they too are fair game for the hunters of hypocrisy and sensationalism. The disjunction between public role and private self is reminiscent of when the terrifying Wizard of Oz was unmasked to be the genial showman.

Structure, Society, and Culture

From a macrosociological perspective, a society can be defined as a historically bounded population that shares a unique configuration of institutional structures and cultural characteristics. Specification of a society's institutional structures is important because those are the contexts within which social life is molded. Specification of a society's cultural characteristics is important because societies with similar institutional structures can differ greatly according to their cultural characteristics—the United States and France share similar institutional structures but differ culturally. Specification of historical period is necessary because the characteristics of societies change over time—the pre–Civil War United States is not the same as the contemporary United States.

When sociologists speak of institutional structures they usually mean configurations of institutions within given areas—the total of economic institutions in a society constituting its economic structure, all of the political institutions of its political structure, all of the institutions regulating the class relations of its class structure, and so forth. Institutions can overlap and crosscut each other. The institutionalized class structure of a society, for example, encompasses economic, social, and other relationships. The grand total of institutions within a society constitutes a society's overall social structure.

There have been quite clearly a very large number of concretely existing societies in world history which can be separately identified and described according to their internal institutional structures. But sociological analysis of societies goes beyond those identifications and descriptions. It places societies with similar institutional structures into categories that are marked off from societies of different structures. The units of analysis become types of societies rather than particular societies. This enables comparative macrosociological analysis within and between types of societies.

Societies can be categorized according to any one of their economic, political, kinship, religious, military, or other institutional structural characteristics depending on the purposes of the research. Societies which share one of those structural characteristics do not necessarily share others. Societies which share the same type of economic structure, for example, can have different political structures. Capitalist societies, thus, have varied greatly according to their political structures, with some being relatively democratic and others dictatorial. What has been most common in sociological research has been to classify societies primarily according to their economic structures, and that is the approach that will be followed in the next three chapters.

One of the advantages of categorizing societies according to their economic structures is that those structures are the most powerful determinants of class relationships which are a central focus of sociological research. What has been of interest to sociologists has been the fusions of economic and class structures, which we call *socioeconomic structures*. The nature of what we are calling the socioeconomic structure is, in short, the most fundamental feature of a society and the basis from which to compare it to and distinguish it from others.

Classifying societies according to their dominant economic and resulting class structures is an important step in research. It enables comparison of societies with like economic structures—such as the United States and Great Britain. But it does not exhaust analysis since, as mentioned, there is an additional characteristic of societies to be considered—their cultural dimension. Societies with similar economic and class structures most often have distinct cultural characteristics. No one would argue that the cultures of the United States and Great Britain are identical.

All societies thus have distinguishable cultural identities. By that it is meant that they have their own particular ways of life. They have their own distinguishable material goods, such as food, buildings and handicraft, nonmaterial values, customs, myths, songs, and languages. And cultural characteristics infuse institutional structures, making it impossible to rigidly separate the two.

Nineteenth- and twentieth-century anthropology pioneered employment of the concept of culture as a way to describe and explain value differences between societies. Societies, in the words of the anthropologists, had different cultures. To understand how they functioned, it was necessary to determine the contents of their cultures. In doing so it was important to avoid ethnocentrism—using the perspectives or biases of one's own culture to judge the values and practices of another.

Sociologists inherited the concept of culture from anthropology and proceeded to investigate the ways in which societies inculcated cultural values into their members. In studying overall cultural dimensions of societies, sociologists, however, became increasingly aware of the need to distinguish the subcultures of different internal class, regional, and minority groupings.

The concept of a subculture is particularly important in societies which contain different ethnic and racial peoples or minorities. Such multicultural societies show clear internal differences of customs, values, and general points of view between peoples. In the United States, being brought up in minority (such as black, Mexican, Puerto Rican, or Native American) families and neighborhoods results in socialization into values and lifestyles which overlap with those of the majority but which still retain important differences. Such differences are manifested in language (Spanish rather than English, for example), dialects (black English), forms of music with different beats and syncopation structures (salsa and soul music), and general values. The more a group leads a separate existence within a society, the more it develops its own unique cultural identity.

Sociologists also speak of class subcultures, as in working-class and middle-class cultures. If classes lead separate lives and lifestyles, then it makes sense to refer to them as having separate subcultures. People from working-class backgrounds share forms of speech—more pronounced in some countries such as England than others, values, and lifestyles which are different from those of middle and upper classes. For that reason people tend to feel at least vaguely uncomfortable, of not really belonging, when attending social gatherings of classes above or below their own.

There are also regional subcultural differences. The less territorially or culturally integrated a country, the more subcultural particularities of regions stand out. In the United States there are clear subcultural differences between southerners and northerners, Appalachians and New Englanders, and Californians and Iowans. These are marked by speech accents, values, and lifestyles. The same holds for regions within Mexico, where there are subcultural differences between *norteños* and *sureños*. In the extreme, regional subcultural differences result in the fragmentation of countries, as when the Central American republics broke away from Mexico in 1823. But it seems likely, as roads and mass media reduce the physical and social distances separating regions within countries, that national cultures will develop more fully at the expense of regional subcultures. In the same respect, it also seems likely that globalization of economic relationships and communication networks will eventually undermine national identities themselves.

SUMMARY

The basic goals of sociology are to understand how humans function within their social environments and how whole societies, in and of themselves, function. Concepts are the basic intellectual tools for pursuing these goals. It follows that the concept of the human being is a key building block for sociological knowledge.

All biological explanations of the human species stress its unique thinking capacity as differentiating it from other species. Humans can think abstractly and creatively. This thinking capacity has social importance in that it allows humans to create their social existences and societies developmentally. There is little controversy over this point. The early twentieth-century sociological theorist George Herbert Mead emphasized that the capacity to think abstractly allows humans to imagine themselves in the position of the other to whom they are socially communicating. Human communication thus involves internalization of social meanings and experiences. Most importantly from a sociological perspective, the human being is a social being who also incorporates creative individuality.

While there is general agreement that the capacities for abstract and creative thought are species-defining, there is considerable dispute over other presumed innate human characteristics that have social importance. One of the most famous controversies of this century, in that respect, concerns Sigmund Freud's contention that human instinctual gratification contradicts the needs of societies to maintain order; and thus that a certain quotient of misery necessarily must accompany the march of civilization.

However one might define the basic meaning of human existence, it is clear that humans socially interact. In order to capture this dimension of human existence, sociologists have developed a set of basic analytical concepts. The microsociological tradition concentrates on the linkages between individuals and the direct social conditions of their existences. The macrosociological tradition concentrates on whole societies as the basic units of analysis.

Roles, institutions, and the self are the basic concepts of the microsociological tradition. Social interaction objectively takes place within settings among people who occupy social positions and perform appropriate roles. Norms, encouraged or enforced by sanctions, are the values which govern role performances. All participants in social interaction—that is, ipso facto all human beings—have internal senses of their own identities. They have, in the words of classic sociology, a sense of self. This sense of self is greatly influenced by outside social factors and the person's own unique way of acting and reacting. Particular character structures or personalities emerge from the interplay of roles and selves. Role behavior occurs within institutional contexts, with institutions being configurations of social positions, roles, and norms which have been created to accomplish particular ends within societies. The most central institutions within most historical societies have been concerned with economic, kinship, political, and religious needs.

Societies, institutional structures, and cultural characteristics are the basic concepts of the macrosociological tradition. Societies are populations that share unique configurations of institutional structures and cultural characteristics within given historical periods. Institutional structures are composed of all of the institutions within given areas—as in the economic, political, and class structures of societies—with the term *social structure* usually meaning the grand sum of all institutions within a given society. In addition to institutional structures, societies also evidence unique cultural characteristics which can include distinct types of material products and values, customs, or languages. Many societies also contain regional, class, ethnic, and other types of sub-groups with their own distinct subcultural characteristics.

The concepts just enumerated constitute the basic language of sociological analysis and are applicable to descriptions and explanations of all historical societies.

In the next three chapters, historical and contemporary societies will be classified most fundamentally according to the criteria of their dominant socioeconomic structures which are complexes of economic and class relations. This form of classification follows from the widely held premise that the economic structure, from which class relations arise in most societies, has the greatest influence in determining the overall social structures of societies. Thus different types of economic institutions structure different types of societies.

Key Terms and Concepts
(in order of presentation)

Human being	Self
Social being	Looking glass self
Instinct	"I" and "me"
Eros and Thanatos	Self-esteem
Social	Character structure
Objective social life	Institution
Subjective social life	Kinship
Setting	Institutional structure
Social position	Social structure
Status	Society
Role	Culture
Norm	Ethnocentrism
Socialization	Subculture
Sanction	

Endnotes

1. Sociologists have applied the concept of the institution in two different ways. In the first case, it refers to only the abstract pattern of social behavior itself and not to particular instances of it. According to this usage, the General Motors Corporation would be categorized as an organization which embodied the institution of capitalist enterprise rather than as an institution itself. In the second case, which we will follow, institutions refer to both abstract patterns of social behavior and particular organized manifestations of those patterns. General Motors, according to this usage, would be both an organization and an institution.

2. Cooley and Mead were classic exponents of what came to be known as symbolic interactionism. This microsociological approach investigates the interaction processes between individuals and their social surroundings. Its key postulate is that social interaction is carried on through symbols—language and gestures—and that individuals are involved in ongoing processes of interpreting and reinterpreting these social symbols. It follows, according to this school, that social reality is continually being transformed through the changing meanings that individuals attach to the social symbols that they receive.

3. As the wary reader will have realized by now, the concept of status is used in two not entirely consistent ways in contemporary sociology. In the first case, it means any position within a hierarchy. In the second it means prestige. According to the first usage, sociologists speak of statuses as the positions themselves within a hierarchy, such as the statuses within a particular corporate structure. In the second, sociologists refer to status as an attribute—the level of prestige—which may be attached to a particular position, as in "the presidency is a high-status position," or person, as in "John Smith enjoys high status because of his charm."

Chapter Three

Classifying Societies

Human societies began between 40,000 and 100,000 years ago. Over the succeeding millennia tens of thousands of societies have appeared and disappeared. For most of them there is no recorded information, since they existed before the relatively late invention and spread of writing, about 5,000 years ago. Indirect archaeological evidence has shed some light on how a number of societies in the preliterate era functioned, but for the majority there is no information. They simply developed and disappeared, leaving no clues about how they lived for future historians and social scientists. Any understanding of the different social ways in which people have lived over the millennia of world history relies therefore of necessity as much on logic as it does on direct evidence.

Whether on the bases of logical possibilities or direct evidence or combinations of both, most sociologists tend to classify the varieties of societies that have existed in world history according to two criteria: their technological capacities and their socioeconomic structures. The first yields a vocabulary of such terms as *hunting and gathering, agricultural,* and *industrial societies*; the second a vocabulary of such terms as *slave, feudal,* and *capitalist societies*.

TECHNOLOGICAL ERAS

Technology (from the Greek *techne,* or "technique" and *logos,* or "knowledge") means literally "knowledge of techniques." In our context, technology means knowledge of techniques of production. The degree of sophistication of a society's techniques for producing food, shelter, clothing, and other survival necessities indicates its stage of technological development. There are three different ways in which social scientists have classified societies according to their technological stages of development.

In the first, archaeologists have based classifications—primarily of early societies—on the materials from which tools and weapons were constructed. During the Stone Age, people shaped their tools and weapons, as literally indicated by the name, out of available stones. As technology increased over thousands of years, copper and bronze replaced stone as the main tool- and weapon-making material. Use of metals indicated a tremendous technological advance over use of stone because it required the knowledge and skill to smelt iron ores into malleable materials, resulting in tools which were far superior in strength and precision to those fashioned out of stone. In large part, archaeologists used tool materials to classify societies because those materials survived the ravages of time long enough to be found in the nineteenth and twentieth centuries and thereby offered direct physical evidence which could be examined.

Second, historians and others have distinguished, partly on technological grounds, historical and prehistorical societies. Historical societies are those which have developed the communications technology of writing, while prehistorical societies were preliterate. Writing first developed in some regions about 5,000 years ago, indicating that most of the 40,000 to 100,000 years of world history have been in fact prehistorical according to this use of the term. For this work though we will use the term *world history* to cover both history and prehistory.

The third approach, which is now conventionally used in sociological writings, classifies stages of development according to dominant types of production-oriented technologies. Sociologists and other social scientists now agree on a fairly standard vocabulary that classifies development into hunting and gathering, pastoral, horticultural, agricultural, industrial, and postindustrial types and stages (see Lenski and Lenski, 1982).

As the name *hunting and gathering* indicates, the earliest peoples survived by literally hunting animals and gathering ready-made nuts, vegetables, and fruit. It took tens of thousands of years for human societies to advance beyond hunting and gathering to more sophisticated production technologies. Hunting and gathering continues to be the major technology of only a few peoples in remote regions of the world today. Societies have also existed which resorted mainly to the related technology of fishing as their means of survival. Such societies continue today on many continents.

Deer Hunt.
Castellón-Spain...

Herding, or pastoralism, and horticulture were the first technological advances beyond hunting, fishing, and gathering. Pastoralism is based on keeping and producing out of a herd of animals (such as goats, cattle, and sheep) meat for food and skins for clothing and tents. Pastoralism continues to be the main technological means of subsistence for peoples in several regions of the world.[1] Horticultural (from the Latin *hortus*, meaning "garden," and *cultura*, meaning "cultivation," thus literally "garden cultivation") technologies are based on people using hoes to cultivate small plots of land or gardens. The earliest evidence of horticulture being practiced is from about 9,000 years ago in Mesopotamia, Palestine, and Asia Minor (Lenski and Lenski, 1982, p. 137). Horticulture has continued to be the dominant technology of a number of peoples down to the present.

Agriculture (from *ager*, meaning "field," and *cultura*, meaning "cultivation," thus literally "field cultivation") is a more advanced technology than horticulture for cultivation of the soil. Instead of human energy driving hoes to cultivate small gardens, humans use animal energy (oxen, horses, cattle) to drive plows to cultivate fields. Mesopotamia and Egypt were the first sites of the agricultural revolution, about 5,000 years ago. Agriculture marked a tremendous technological advance over horticulture because in it humans employed nonhuman sources of energy to drive their tools. The later incorporation of wind and river power to drive mills was related to technologies of using readily available natural energy sources.

Industrialization, dating from about 1750, represents both an advance in technological sophistication and a shift of populations away from the land, that is, an urbanization of populations. In industrial production, humans use fossil fuels, electricity, steam, and now controlled nuclear fission as energy sources and machines as tools. At the same time, industrial production takes place in factories around which grow city populations of workers and others. While the factory was the primary location of industrial production, the invention of tractors and other motorized farm machinery has also brought about an industrialization of agriculture. (Hoe, plow, and tractor are the most useful symbols of the technological development of growing food.)

Many social scientists argue that today most of the First World countries of Europe and North America have advanced beyond a strictly industrial technological base to their economies. In general developmental stages, as agriculture becomes more productive, fewer laborers are needed on the land, freeing up labor to be employed in industrial production. A society can be considered to be at an industrial stage of development when it has more industrial than agricultural employees and when the two together constitute a majority of all employees. But these conditions no longer prevail for most of the European and North American labor forces where service employees in health, education, recreation, and other sectors now constitute the majorities. What has occurred is that labor-saving productivity gains in industry have freed up labor to be employed in services, as previously productivity gains allowed labor to be shifted from agriculture to industry. For that reason a number of social scientists (see Chapter Five) now refer to most of

Agriculture in Germany, 1473, Johann Zainer, artist

Agriculture in the United States, 1936

Europe and North America as being at a postindustrial rather than industrial stage of development.

While it is generally agreed among historians and archaeologists that technological progress has been a central feature of grand historical development, there has been less agreement over whether the consequences of that type of progress have brought unmitigated benefits. Many argue that there is no evidence that people in technologically advanced societies lead any happier or more fulfilling lives than those in less advanced societies. The most that can be said is that technological advance has always brought with it the capacity for reducing misery. Development of technological means of producing more food has the potential of reducing malnutrition, starvation, sickness, and death. Increases in medical knowledge have a similar potential for reducing sources of misery. On the other hand, there are also increases in the technological means of producing misery, such as military means of destruction, which may have proceeded as fast as or faster than the means of reducing misery. Like most everything else in history and societies, what becomes of technological advances—whether they produce better lives or cause more misery—depends on what humans make of them. Technology in and of itself is not a cause. It is how it is used by humans that is the cause. Technological development, both in world history and in the Third World today, thus brings the possibility of material improvements in living conditions, but it does not necessarily produce positive social development. For the latter, other conditions are necessary.

SOCIOECONOMIC STRUCTURES

Societies that share the same level of technological development need not share the same type of socioeconomic structure. Agriculture, for example, was the dominant technology in both ancient Rome and nineteenth-century New England. But in the first, slaves were the major labor force, while in the second, free farmers predominated. Despite sharing a common agricultural technology, ancient Rome and nineteenth-century New England had essentially different socioeconomic structures—one slave and the other capitalist. Similarly, the postwar United States and Soviet Union were both at industrial stages of development, but one had a capitalist and the other a socialist socioeconomic structure. It follows that it is necessary to classify societies both in terms of their socioeconomic structures and technological stages of production.

Socioeconomic structures are composed of the institutionalized ways in which societies carry out the production of their necessities. These institutionalized ways, called *modes of production* in some accounts, contain typical economic and social role configurations.[2] The first type of socioeconomic structure in world history incorporated essentially equal social roles; all subsequent ones have incorporated unequal class roles. The history of types of socioeconomic structures, beyond the first, has thus been largely the history of different types of class structures.

In communal societies, which were based on the earliest and simplest types of socioeconomic structures, people equally cooperated in producing their necessities and equally shared what they had produced. Most communal societies were no more than small bands of nomadic peoples that eked out bare subsistence existences with primitive techniques of production. The communal type of economic structure, however, was both the earliest and the longest-lasting in world history. Communal peoples have continued to exist in remote parts of the world down through the present century.

The earliest types of class-based economic structures emerged in ancient empires in which a central ruling state authority, composed originally of leading warriors and often priests, dominated and taxed

TABLE 3-1 Technological Eras and Socioeconomic Structures in
World History

	TECHNOLOGICAL ERAS	SOCIOECONOMIC VARIETIES
1750	Industrial	Capitalist, Socialist
3000 B.C.	Agricultural	State, Slave, Feudal, Capitalist, Socialist
7000 B.C.	Horticultural	Communal, Village Communities
100,000 B.C.	Hunting and Gathering	Communal

outlying peasant villages for labor, products, or money. These state societies began perhaps 5,000 years ago and existed in many parts of the ancient world, including Mesopotamia, Northern China, Egypt, and India. They also existed in the Aztec, Inca, and other empires of the pre-Columbian Americas. What had been largely isolated communal and semi-communal peoples were drawn into larger, more encompassing nets of social and economic relationships, the grand total of which comprised a state-based socioeconomic structure.

Out of the ancient world, slavery-based economic structures eventually developed, most prominently in ancient Greece and Rome. Slave structures were, as the name indicates, based on the use of slave labor to produce. In addition to their ancient world existence, they also figured prominently in the economic development of the Americas from the sixteenth to nineteenth centuries.

After the decline and end of the Roman Empire a type of socioeconomic structure, feudalism, emerged in Europe that was based upon landlords expropriating tax payments from peasants. Feudal or at least semi-feudal socioeconomic structures have also existed in parts of Africa, Asia, and Latin America.

The present capitalist era has roots which go back until at least the thirteenth century in Europe. By the beginnings of the sixteenth century it had developed into a coherent economic and social system and spread to other parts of the globe. Capitalism, as a socioeconomic structure, is based upon owners of private enterprises (factories, mines, banks, stores, etc.) employing workers to produce commodities for sale on markets.

During the twentieth century as many as one-third of the world's peoples have lived in societies with socialist socioeconomic structures, that is, types of socioeconomic structures in which states or governments, rather than private individuals, were the major owners of means of production, such as factories and mines.

SUMMARY

Most sociologists classify societies according to two complementary criteria: their stages of technological development (hunting and gathering, pastoral, horticultural, agricultural, or industrial) and their types of socioeconomic structures (communal, state, slave, feudal, capitalist, or socialist). Both forms of classification are necessary, since each focuses on a different essential societal dimension.

Technological classifications are useful in part because there is little disagreement among social scientists that world history has developed through clear technological stages that are relatively easy to identify—from hunting and gathering to agriculture to industry. Technological classifications of societies thus have the advantage of being unambiguous and noncontroversial. They are also widely used today in studies of economic development in the Third World, with development being identified with industrialization and underdevelopment with overabsorption of labor forces in low-yield agricultural work.

Socioeconomic classifications shed light on the different institutional characteristics of societies. Societies at the same stages of technological development can have very different socioeconomic structures. Agriculture can be practiced under conditions of both slavery and free labor. Industrial societies in this century have functioned with both capitalist and socialist socioeconomic structures.

Used together, the technological and socioeconomic forms of classification form a complementary whole in the classification of a given society as, for example, industrial capitalist.

In the next two chapters we will trace in more detail the varieties of societies in world history. But we must now reorder the priority of our analytical concepts—technology and socioeconomic structure—because socioeconomic characteristics are of more direct interest to sociologists than are technological characteristics per se. Thus, instead of seeing socioeconomic structures as varieties of technological types of societies, we will classify societies primarily according to their socioeconomic structures.

Key Terms and Concepts
(in order of presentation)

Technology
Prehistory
Hunting and gathering
Pastoral
Horticultural
Agriculture
Industrial

Socioeconomic structure
Communal society
State society
Slave society
Feudalism
Capitalism
Socialism

Endnotes

1. The best examples of recent or contemporary peoples who have subsisted on the bases of pastoral technologies are in East Africa, including the Borana, Maasai, Nandi, Turkana, and Jie peoples (Huntingford, 1953; Gulliver, 1955; Dahl, 1979). The Maasai are the best-known examples of pastoralists. For an account of the problems that they had in maintaining their traditional way of life in the face of development pressures to use grazing lands more productively for food growing, see Hunt (1988).
2. For greater elaboration of the concept of mode of production as well as of types of modes of production, see Russell (1989).

Chapter Four

Past Societies

There are at least two reasons why the analysis of past types of societies is important to contemporary sociology. First, it is important to understand these societies in their own rights in order to have an accurate accounting of the social ways in which humans have lived over the 40,000 to 100,000 year span of world prehistory and history. Second, communal, state, slave, and feudal societies have continued to exist in some regions of the world up to the present or at least recent past. Part of the logic of world capitalist development from the sixteenth century forward has been determined by its encounter with state societies in the Americas (the Aztec and Inca empires), absorption and destruction of communal societies in many areas, struggle with feudal institutions in Europe and other areas, and initial articulation with slave modes of production. The encounters and articulations of rising capitalist modes of production spreading outward from Europe with precapitalist modes of production in other areas has been a significant thematic element of the construction of modern world history.

COMMUNAL SOCIETIES

At the beginning of world history, humans lived in small communal groups and bands that roamed over territories in search of food and other means of survival. Because of their ability to adapt creatively, they were able to improve their survival skills and tools. Unlike other animals who were unable to accumulate and pass on technological knowledge to succeeding generations, humans were able to make developmental technological progress a unique feature of their historical experience.

The communal nature of these societies is beyond doubt. Virtually all anthropological, archaeological, and prehistorical studies confirm that they were composed of peoples who cooperated in their production tasks and shared what they produced. Such vertical role differences as there were were not enough to produce class differences, and there were little horizontal role differences or development of different specialized production tasks. These were societies in which there was genuine equality among members. No one worked for anyone else. Each worked instead for the survival of the whole community, and no one received a larger share of the communal product. Equality was thus the primordial social condition of humanity. They were equal products of nature, equally weak before nature's awesome storms and harsh living conditions, and equal among themselves as they tried to eke out usually meager existences.

The first of these communal societies began with the final evolution of the subspecies, between 40,000 and 100,000 years ago. For tens of thousands of years, up until the advent of class-based societies, which came relatively late in world history, these were the only types of societies in existence. Communal societies have therefore predominated for well over 90 percent of world history. There is no evidence on any continent that they were preceded by other types of societies. The commonplace saying that there have always been rich and poor is simply wrong. For most of world history there was no division between rich and poor within societies.

After the beginning of class-based societies in some regions of the world, communal societies continued to exist in other regions. Down to the nineteenth century they were still numerous in many parts of the world. The Americas, for example, were home to large numbers of communal societies of indigenous peoples. Such societies exist today in remote areas of Ecuador, Botswana, New Guinea, and elsewhere, but their numbers are rapidly dwindling.

The early societies were nomadic, moving from area to area, in continual search for better hunting and gathering possibilities. Over generations, nomadism became migration as peoples wandered thousands of miles in search of easier living conditions. The luckiest found lands with temperate climates, lush vegetation, and bountiful game. There is now reason to believe that some of these fortunate early communal peoples led lives of relative ease. Because of the favorable conditions in which they lived, they could produce their necessities in a short amount of time and devote the rest of their days to leisure and cultural activities.

Studies (see Sahlins, 1972) among some Australian aborigines indicate that despite having working days far shorter than those commonplace in contemporary First World societies, they managed to secure enough to enjoy a relatively healthy diet. But these were exceptions. Most of the early communal societies led unenviable poor existences. They were by no means utopian societies. Most were at the technological stage of hunting and gathering and materially poor. Their tools and knowledge of production techniques were primitive, enabling them to produce only a miserable subsistence standard of living. Most children did not survive infancy, and adults died at early ages.

What stands out economically about these societies is that there was equal access to means of production—land, tools, raw materials, and other necessary prerequisites for producing. Each member was free to hunt and gather in surrounding forests and plains. The land, the central means of production of societies which subsisted through hunting and gathering, was the property of no one. Land was a means of production in the sense that it was where animals existed to be hunted and wild plants to be gathered. Without land on which animals and wild plants existed, there could be no production of food through hunting or gathering.

What also stands out economically about communal societies is the subsistence character of production and lack of accumulated wealth. Virtually all that was successfully hunted or gathered was consumed, with nothing left over for storage or that could be turned into wealth for accumulation. Personal items may have been prized, but there was no wealth in the economic sense of that word. Nomadism itself precluded wealth formation, since there was little possibility of carrying more than a few light-weight personal items from place to place.

Socially, equality reigned in the communal societies. There could be status differences—as between leaders and followers, medicine men and ordinary members, and elders and others—but these differences were not so great as to become economic class differences. Leaders, medicine men, and elders were workers like everyone else. All that was different about them was that they were looked up to. They did not have privileged access to or ownership of means of production.

Politically, the earliest societies were undoubtedly small-scale democracies. Their small size made it possible for everyone, or at least adults, to participate in decision making. Since there were neither economic nor social differences, it is unlikely that there would have been sharp differences between political decision makers and those whom they dominated. They were prestate societies in the sense that they had no permanent group of full-time governing officials. Nor did they have standing armies. When fighting was required, the adults suspended temporarily their economic roles as hunters and gatherers and assumed military roles. When the conflict was over, they returned to their usual roles. The existence of full-time governing officials and armies would not have been possible in subsistence societies, since there was not enough surplus production to support them. There was thus governance in the sense that people met and agreed upon rules and courses of action for their common affairs. But there was no state apparatus in the sense of an identifiable group of full-time governing officials. There may have been chiefs or head persons. But these worked and participated alongside of everyone else in producing the collective subsistence. Only in relatively late history, after tens of thousands of years of communal stateless existence, were chiefs able to begin to devote their full time to governance.

In the early communal societies there is little reason to believe that there were any separate families or kinship units. Children were most likely seen more as offspring of whole peoples or societies than of particular individuals. They grew up and identified primarily with their bands and knew no separate family loyalty or bonds of affection. Adults viewed children in an undifferentiated manner, making and knowing no distinction between their own progeny and those of other individuals.

One hypothesis holds that kinship units could not form in the earliest of societies because there were free sexual interrelationships between adults. If what nineteenth-century anthropologists labelled as promiscuous relations were institutionally acceptable, then it would have been impossible to determine the unobservable biological link between fathers and offspring. Free sexual relations would have functioned to strengthen communal responsibility for children and would have blocked division of the society into separate kinship units.

There is, however, no direct evidence that either supports or disproves this intriguing hypothesis that such a stage of communal sexual relations ever existed. As with much about the characters of early societies tens of thousands of years ago, the evidence necessary to confirm or reject hypotheses has long ago disintegrated. There are no known examples of contemporary communal peoples with completely free sexual relations.

What is known from the earliest societies from which there has been accessible evidence is that blood relationships became very important at some point in the institutional ordering of societies. As societies grew larger and transcended being small bands, kinship units differentiated themselves. Why they differentiated, causing the origins of the family, remains an area of mystery and great dispute.

One of the leading hypotheses, which was endorsed and spread widely by Frederick Engels (1884), was that the origins of the family and private property were interrelated. According to Engels, once private control over property in land or herds of animals became important, men who had accumulated such property wanted to be able to pass it on to their biological offspring. They could only do that if they had their own exclusive wife from whom they could be sure that births were their own progeny, hence the origin of monogamy. But as Engels observed, it was monogamy only for the woman because prostitution correspondingly arose as an institution available to the man.

Whatever their origins, once kinship units were established, they began to play key roles in the institutional ordering of societies. Through these kinship units property was accumulated and passed on. Within them, primary identities were formed. As societies grew, they divided themselves up into clans of interrelated families and individuals. Clans included those who could trace their biological descent to a common individual. Mates of biological clan members became members also, as their offspring would add to the pool of biological descendants. In clan-structured societies, the clan itself was a political structure within and through which decision making occurred.

For large parts of world history, religions have been central to the institutional makeup of societies. Religion, as Gerth and Mills (1953, p. 230) defined it, involves the use of "supernatural means—prayer and sacrifice, for example—in an effort to attain supernatural ends." The further back we move historically, the more religions and religiosity appear as centers of social gravity. It is of course impossible to know what the early communal peoples believed. What is known, or at least what can be reasonably assumed, is that they quickly developed explanations for the mysterious and awe-inspiring natural conditions that surrounded them, and magic and animism were among the first forms of explanation. In magic, supernatural means are used to control natural phenomena. The communal practitioner of magic invoked a chant or used an object assumed to be invested with supernatural powers to attain a naturalistic end—to ensure success in a hunt, to make it rain, or to cure a sick person. The more the end was achieved, the more the practitioner was believed to have access to supernatural powers. If the practitioner failed to achieve the end often enough—if the medicine man could not cure the sick or the rainmaker not make it rain—then he or she lost the presumption of having that power. In such societies, magic existed as a potentially available means for controlling a natural world in which humans with their primitive means of production and knowledge were largely powerless. Magic thus represented wishful thinking, a compensatory belief in potential power for humans who, at their stage in their technological development, were quite weak in the face of the thundering powers of nature. In animism, all elements of the physical world—humans, animals, rocks, trees, and so on—were believed to have indwelling spirits which gave them life. In some cases, the spirits were all different with each having its own separate identity. In others, the spirits were all emanations from one source that united every human and other creation in nature. Animism, like magic, arose in conditions where the low state of technological development condemned humans to little knowledge of and feeble control over the natural world that surrounded them. Instead of being able to gain knowledge of what constituted a tree, for example, myths were invented and then believed about the indwelling spirits of trees. Animism and magic went on to outlive the social and technological conditions which gave rise to them and continued as secondary thought currents within later social formations.

Formation of Surplus Products

The great economic and technological watershed of world history occurred when early societies began to be able to produce beyond their subsistence needs. Production of economic surplus products—products in excess of subsistence necessities—enabled them to grow into more complex societies. If food producers had surpluses, they could trade them to nonfood producers, such as tool makers, for their products. The more food surpluses there were, the more they made possible the development of specialized production roles within a widening horizontal division of labor. The more specialization of production roles became possible, the more time laborers had to devote to particular tasks, the more skill they developed, the more technology advanced, and the more overall production increased. Food surpluses also made possible the development of vertical class role differences and the support of state apparatuses. Dominating classes could live off surpluses that they expropriated from dominated laboring classes. State officials and armies could be supported from taxing the surpluses.

Development of regular surpluses brought with it population growth. It was out of economic surpluses that nonproducing children, old people, and the incapacitated could be supported. The more surpluses there were, the more they could be supported. Presurplus early societies had had to practice infanticide, since they were unable to support all of the children born. The production of regular surpluses also created more reliable and better diets for producers, resulting in healthier and longer lives. As death rates decreased and people lived longer, overall population increased.

In order for a state apparatus of even the most simple type to exist, the society had to be economically productive enough to produce a regular surplus. Laborers had to be able regularly to produce food in excess of what they themselves needed to subsist. Only from surpluses was it possible to draw taxes which were used to support state officials. Without surpluses, societies could not afford to support state officials who did not directly produce a share of the collective subsistence.

Advances in technological productivity, which took tens of thousands of years to develop, were thus also the necessary conditions for the formations of the first states.

Frederick Engels (1884) advanced the classic hypothesis that the formation of early states was intimately related, like the family, to the formation of private property and internal class divisions. At some point, communal ownership of the means of production broke up, with individuals and households appropriating for themselves exclusive controls over herds and lands. In time some individuals accumulated more herds or land than others. These herd- or land-rich individuals required a specialized organization of armed men to protect their wealth from the rest of society. Thus was born the state. Its birth indicated the definitive end of communal life. The community was now internally alienated. The rich needed and had the power to protect themselves and their wealth from the poor. The formation of private property made the emergences of class divisions and the state both possible and inevitable.

In Engels's account, the formation of regular surpluses, individual appropriation of means of production as private property, and the consequent development of class divisions between rich and poor were the necessary prerequisites and historical steps that led up to the development of the first state apparatuses. States thereafter were simply a necessary and essential facet of class-based societies. Their essential function was to protect privileged from less privileged classes. To protect the privileged, states had to concentrate in their hands military means of control and repression—arms, soldiers, jails, and so on. The core of state apparatuses was thus essentially military.

All of this is not to say that relations between communal societies had necessarily always been peaceful. Raids and plunder among neighboring peoples were common in many regions and periods, necessitating formations of communal militaries. But these were not full-time military forces. Communal warriors were also hunters, herders, and farmers. They were only part-time warriors, whose fighting abilities were called upon when necessary. The military skills of communal warriors were directed against outsiders. They were not used at the behest of an internal class of rich people because such a class did not yet exist. Communal warriors were warriors of whole peoples. Therein lies the difference between them and later state military forces. Only when class divisions forced the development of states would warriors be put to the services of privileged classes as opposed to whole peoples, and only then would they serve on full-time bases. Warriors would now be used both against foreign peoples and to maintain control over peasants, slaves, and other domestic lower classes.

Engels's theory remains as the most provocative account of early state formation. Other theorists may not accept one or another of its features, and they may reject entirely the way in which he tied it to general Marxist theory, but its hypotheses continue to be points of departure in anthropology and the social sciences in general for attempts to explain the formations of early states. There is broad consensus that state formation followed private appropriation of herds or land. There is less agreement over how and why that appropriation occurred. There is also little agreement over whether state formation was a function primarily of the development of class divisions, as Engels held, or more a natural function of growing population sizes and the evolution of complex divisions of labor.

The production of regular surpluses thus was the economic prerequisite for the giant step out of the primordial communal past. It was in many ways, though, a mixed blessing. It opened up the possibilities of extraordinary technological development in all areas. With the production of regular surpluses, the pace of technological innovations quickened greatly. There was now collective time available for thinking about and creating innovative solutions to production problems. But on the other hand, regular surpluses also enabled formations of wealth which could be and were privately appropriated and which were divisive of collective unity. Regular surpluses became the foundations upon which developed class divisions and alienation of humans from each other.

VILLAGE COMMUNITIES AND STATE SOCIETIES

As early peoples learned the techniques of horticultural planting, they settled into small village communities. Many parts of the world at different time periods show this pattern. Use of horticultural techniques of production increased the direct value of land and made possible the first formations of regular surpluses. These developments paved the way for class divisions both within the villages and between the villages and outside authorities.

The increasing value of land for production could and did become a source of class divisions within village communities. The practice of horticulture had of course changed the relationship between humans and the land. Instead of land being merely a surface on which to hunt and gather already existing food and other necessities, it became the irreplaceable direct means of production along with seeds and tools. Its rising importance within production provoked the disintegration of communal relationships. Class divisions emerged between large and small landowners, between relatively rich and poor. In a parallel fashion the same process of private property formation occurred among pastoral peoples and lead to class divisions between herd-rich and herd-poor households.

Regular surpluses, such as in the form of stored-up grain, were available to be taxed by outside authorities. The villages were drawn voluntarily or through conquest into a net of taxing relationships that a central authority, most often institutionalized as royalty, cast over far-reaching territories. Out of taxes collected from the village communities, state authorities supported their households, armies, and the tax collectors themselves. The clearest examples of these types of formations in ancient history occurred in Mesopotamia, Egypt, Northern China, the Indus Valley, and Persia in Asia, and among the Aztecs and Incas in the pre-Columbian Americas.[1]

These early state officials were a dominant economic class in themselves. They expropriated and lived off taxes collected from peasant village communities. Economic and political domination were fused in such state-structured societies. In addition, religious leaders often resided in and presided from royal centers, producing an even greater fusion of domination in economic, political, and spiritual life. By most accounts, the peoples of the ancient state societies were deeply religious. Temples dotted the land, their priests being parts of religious bureaucracies that

Pyramid at Chichén Itzá, Mexico, constructed c. 1000 A.D.

rose up to the very centers of societal power. In many cases the head of state was simultaneously the head of religion—both emperor and high priest. Hence political governance and institutionalized religion were organizationally fused at the top, indicating the importance of religion as a component of overall social control. The fusion of the pinnacles of Aztec religious, military, and political hierarchies is an example. One of the explanations for the depth of religiosity in these societies was that while they were politically centralized, they continued to be largely decentralized economically, producing the need for a strong unitary religion as an arm of state power. The more that people held common fundamental beliefs, the easier it was to govern them. Common, and deeply held, religious beliefs compensated for the lack of economic ties binding people together.

It was within these state societies that the first large cities grew, often around the royal centers of power; and within these cities the first systems of writing were invented, often for the purpose of keeping track of tax collections.

In many areas state authorities performed a clear economic function of overseeing the construction and maintenance of vast irrigation and river control systems, such as around the Nile, Tigris, Euphrates, and Yellow rivers. This led to their identification in some writings (see Wittfogel, 1957 for the classic treatment) as hydraulic civilizations. In some areas they developed to oversee the common defense needs of confederations of villages. In other areas they emerged strictly out of the prerogatives of conquest and empire. In all areas, once established, state rule became institutionalized and intergenerationally reproduced.

SLAVE SOCIETIES

The clearest examples of slave societies—in which slave labor accounts for the most amount of a society's surpluses—were in the ancient world (Greece and Rome primarily) from the sixth century B.C. to the fifth century A.D. and in the Americas (Brazil, the Caribbean islands, and the southern areas of the United States) from the sixteenth to nineteenth centuries. The institution of slavery existed in other societies, but alongside of and subordinate to other labor systems which accounted for greater proportions of the total surpluses produced.

Production of a regular surplus was the absolutely essential prerequisite for the development of slavery. Not even marginal slavery could exist without it. Slaves had to be able to produce enough for their own maintenance and an extra or surplus amount which was exploitable by their owners. Otherwise there would be no incentive to own slaves.

Technically a slave is a person whose labor is owned by another.

Poster, antebellum Missouri

The slave was not free to sell his or her labor to the employer who offered the most favorable terms (wages and conditions of work), as is a modern worker. Nor was the slave free to quit and change employers. Conditions of work need not be harsh for slavery to be in force. To be sure, there is no more accurate symbol of slavery than the whip. But there were also favored slaves—house slaves in the southern parts of the United States—whose treatment was more benign if none the less degrading; and there were owners who—as their descendants endlessly recount—"treated their slaves well." But a well-fed slave was still a slave. Oppressiveness of working and living conditions was a correlative of slave systems which was present in varying degrees. It was not a defining condition. What defined slavery was the treatment of the slave as property which was owned by another.

Chattel (meaning property) slavery was the purest and most literal form of a slave labor system. In it, the slave was unconditionally owned by the master for life or until sale to another master. There were other systems in which the slave condition was either hidden or not imposed as severely or permanently.

Peonage was a system of debt slavery which existed in a number of historical societies, including ancient Greece, Mexico in the nineteenth and early twentieth centuries (Turner, 1910; Meyer and Sherman, 1987), and in the postbellum ex-slave areas of the United States south (Daniel, 1972). In peonage, creditors claimed the future labor of debtors as payment for the incurred debt. There have been a number of cases in which the debt was so high that it could not be paid off during the life times of the people who incurred it. The creditor or succeeding generations of the creditor's family then laid claim to the labor of succeeding generations of the debtors' families.

Indentured servitude and contract labor are semi-slave systems in which labor is owned for a defined period of time. Approximately half of the white colonial working class came to British North America as indentured servants. Their passages from England had been paid for by ship companies and other labor suppliers in return for an agreement to be sold upon arrival as a temporary servant (usually for a period of seven years). After that they were freed. Most of the early Chinese population that migrated to the United States in the late 1840s and 1850s came as contract laborers, having had their passages paid for in return for future labor obligations. The labor of modern prisoners may also be analyzed as having a slavish or at least slavelike character, since they are neither free to quit nor to change employers for better working conditions. Whether or not they deserve to be in prison is irrelevant to the analysis of the economic type of labor that they perform.

Slave societies, as opposed to other types of societies in which there is marginal use of slave labor, exist when slave labor is the largest single source of economic surpluses. In order to account for that, slaves need not be the majority of the population. If the majority of the population were subsistence farmers and slaves were a significant but smaller proportion, as they were in ancient Rome, the antebellum United States south, and eighteenth- and nineteenth-century Puerto Rico, then a society was most accurately defined as being principally driven by a slave mode of production, since subsistence farmers produced little in the way of surpluses, and the numerically smaller slave labor force produced the bulk of societal surpluses.

Paradoxically, ancient Greece is known as both the world's first democratic and first slave republic. Democratic privileges were enjoyed though only by the free population, the slave population had no democratic rights. Estimates of the proportions of slaves in Greece vary considerably from one-third to 80 percent of the population (see Westermann, 1955; Andrewes, 1967; Anderson, 1974a; Vogt, 1975; and Finley, 1980). Most researchers agree that there were proportionately fewer slaves in the Roman Empire, but the scale of the institution was much larger (see Brunt, 1971). The Roman Empire covered a much greater area and included more people than did the Greek city-states. Where slavery was practiced in the Roman Empire it tended to be practiced on a large scale. In Greece, on the other hand, slaves were spread out in small numbers among many free families. In Rome, ownership of slaves tended to be concentrated among the rich. Large-scale Roman plantation slavery, for which there had been no precedent in Greece, became the prototype for slave production systems in the Americas.

Capitalism drove slavery in the Americas from the beginning (for the classic discussion, see Williams, 1944). Slaves produced a number of the early commodities that built early international capitalist trade. Sugar was the first and for many years the most important slave-produced commodity (see Klein, 1986). Slave-produced sugar from Madeira and other areas had been imported to Europe for some time before Columbus made his voyages to the Caribbean. Favorable soil and climatic conditions made the newly discovered Caribbean islands natural sites for the establishment of plantation economies to supply the international sugar market. At first, the local indigenous, or Indian, peoples were enslaved by their Spanish conquerors. But they dwindled as a labor supply within a generation due to disease, being killed resisting enslavement, or overwork on the plantations. At least one million Caribbean Indians perished during the period of establishment of the plantation slave economies. With sources of labor diminished to almost nothing, plantation owners turned to Africa as a more reliable source of labor, thereby stimulating the international slave trade which continued for three centuries more.

The economic effects of slavery were far reaching. In many ways slaves built the foundations of the modern capitalist economy.[2] The profits gathered from the slave trade and slave production contributed to the accumulation of capital which financed the Industrial Revolution. Slave-produced raw materials such as cotton fed the early textile factory systems in England and the northeastern United States. Slavery thus benefited capitalist development in the West. But the effects of the slave trade on Africa were disastrous. At least ten million members of west African societies were kidnapped, causing a continual drain of those societies' youngest and strongest laborers and condemning those parts of Africa to long-term structural underdevelopment and poverty, conditions which are still lived with today (see Rodney, 1972). Slavery also left a continuing legacy of racism and racial tensions in the areas where it was practiced.

FEUDAL SOCIETIES

The classic examples of feudalism developed in Europe between the decline of the Roman Empire in the fifth century and the beginnings of capitalist development in the thirteenth and fourteenth centuries (for the classic account, see Bloch, 1933, 1940). Feudal societies, or at least semi-feudal characteristics, have also been noted in Asia (Japanese history offers the closest examples), Africa, and Latin America.

European feudal societies had military origins. As the Roman Empire disintegrated, leaders of military bands took control over areas. They institutionalized their control by granting land to subordinate officers in return for loyal past deeds and the promise of loyal future service when needed. These land grants, or fiefs, came with the peasants who were living there. Loyal subordinate officers were essentially granted income-producing estates in return for pledging military support to the grantor in times of conflict or other need. The bond between grantor and grantee was intensely personal and theoretically the grant could be revoked at any time for acts of disloyalty. Landlords controlled their estates, but not as private property. Paradoxically, they had almost complete control over the peasants who worked on the estates, but they were not as free to do with the land as they pleased. They could not, for example, sell the land to another, since it was not ultimately theirs to sell.

The largest part of feudal surpluses was rent payments which landlords extracted from peasants. Historically, there have been three ways in which feudal peasants have paid landlords for the use of land. In the first, they have paid through their labor. That is, they have met rent obligations through working on land set aside for providing the landlord's household. This system, called *corvée* labor, prevailed in medieval Europe, where peasants usually worked for three days a week on their own plots and three days on the landlord's. In the second form of rent payments, quitrent or payment in kind, peasants delivered to the landlord a set quantity or proportion of the harvest. In the third, the peasant paid the rent directly in money.

In feudal economies there was very little actual buying and selling of products. These were essentially precommodity economies. Put differ-

Albrecht Dürer, Peasants at Market

ently, most of the goods that people produced did not become commodities, that is, items which are exchanged through market transactions. There could be village markets and traveling merchants, but their merchandise represented only a small proportion of total societal production. Most of what was produced was either directly consumed by peasant households or turned over to landlords as rent payments.

Strict hierarchy, ascription, and rigidity characterized feudal class relations. Landlords, through the control of the key means of production for agriculturally based societies—the land—were able to dominate majority peasant classes. Landlords saw themselves socially and ideologically as nobles and aristocrats (from Latin and Greek *aristos*, meaning "best," and *kratein*, meaning "rule"—hence "rule of the best"). The contemporary identification of aristocratic attitudes with snobbery is a carry-over from feudal days of landlords' self-rationalization for their class domination. Feudal ideologists assumed that people were born into their class positions, whether high or low, due to natural differences of superiority and inferiority, and that there they should remain. Contemporary notions of class mobility from humble to exalted positions or of the virtue of becoming a self-made millionaire were completely absent in feudal societies. Born a peasant, die a peasant was the rule. It was very exceptional for people to move out of the class position into which they were born. The attitude that lower classes are innately inferior is a feudal carry-over that continues in areas where feudal traditions are still strong.

Decentralization and personal loyalty characterized feudal political relationships. There could be centralized states which nominally covered large territories, but substantive political authority was seated and exercised locally by landlords who often organized their own private armies. The complete hegemony of local over central authority included legal affairs. Each feudal estate and area had its own law, which was made, interpreted, and enforced by the local landlords.

The Roman Catholic church monopolized the religious terrain of medieval European feudalism. As has been commented upon many times, by the ninth-century apogee of feudalism, the church's fundamental doctrines and even structures harmonized greatly with the basic feudal socioeconomic and political structures. Church doctrine was essentially conservative, advocating peasant docility and acceptance of the social order as natural. It placated their earthly misery with the promise of better things to come in the next life. In many ways the organization of the church, with hierarchical levels for priests, bishops, archbishops, cardinals, and the Pope, paralleled the hierarchical social and political organization of feudal society. The church also was a great landlord. One of the intended or unintended consequences of priesthood celibacy was that there were no heirs other than the church itself for the property that accumulated or otherwise fell into its hands.

Feudal societies were the contexts out of and against which capitalist societies developed. As such, it is not possible to understand how capitalism originated without an understanding of the European feudal past. For long periods of time, feudal and capitalist regions existed side by side within and between countries. Within countries, capitalist developments took place first in cities—the locations of markets—while estate economies dominated the countrysides. Capitalist developments proceeded at a much faster pace in some countries, resulting in uneven development. Today there are still countries with semi-feudal institutions. Class relations in most parts of Latin America, for example, have a much more feudal character than do those of the United States.

SUMMARY

The first societies developed between 40,000 and 100,000 years ago with the evolutionary emergence of the subspecies *homo sapiens sapiens* to which humans belong. These were technologically primitive and, for the most part, materially poor communal societies in which there was equal access to means of production and consumption of items. As such, they were preclass and prestate societies.

Most likely there was a long period in which communal bands lived together and took joint responsibility for children. At some point, for reasons that are the subject of continuing research and debate, individual families and clans became distinguishable. These families and clans then increasingly assumed key roles in the institutional ordering of societies.

Development of regular economic surplus products was the absolutely necessary prerequisite for the formation of societies with class divisions and state apparatuses of full-time governing and military officials. With developments of regular economic surplus products also came increases in rates of technological innovation and population growth.

There were three major precapitalist forms of class societies. In state societies, which covered large parts of the ancient world, a state apparatus made up of governing political, military, and often religious figures taxed peasant villages. In slave societies, which have existed in both the ancient and New Worlds, slave owners exploited surplus labor from their slaves. In feudal societies, which developed in Europe with the decline of the Roman Empire and have existed in various forms elsewhere, landlords dominated rent-paying peasants.

Key Terms and Concepts
(in order of presentation)

Communal society	Chattel slavery
Means of production	Peonage
Subsistence production	Indentured servitude
Nomads	Contract labor
Kinship	Feudalism
Clan	Fief
Religion	*Corvée* labor
Magic	Quitrent
Animism	Commodity
Surplus product	Ascription
Village communities	Peasant
State society	Landlord
Hydraulic civilization	Aristocracy
Slavery	

Endnotes

1. There is a long and controversial literature which identifies these as Asiatic modes of production. Karl Marx (1858) introduced somewhat in passing the concept of the Asiatic mode of production, touching off debates over its validity and usefulness which continue today in both Marxian and non-Marxian circles. For approaches which use the concept of the Asiatic mode of production, see Godelier (1969, 1978) and Krader (1975). For an interpretation of pre–Soviet Russian society as an example of an Asiatic mode of production, see Kagarlitsky (1988). For an analysis which rejects the validity of the concept of the Asiatic mode of production, see Anderson, (1974b). The term *state mode of production* confers the same general meaning but has the advantage of not being geographically restrictive.
2. For an interpretation that slavery was not instrumental in capitalist development, see Weber (1923).

Chapter Five

Contemporary Societies and the World Economy

In the half-millennium since 1500—the year marking both the entrance of developed capitalist socioeconomic structures on the world stage and the beginning of modern world history—two large-scale socioeconomic dramas have taken place. In the first, rising capitalist societies overcame the obstacles and resistance of precapitalist orders. In the second, capitalist societies confronted and ultimately prevailed over the challenge posed by socialist societies during this century.

ORIGINS AND SPREAD OF CAPITALIST DEVELOPMENT, 1500–

Capitalist societies are market societies in which a private class of individuals and families owns the major means of production—factories, banks, land, retail outlets, and so on—and employs laborers for wages or salaries with the primary goal of reaping profits. In capitalist societies all elements of production processes—raw materials, tools, land, buildings, and products—take the form of commodities which are exchangeable through market transactions.

Elements of capitalistic organization had existed on the margins of precapitalist societies for thousands of years. Ancient Greece and Rome, for example, had had some market trade and employment for wages of laborers in urban workshops. But in precapitalist societies, the majority of products were not sold or exchanged through markets—they were instead consumed by their producers or simply handed over as payments to landlords or tax collectors—and the majority of labor was not performed for wages.

The first societies that were substantially capitalist emerged in the sixteenth century in Europe after a protracted and successful struggle to transform feudal conceptions of labor, land, and production. Peasant labor in feudalism had been tied to particular estates. Peasants neither worked for wages nor were they free to change landlords. Feudalism, hence, knew no markets for peasant labor. Land, the central means of production of feudal societies, was not considered to be private property which could be bought or sold. It was rather a grant or fief from an over-lord that had to be continually renewed. The landlord was not free to sell it. Finally, with most goods being directly consumed by peasant households or turned over to landlords as rent, feudal economies saw lit-tle distribution of products through markets. For capitalism to become entrenched as a way of life, peasant labor would have to be released from the estates and become available for employers to hire for wages, land would have to become privatized and available for sale, and goods would have to be distributed through markets. Put more succinctly, labor, means of production, and goods would have to be commodified.

For several centuries capitalist development proceeded unevenly in Europe. Cities were its stronghold, while the countryside remained backward and feudal, resulting in a European social landscape that was a patchwork of capitalist cities surrounded by feudal rural estates. The cities formed at port and crossroads locations. Some were complete-ly new, forming around commercial activities which began to increase in the late feudal period. Others were revived old Roman cities which had declined greatly in size and importance in the feudal period. In time, city-based commercial, productive, and financial activities gained enough hegemony to pull the countryside into the vortex of capitalist development. By the sixteenth century, many European countries could be described as having predominantly capitalist socioeconomic structures.

But at the same time, the political structures of these early European capitalist societies were still largely feudal. They had been formed during the feudal period and were occupied by the landed aris-tocracy, producing a contradiction between rising capitalist and old landed interests over state policies. Further capitalist development required transformation of the state, which was accomplished through revolutions and civil wars in England in the seventeenth century, France in the eighteenth century, and Germany in the nineteenth century.

Externally, the capitalist world market took shape by the early six-teenth century and drew into its vortex widely disparate countries and regions. Its centripetal pull was felt far and wide. Western Europe was its original center. As capitalist production and market activities developed there into a solid system, traders, explorers, soldiers, and mission-aries ventured out into Asia, Africa, and the Americas establishing peripheral markets and production sites. The world capitalist system thus developed at first with Western Europe as its center and Asia, Africa, and the Americas as its periphery. By the early twentieth centu-ry, the United States and Japan had joined Western Europe as centers of world capitalist development.

Today, capitalist societies continue to be based on commodity-pro-ducing economies in which the dominant class exercises power by own-ing and controlling the most important means of production, including factories, mines, banks, and stores. Wealth invested or available for investment in the means of production is capital. Those who own signifi-cant shares of capital are capitalists. The major part of the labor force of developed capitalist societies is made up of workers who are obliged to work for private or state employers because they do not own their own means of producing an income. Aside from the class positions of capital-ists and workers, which arise from the central class division of capitalist societies, there have also been other class positions occupied by peas-ants, small-business owners, and employed professionals and managers (see Chapter Eight).

There seems to be no necessary political form to the state for capi-talist economies. Historically, they have functioned under governmental systems which have ranged widely from highly autocratic to relatively democratic. The most essential task of the government of a capitalist society is to have economic policies that protect and promote the general business climate. Whether that is done through autocratic or relatively democratic means is secondary. In a parallel sense, the economic poli-cies and programs of the governments of capitalist societies have widely varied depending on the parties in power. Conservative parties, such as the Republican Party in the United States and the Conservative Party in Great Britain, use capitalistic means as much as possible. Their pri-mary goal for government policy is to improve the operating conditions for private businesses. Liberal parties, such as the Democratic Party in the United States, and social democratic parties, such as the Socialist Party of France, on the other hand, have used semi-socialistic means. That is, they have at times adopted policies leading to state ownership of some industries and the establishment of publically financed services, such as socialized health care systems.

In reality, there are no purely capitalist countries, since in all of them the government to one degree or another participates in economic planning, ownership, or provision of services. Countries where state par-ticipation is relatively high, such as Sweden, can be justifiably classified as having to some extent mixed economies. But so long as private inter-ests own and control the largest share of a society's major means of pro-duction and state ownership is secondary, the society retains a predominantly capitalist economic structure, albeit mixed with significant state ownership and economic participation.

The universal market is a central characteristic of predominantly capitalist societies. The more capitalism initially developed, as we have seen, the more it transformed the fundamental elements of production— labor, means of production, and produced goods—into commodities, resulting in the eventual institutionalization of the labor, capital or stock, and goods markets which are now central features of all capitalist societies. This commodification of all central economic activities has had far-reaching cultural consequences. Many critics argue that consumerism has become a central feature of daily life, reducing all other life goals to secondary importance. Massive advertising campaigns inflate consumer desires and divert attention from more substantive life questions.

Capitalist firms have two primary goals: to make as much profit as possible in the short run and to grow through accumulating capital in the long run. The two goals are related since profits are the immediate source of capital formation. Corporate executives may be personally concerned about the public interest, but they believe that they can only serve it if their companies are profitable. But it is not necessarily clear that, as Charles Wilson, secretary of defense for the Eisenhower administration and a former top corporate executive once put it, "What's good for General Motors is good for the U.S."

Class and social inequality are structural principles of all capitalist societies. Some, such as Durkheim (1893) and, more recently, Herrnstein and Murray (1994) argue or imply that such inequality simply reflects natural inequalities among people. Others argue that unequal distributions of income and wealth function to stimulate labor productivity.[1] Inequality as a motivating force, by implication, means that one strives to become rich both for its own sake and also to avoid the penuries of being poor. It is a race and competition which in the extreme encourages each man or woman to be out ultimately for himself or herself alone. Inequality and individualism thus come together as guiding capitalist principles.

The more relative income and wealth upper classes receive, the less relative income and wealth lower classes receive. Upper-class standards of living are, it follows, to some extent gained at the expense of other classes' standards of living. In the United States, the richest 10 percent of households receive more income than that of the combined bottom 50 percent. But the distribution of income for the total world population is even more unequal. The richest countries, with about 10 percent of the world's population, have more income than countries which contain 85 percent of the world's population (World Bank, 1994, pp. 162 and 220).

However, despite inequality being a firm principle of capitalism, individual capitalist societies vary considerably in terms of the actual extents of inequality that exist within them. In distribution of income terms, Brazil, where the richest 10 percent of the population take 46 percent of all national income, is the most unequal society. By way of contrast, in Sweden, the richest 10 percent take only 21 percent of the national income, less than half of what their Brazilian counterparts take (World Bank, 1994, p. 236).

Large corporations and the state are today the major actors in developed capitalist economies. Up through the nineteenth century, family-owned capitalist firms were the dominant actors. By the early twentieth century, the family-owned firm had been supplanted in importance by the joint stock corporate form. The corporate form arose as a result of fierce competitive struggles among individual capitalist firms in the middle and late nineteenth century for dominance over markets. By combining the capitals of many individual capitalists, corporations could achieve greater size and economic power than family-owned firms. By the early part of the twentieth century, governments became increasingly involved as accumulators of capital through taxation and as employers in the otherwise capitalist-directed economies. State and private economic activities are now thoroughly intertwined, with state-collected taxes often being used to finance private corporate activities. State contracts, such as for the production of military goods, are one of the major sources of business for private corporations. James O'Connor (1973) estimated that in the United States as much as one-third of the labor force was employed directly or indirectly (through private employers financed by government contracts) by local, state, and federal government. Even between 1980 and 1992, when the conservative Reagan and Bush administrations attempted to cut back government spending, federal spending as a proportion of gross national product actually rose from 18.2 to 25.5 percent (World Bank, 1994, p. 181). Thus, regardless of whether governments increasingly adopt policies of engaging private contractors to perform functions that they formerly performed directly themselves—for example, engaging a private contractor for garbage collection rather than using city-owned trucks and employees—it is still state revenue that is financing the economic activity.

THE SOCIALIST CHALLENGE, 1917–1989

The eruptions of the 1917 Bolshevik and 1949 Chinese revolutions, in the world's largest and most populous countries respectively, challenged the continued development of the capitalist world economy. The subsequent spread of socialism to other countries in Asia, Africa, and Latin

America further constrained capitalist development. Through the 1950s, those countries largely developed outside of the parameters of international capitalism, leading to the sharp demarcation of separate capitalist and socialist worlds.

In the socialist countries the state, rather than a private capitalist class, owned and managed the majority of the major means of production (factories, banks, large stores, etc.), and pursued policies directed in the short run toward narrowing the range of social inequality and in the long run toward establishing full social equality.

Socialism and communism as ideologies had roots which went back several centuries. They developed as coherent alternatives to capitalism in the early nineteenth century and received their greatest intellectual development with the epochal works of Karl Marx and Frederick Engels (see Chapter Six). By the late nineteenth century, Marxism was firmly established in Europe as a major ideological and political alternative. Everywhere Marxist ideas and political parties struggled openly or clandestinely, as circumstances dictated, against the capitalist organization of society. By the early twentieth century, large socialist or socialist-oriented opposition parties had developed in Germany, France, England, Italy, and other countries.

In Russia, V.I. Lenin (1870–1924) led the Bolshevik Party through two decades of a mostly illegal and underground existence against the decrepit and highly repressive Czarist state to the successful 1917 revolution. The Bolshevik Revolution inaugurated development of the world's first socialist society. Since 1917, revolutions in China, Cuba, Vietnam, and other countries were either led by Marxists or adopted Marxist ideas in the aftermaths of their triumphs. Following World War II, the Soviet Union used its military power to dominate Eastern Europe and ensure that those republics would be both allies and socialist. After their devastating experience in the war, in which upwards of thirty million of their citizens were killed during the Nazi invasion and occupation, the Soviets sought to create in the Eastern European countries a buffer zone between themselves and the hostile NATO (North Atlantic Treaty Organization) countries. Of the Second World countries, however, socialist policies enjoyed the least support in Eastern Europe, owing to the experience of having had it imposed upon them out of the geopolitical needs of a nearby superpower rather than having freely adopted it as a result of their own revolutionary experiences.[2]

The original conception of socialism, as envisioned by Marx, Engels, and Lenin, was that it would be a transitional form of society between class-based capitalist and classless communist modes of production. The future communist mode of production would be based on common or state ownership of means of production, altruistic motivation (the new communist man or woman), full social equality and highly developed forces of production which would allow goods to be distributed according to need—"from each according to their ability, to each according to their needs." The future communist mode of production would represent the overcoming of the major problems that have plagued societies for millennia—scarcity and class division. Material abundance and human solidarity would make a higher level of social existence possible. That was the promise. But neither Marx nor his followers thought that it would be possible to immediately construct a communist mode of production after the overthrow or collapse of a capitalist society. It would require decades, perhaps centuries, of preparation through the buildup of forces of production (including technological capacities) and transformation of overall social consciousness from individualistic to altruistic motivational bases.

There would thus have to be a socialist transition period between the end of capitalism and the achievement of communism. The state would own and manage according to central planning of society's major means of production, but neither full equality nor distribution strictly according to need would yet be possible. "From each according to their ability, to each according to what they produce" would be the principle of necessity that guided production and distribution in socialist modes of production. At the same time though, it would be possible to progressively narrow gaps in class standards of living and distribute some necessities such as food, health care, and education according to need rather than market principles. But, according to Lenin (1918), capitalist interests would never peacefully permit such changes to take place. Therefore, in order to carry them through, the revolutionary state would have to be able to force them through by taking the form of a dictatorship of the proletariat.

Up through the end of the 1980s, socialist countries were primarily structured according to those economic, social, and political principles. The various socialist states owned and managed according to central planning their societies' major means of production. Class differences remained, but in diminishing proportions. Extensive social programs were constructed to allow free access to health care and education. Food prices were subsidized, making food affordable to all citizens. Though supplies of many types of food fell short of demand, resulting in long lines at stores, those supplies were relatively equally distributed. One of the most notable achievements of socialist—compared to capitalist—societies was that they succeeded in effectively eliminating unemployment.

Overall, the socialist countries achieved impressive health standards, as Table 5–1, based on World Bank data, indicates. In comparing world health conditions in 1988, the year before the Eastern European countries began to abandon socialism, it was clear that the level of income of a country was related to the health conditions that it could afford. But the type of socioeconomic structure, whether capitalist or socialist, also significantly affected average health conditions. By far the high-income capitalist countries enjoyed the world's highest average health conditions. But in the low- and middle-income levels where there were socialist societies, those societies had significantly better health conditions, as measured by infant mortality rates and life expectancies, than did their capitalist counterparts.[3] The differences were especially significant in low-income countries. Socialist low-income countries had average infant mortality rates less than one-third those of the low-income capitalist countries (32 compared to 99), and people lived on average 16 years longer. Much of these differences were due to China, which both had a large population and a well-developed public health system, being classified as a low-income country. Thus, socialist public health systems impressively outperformed their capitalist counterparts in middle- and low-income countries. At the same time, though, socialist economies were not as impressive in meeting other, less essential consumer demands.

The Soviet Union and its Eastern European allies ran into deep troubles in the 1980s. Communist leaders had originally assumed and promised that the standards of living in those countries would catch up

TABLE 5-1 Countries of the World, 1988

	Population		Average infant mortality rate (per 1,000)	Life expectancy at birth (years)
	(millions)	Percent		
High Income				
Capitalist	784.2	15.4	9	76
Socialist	0.0	0.0		
Middle Income				
Capitalist	995.9	19.5	54	66
Socialist	434.1	8.5	22	71
Low Income				
Capitalist	1,727.5	33.9	99	54
Socialist	1,158.5	22.7	32	70
World	5,100.2	100.0	57	64

Note: Identified as middle-income socialist countries were the Union of Soviet Socialist Republics, the Democratic People's Republic of Korea, the German Democratic Republic, Czechoslovakia, Cuba, Bulgaria, Albania, Poland, Hungary, and Yugoslavia. Identified as low-income socialist countries were China, Vietnam, the Lao People's Democratic Republic, and Mongolia.

Source: Calculated on the basis of data in The World Bank (1990, pp. 178, 232, and 244).

to those of the prosperous West. But by the 1980s, it was clear that this goal was increasingly elusive for a number of perhaps historically unavoidable reasons, causing socialism to increasingly lose public credibility. In the 1970s, socialist countries, such as Hungary, began to take out Western loans to finance projects that would speed up development and increases in standards of living. These projects though failed to live up to expectations, resulting in their loan repayments becoming extra burdens in the 1980s on already shaky economies (see Phillips, 1990). In addition, in the Soviet Union economic growth slowed down considerably during this period (Sweezy and Magdoff, 1990), thereby stagnating improvements in public standards of living.

In large part, the 1980s economic downturns in the Soviet Union and Eastern Europe followed a pattern in the world economy: The rich economies grew and prospered while poor economies and those of the socialist countries suffered sharp reverses. The response within significant proportions of the public in the Soviet Union and Eastern Europe was to blame the economic downturns on the socialist structure of the economy and the governments in power. In low- and middle-income capitalist countries, the response was to blame whatever political party was in power. In the late 1980s and early 1990s, for example, not one incumbent regime was electorally returned to office in Latin America.[4]

The pivotal year 1989 saw the unleashing of massive economic and political changes in Eastern Europe and the Soviet Union. Facing perceived stagnations in economic growth and other problems, those countries loosened their states' grips over economic life, hoping that this would lead to economic revival. In some cases that included significant privatization of state-owned companies, in others it was restricted to allowing market forces to operate in areas that had formerly been managed by central planning. In some countries, such as Poland, the goal was an all-round restoration of capitalism, in others, it was the establishment of a larger private sector within a mixed economic structure. In 1990, the German Democratic Republic (East Germany), the most prosperous of the Eastern European socialist countries, ceased to exist as an independent country after essentially allowing itself to be annexed by West Germany. In 1992, the Soviet Union dissolved itself as an entity with its major component parts, including Russia, Ukraine, Belarus, and Georgia, reforming themselves as independent countries. Politically, the republics of the old Soviet Union and Eastern Europe abandoned the one-party concept of the state and instituted multiparty parliamentary forms. All of these changes, taken collectively, resulted in a significant restructuring of the postwar world political order and the strengthening of capitalist tendencies within it.

At the same time that epochal changes swept through the Soviet Union and Eastern Europe, the major Third World socialist countries,

China, Cuba, and Vietnam, maintained independent courses of action. All three continued as one-party states, though allowing significant private sectors of their economies to develop.

THE WORLD ECONOMY AFTER 1989

It has thus become an increasingly capitalist new world order since 1989. But it is not a homogeneous world order. There remains a steep stratification of the just over two hundred countries in the world today that stretches from First World comfort and opulence to Third World misery and squalor. At the same time, the global poles of wealth and poverty intersect within countries as well, for rich countries contain poverty and poor countries contain elites who are rich by anyone's standards. Together, all of these societies make up the contemporary variegated world economy, an overall economy within which the economies of all societies have been increasingly drawn together and subsumed.

Theories and Classifications

From the 1950s until the 1980s, the divisions in the world economy between capitalist and socialist countries on the one hand and between rich and poor countries on the other led to the practice of speaking in terms of distinct First, Second, and Third World countries. The tripartite conceptualization of the world economy originally contained five connotations: political alliances in the cold war, type of socioeconomic structure, technological stage of development, geographic location, and standard of living. First and Second World countries were politically and militarily aligned with the United States and the Soviet Union, respectively, while Third World countries were nonaligned. The superpowers competed for influence within Third World countries and for their votes in international forums such as the United Nations. First World countries had capitalist economies, Second World countries had socialist economies, and Third World countries were largely capitalist. Technological stage of development, geographic location, and standard of living were thought to largely overlap. Western countries—those in North America and Western Europe—were industrial and enjoyed the world's highest standards of living. The Eastern countries—the Soviet Union and its allies in Eastern Europe—were also industrial and had the world's second highest standards of living. Third World countries, which were located in Asia, Africa, and Latin America, were mainly agricultural and poor by international standards.

Three-worlds terminology was evocative of much of the bases of international divisions between countries within the world economy, but it was not without ambiguities and problems. Political alliances, economic systems, technological stages of development, geographic locations, and standards of living ceased to be as clearly correlated as they were in the immediate postwar years. Japan, in Asia, became one of the world's most prosperous countries. Many formerly agricultural Third World countries industrialized rapidly but still remained poor. It was always unclear where to place underdeveloped socialist countries, such as Cuba and China. They were politically and economically in the Second World, but technologically and geographically in the Third World, and their standards of living varied greatly. South Africa was both a First and Third World country. The minority white population enjoyed First World standards of living, while the majority black population had Third World living standards. And, since the 1989 and early 1990s transformations of the Soviet Union and Eastern Europe, there was no longer a separate Second World or socialist camp.

The strength of the three-worlds classification was its evocation of the reality that contemporary societies differed significantly both according to their socioeconomic structures and their standards of living. Those differences could be seen statistically through the 1980s. Of the 163 countries in the world in 1986, 148 with just over two-thirds of the world's people were capitalist, and 15 with nearly one-third of the world's people were socialist. But after 1989 the percentage of the world's population in socialist societies declined dramatically and with it a large part of the utility of the three-worlds classification. The term *Second World* is now completely obsolete except for historical uses. The terms *First* and *Third World* continue to be used though less so than in the past.

A number of sociologists also conceptualized international differences in terms of First, Second, and Third Worlds (see, for example, Horowitz, 1966), and today the terms *First* and *Third World* continue to be ingrained in international social science. But other sociologists classified international differences in different, more directly sociological, terms.

Since its inception, modern sociology has been concerned with the steep stratification of the world's countries. Just as societies are stratified along the lines of upper and lower classes, the world's societies are stratified along the lines of rich and poor countries. But as with many other issues in sociology, there are sharp disagreements and controversies regarding the causes and policy implications of this stratification.

On one side of this debate stands what can be loosely termed the *modernization approach*. According to its proponents—which include the World Bank, the International Monetary Fund, and the U.S. Agency for International Development, as well as a number of sociologists, countries are poor because they remain institutionally mired in premodern, largely agrarian-based structures. If they wish to develop and achieve more prosperity, they must modernize their institutional structures according to the already proven institutional structures of the advanced industrial societies. Among the policy implications of this approach are that poor countries should increase their economic integration with the modern dynamic parts of the world economy through export-oriented trade and hosting foreign investments. The latter will facilitate technology transfers from the advanced countries which will serve to accelerate economic modernization.

Beginning in the 1960s, a number of other sociologists began to increasingly challenge key premises of the modernization school. In particular, they questioned whether the motives of the rich countries for being involved in the poor countries were as benevolent as the modernization theorists assumed, arguing instead that the rich countries had for centuries economically exploited the poor countries and continued to do so. By the 1970s, many of the proponents of this latter perspective developed what came to be known as the *world-system approach*.

Shannon (1989, p. 20) states that the world-system approach begins from the premise that "an identifiable social system exists that extends beyond the boundaries of individual societies or nations." It is therefore "a mistake to view the world as a set of independent societies that can be analyzed by focusing solely on events internal to them." Sociologists who work within this perspective generally also view the contemporary world-system as having begun to take shape in the sixteenth century; as being stratified between core, semi-peripheral, and peripheral countries; and as having exploitative relations between the core and other countries.

The core countries in the world-system now include the United States, most of the Western European countries, and Japan. As the world's most economically and militarily powerful countries, they are able to dominate the world economy and international politics. This domination has allowed them to economically exploit other countries, the proceeds of which have significantly bolstered their own economic development and prosperity. During the development of the world-system from the sixteenth century to the present, different countries have occupied the center of the core, such as Holland in the seventeenth century, Great Britain in the nineteenth century, and the United States in the twentieth century. At the other extreme are the peripheral countries which include most of the countries of sub-Saharan Africa, China, India, and other Asian countries, and some Latin American countries. They are the world's economically weakest as well as poorest countries. Their main importance for the world economy has been mainly as agricultural and raw material exporters. In between the two extremes in the world-system are semi-peripheral countries, which include the major Latin

American countries, the poorer countries of Western Europe, the former-ly socialist Eastern European and Soviet countries, northern African and Middle Eastern countries, and the rapidly industrializing countries of Southeast Asia (Taiwan, South Korea, Hong Kong, Singapore, and Malaysia). These countries contain both core-like and peripheral-like features. A minor but significant part of their economies is industrial-ized, while other parts remain agricultural or labor intensive.

Most world-system theorists (such as Amin, 1980; and Wallerstein, 1974, 1984) thus contend that it is no longer valid to think in terms of entirely separate national economies. Rather, they contend, there is now essentially one international capitalist economy—the world-system—which is the basis on which national economies function. Individual countries have progressively lost sovereignty over their own economies. The more powerful the capitalist world-system grows, the more it, rather than national economies, becomes the arena of economic interests and class forces. The core economic powers seek to remove remaining barriers to the complete unification of the market by promoting free trade policies. By lowering tariff walls they seek complete access to all markets. At the same time though, political power continues to be based in states. In a sense, a fragmented political order of different state pow-ers overlays the increasingly unified capitalist world-system.

Uniting all attempts to classify and understand international dif-ferences is a concern over development. In general terms, a developed society is one that has an economy that is productive enough to generate sufficient national income to ensure average standards of living that meet modern expectations. However, there is no international consensus on how exactly to define what constitutes development for statistical purposes. One of the major indicators of development is gross national product per capita, but it is not a sufficient indicator, since an economy can, for example, have high oil revenues without having developed an industrial base. Average health conditions, including infant mortality rates and life expectancies, are other indicators of development. But here a developing country can achieve health conditions equivalent to those of the developed countries without having an equivalent industrial base. Cuba's impressive public health system, for example, has resulted in Cubans enjoying First World health standards, but its economy is not sufficiently developed to insure First World living conditions in most other respects. There are thus multiple issues involved in defining the development of a society. Consequently, there are also multiple statisti-cal indicators of the degree to which a society is developed in different respects with there being no consensus on which or which group is the most important.

The World Bank and the United Nations are today the two major international agencies involved in development and the major sources for international comparative statistical information. The World Bank (1994) classifies countries as upper, middle, and low income on the basis of their gross national product per capita. Over one-half (59 percent) of the world's people live in low-income countries, a little over a quarter (26 percent) in middle-income countries, and a relatively small minority (15 percent) in upper-income countries. As Figure 5–1 illustrates, there is a sharp inequality in the distribution of world income. The high-income countries, with just 15 percent of the world's population, receive 79 percent of total world income while the low-income countries, with 59 percent of the world's population, receive a slight 5 percent of total world income. Over the last several decades, world income inequality has been growing significantly, as indicated in Table 5–2. Between 1970 and 1991 the share of the gross world product—an indicator of share of world income—associated with the richest 25 percent of the world's population increased by 9 percent while that associated with the poorest 25 percent decreased by 37 percent. According to another study (United Nations Development Programme, 1994), between 1960 and 1991 the ratio between the income shares of the richest and poorest 20 percents of the world's population rose from 30 to 61 to 1.

Here it is important to make two mitigating observations. First, growing income inequality does not necessarily mean growing misery at the bottom. The material living conditions of the poorest members of the world economy have, on average, improved over the last decades, as they have had greater access to basic survival necessities of food, shelter, and medical care. Second, a 61 to 1 ratio between the incomes of the richest and poorest 20 percents of the world's population does not produce a similarly large ratio between their standards of living. Greater income, after the point at which basic necessities are provided for, only produces a marginal improvement in living conditions. The average rich person cannot live 61 times as long as the average poor person. Similarly, a low income will usually go a lot further toward the provision of food and housing in a poor country than it will in a rich country.

TABLE 5–2 Changes in the Share of Gross World Product by Quartiles of the World Population.

	1970	1991
Poorest 25 percent	2.7	1.7
Second 25 percent	3.2	1.9
Third 25 percent	13.6	9.0
Richest 25 percent	80.5	87.4
Total	100.0	100.0

Source: United Nations (1994, p. 249).

FIGURE 5–1 The World Economy by Income Class, 1992

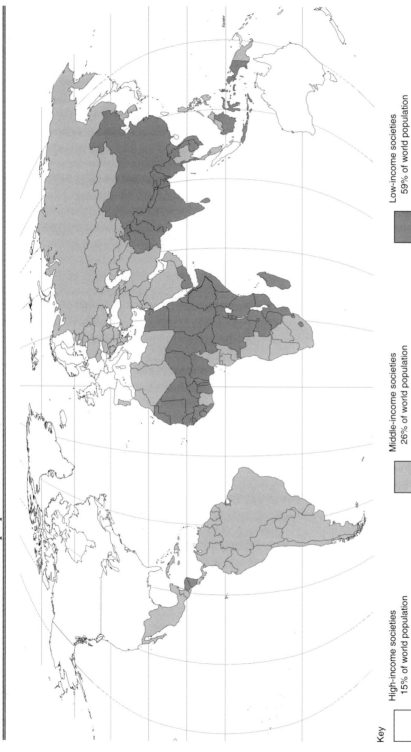

Key

High-income societies
15% of world population
79% of world income

Middle-income societies
26% of world population
15% of world income

Low-income societies
59% of world population
5% of world income

Source: Calculated on the basis of data in The World Bank (1994), pp. 162 and 214.

Nevertheless, between high- and low-income countries in the 1990s there are vast differences in health conditions, one of the central indicators of standards of living. The average infant mortality rate for developed societies in the 1990s is seven per thousand live births, while that for low-income developing societies is seventy-three, over ten times as high. Life expectancies correspondingly rise and fall according to prosperity and level of development with people in developed societies living fifteen years longer on average than people in low-income developing societies (World Bank, 1994, pp. 162 and 214).

Up until recently, the United Nations classified countries as either developed or developing, largely on the basis of international convention. This was because of the difficulties and controversies involved in establishing an exact statistical criterion. Until the beginning of the collapse of the socialist economies, the UN included as developed countries both what were then called First and Second World countries. Currently, the UN (1993, 1994) classifies economies as developed market, in transition, Asian socialist, developing, and least developed.[5] The developed market economies are the traditional First World economies.[6] The economies in transition are the formerly socialist countries of Eastern Europe. The Asian socialist countries are China, North Korea, Vietnam, and Mongolia. The developing countries are the rest, with the UN singling out forty-seven countries as "least developed." For the discussion that follows, we will follow this classification.

Developed Societies

Since the end of World War II, there has been a general movement toward equalization of living conditions in most of the developed societies—the U.S., Canada, U.K., the Western European and Scandinavian

TABLE 5–3 Countries of the World, 1992

	Population (millions) Percent		Average infant mortality rate (per 1,000)	Life expectancy at birth (years)
Developed Market	851.8	15.6	9	76
In Transition	394.5	7.2	27	70
Asian Socialist	1,282.4	23.5	35	70
Developing	2,399.1	43.9	66	63
Least Developed	537.0	9.8	112	50
World	5,464.8	100.0	52	66

Note: For information on individual countries, see appendix.

Source: Calculated on the basis of data in UNICEF (1994, p. 65).

countries, Japan, Australia, and New Zealand. In the immediate post-war period the average standard of living in the United States was much higher than that of any other country. Since none of the war was fought on its soil, the industrial capacity of the U.S. emerged from the war unscathed and poised to capitalize on that advantage in world trade for the next two decades. During the 1960s though it became increasingly clear that Japan and the other developed countries had largely rebuilt their industrial capacities to the point that their products could seriously compete with those of the U.S. in world trade. As a result, from the 1960s forward, the gap between average living conditions in the U.S. and the rest of the developed countries steadily closed to the point where today, the U.S. has dropped to sixth place in average incomes behind Switzerland, Japan, Sweden, Denmark, and Norway. Some interpret this development as representing a decline in the economic power of the United States, others see it more as the intentional result of U.S. political policy. According to Nau (1990), U.S. policy makers sought to construct a postwar relationship of relative equality with the other developed countries in order to avoid debilitating conflicts in their common cold war struggle against the Soviet Union and the other members of the socialist bloc.

Overall, the developed countries today tend to have the following common characteristics:

(i)   high gross national products per capita, average incomes, and capital accumulations;
(ii) in many cases, a history of having held colonial possessions;
(iii) labor forces that are increasingly concentrated in service production as opposed to industry or agriculture; and made up of employees as opposed to small business owners, including farmers;
(iv) significant exports of finished goods and capital.

The economic strength of the developed countries results from the accumulated capital and economic infrastructure (roads, underground pipes for delivery of water and removal of sewage, energy delivery networks, etc.) that they have built up over several centuries at advanced stages of technological development. The accumulation of capital and buildup of economic infrastructure which now underwrite high standards of living in the developed countries took at least two hundred years of grueling labor by their working classes in which upwards of sixteen- to eighteen-hour workdays were common, occupational death and maiming rates were high, and wages were low. There is also considerable evidence that through conquest, colonialism, and slavery, the contemporary developed countries pumped profits and resources out of the Asian, African, and Latin American areas that they dominated which significantly augmented and quickened the rates of their total accumulations of capital.

Two great shifts have occurred in the distributions of labor forces in developed countries.[7] The first shift was from agricultural to manufacturing employment. Rising levels of agricultural productivity decreased the need for labor in the countryside and thereby made it available for employment in urban-based factories, a shift that was accompanied by considerable social trauma, including the ruin of many small farmers and their families. The second shift has been from manufacturing to service, administrative, and sales employment. Rising levels of industrial productivity have decreased the need for factory, mill, and mine labor, making it available for employment in services (entertainment, recreation, restaurants, repair) and administration (clerical and managerial), and sales. The two shifts in the distributions of labor forces have occurred unevenly across the developed economies. They are more advanced in some regions and countries than others. The United States economy has progressed farthest in this direction.

As a result of the second shift—from manufacturing to service, administrative, and sales employment—the developed countries are at advanced industrial or what some, such as Bell (1973), call postindustrial stages of development. Production of virtually all necessities of food, clothing, housing, and even health has become industrialized. Tractors, harvesting machines, and food-processing machines make food production a literal industry. Workers operate sewing and sophisticated computer-guided cutting machines to mass-produce clothing. House builders no longer dig ditches and frame houses completely by hand. They have machines that speed and simplify those processes. First World hospitals are now loaded with testing and other types of machinery. Bell (1973) and others argue that the Western economies are no longer properly industrial. They have rather become postindustrial because the labor saving caused by the application of machinery to the production of material goods has resulted in the shifting of the majority of the labor force away from basic production tasks. Factory workers, for example, increased steadily in the early stages of industrial development, but now with more productive machinery it takes fewer to maintain the same and even higher levels of production. Factory workers therefore have begun to decrease as a percentage of total First World labor forces. As their per capita production has gone up, owing to better machines, fewer of them are needed in the economy.

Just as mid-nineteenth-century England had the most advanced industrial economy in the world for that time and therefore showed other countries what the main outlines of their economic futures would bring, the postindustrial distribution of the United States labor force today portends what is likely to come in most First World countries.

The economic significance of postindustrial labor force distributions though can be misleadingly overestimated. Regardless of where a labor force is distributed, agricultural and industrial production are still the essential components of any contemporary economy. No economy, no matter how advanced, can exist without food and other material goods. It is precisely because of the high productivity of agricultural and industrial workers that economies have surplus capital to invest in services, administration, and sales.

Virtually all economic sociologists note rising rates of corporate concentration across the developed economies. As dominant corporations have grown larger, they have become more powerful, allowing them to squeeze out competitors and capture increasingly greater market shares. At the same time, as large businesses have grown larger they have taken over markets that were formerly served by small businesses, resulting in sharp declines in the proportions of farmers, retail store and restaurant owners, and other small business owners in labor forces. Correspondingly, as the proportion of small business owners has declined, the proportion of employees has grown. Over 90 percent of the labor forces of the United States and Canada, for example, are now made up of employees. A century ago in both countries farmers, Main Street merchants, and other independent owners predominated in the labor forces. But the twin forces of capital accumulation and corporate concentration progressively squeezed most of them out.

The growing power of top corporations has significantly restructured the economic landscape of the twentieth century. Top corporations dominate national and often international economies as multinational or transnational corporations. The more dominant a First World corporation is in its own domestic market, the more likely it is to have extensive investments and sales abroad.

Corporate power is exercised internally as well as externally. That is, owners and managers in a private property and market society have considerable power to design and control the workplace according to their interests. In 1914, Henry Ford revolutionized factory production by developing the assembly line, which enabled the mass production of a single standardized product at low cost. He coupled that innovation with paying his workers the then relatively high wage of $5 for an eight-hour workday. Ford challenged the old Robber Baron practice in the United States of paying workers as little as possible with the argument that for his company to prosper his workers had to be able to afford to buy the cars that they built (Harvey, 1989). Ford's argument was similar to that of the economist John Maynard Keynes who urged central governments during the Great Depression of the 1930s to redistribute some income to the lower classes in order to allow them to become effective consumers and thereby stimulate the market for factory products.

Ford's assembly line innovation spread from automobiles to other industries rapidly with resulting all-round increases in production and overall factory wages for the next several decades, but increases in production and wages were at the expense of workplace satisfaction. Sociologists, such as Blauner (1964), interviewed workers and found that assembly line work was highly alienating. The restriction of each worker to performing a simple, repetitive motion—once a minute on most automobile assembly lines, day in and day out—produced boredom and precluded any sense of creative satisfaction with the work done. Accounts by workers themselves, such as Boggs (1963) and Hamper (1991), provided further confirmation that assembly line work was inherently alienating.

Since the 1970s, a number of sociologists and other commentators have used the term *Fordism* for this period of capitalist development which was characterized by mass assembly line production of standardized products for mass markets. These commentators detected the beginning of a shift in that decade in some industries in the developed countries toward *post-Fordist* strategies. By that, they meant retooling assembly lines so that they could vary their products to satisfy different consumer demands with shorter production runs for each. Instead of producing one standardized car, an automobile factory now attempted to develop a number of different models that appealed to different segments of a more diversified market.

The concept of post-Fordism, as it is used to characterize the leading edge of the present period of industrial development, is similar to the concept of *flexible accumulation*. By that it is meant that corporations now must increasingly develop ever-changing strategies to remain competitive and profitable as the global economy becomes more competitive. In large part, the shifts from Fordism to post-Fordism and from fixed to flexible accumulation began to occur in the 1970s because Western European and Japanese industry had recovered enough from the damages of World War II to seriously challenge U.S. industry for domination of the world market. U.S. industry had been the undisputed leader of world industrial production for the two decades following World War II, precisely because it had emerged from the war unscathed. With the world economy by the 1990s even more competitive, industrial survival came to depend upon ever more efficient production techniques.

In this context, Japanese industry developed the concept of *just in time production*. Factory production traditionally relied on keeping a warehouse well stocked with its raw materials so that they could be used as needed—*just in case production*. But Japanese managers observed that this was a costly practice that drove up overall production costs. They accordingly developed a new system whereby a factory ordered only the quantity of materials that it needed and only when it needed them, thus avoiding the costs of over-ordering and warehousing. With lower production costs, the company could sell at a more competitive lower cost.

On one level, flexible accumulation strategies have produced more efficiency and a greater array of products that are tailored to meet increasingly diversified consumer demands—the great diversity of clothing colors and styles is one example. But, it was only a logical next step to adopt a flexible policy toward worker security. If corporations are flexible in how they design products and their production, they are also increasingly flexible with where they produce, with which workers, and under what conditions of job security.

In the former, more fixed accumulation, period factory production was rooted in particular communities. Once the factory was built, the corporation had to remain there. Thus, generations of workers enjoyed a certain stability and job security. There might be layoffs during recessions, but these were only temporary. The factory remained in town and rehired its laid-off workers once the economy improved. But as the global economy has become more competitive and the costs of constructing new factories have decreased, corporations have found that they can lower labor costs by moving from high- to low-wage areas. In the United States this has meant a shift of industrial production from the largely unionized high-wage northeastern and midwestern states to the largely nonunionized low-wage Sunbelt areas of the south and southwest. Internationally, it has meant the shift of labor-intensive industries, such as those in clothing and electronics, from relatively high-wage First World countries to Third World areas, including Mexico and the Caribbean islands.

Even where corporations maintain workplaces in the same communities, they have increasingly used rising proportions of temporary and part-time workers, who are paid low wages, receive few if any benefits, and have little if any job security, in order to lower labor costs. In the United States labor force as a whole the proportion of temporary and part-time workers has grown. Thus, a decreasing unemployment rate—which has traditionally been taken to be an indicator of economic recovery and increasing prosperity for the labor force—may mask deeper problems, as when a laid-off $17-an-hour worker, who had had a relatively secure job for twenty years with medical, retirement, and other benefits, is only able to find a new job that is part-time at $8 an hour with little security and no benefits. In visual terms, the labor force can be regarded as having a core of full-time workers with relatively secure positions that pay enough to maintain a relatively decent standard of living and a periphery of low-paid part-time and temporary workers. Flexible accumulation has been accompanied by a growth of the periphery at the expense of the core.

Workers have two traditional avenues to mitigate their employers' power and pursue their own workplace interests. First, they can form their own labor unions, which directly negotiate working conditions and rates of pay with management, reserving the threat of laying down their tools and striking as their ultimate bargaining chip. Rates of labor force membership in unions vary considerably between the First World countries. The United States has the lowest rate of membership, 19 percent, which is down from a high of over 30 percent after World War II. The comparable rate for Spain is 40 percent, Italy 45 percent, England 50 percent, and Sweden 90 percent (Hayward, 1980, p. 4). Second, they can pursue political action to pressure elected government representatives to pass legislation favorable to their interests, such as government-enforced minimum wage and occupational health and safety standards. In both cases, their effectiveness largely depends on their degree of organization.

Economies in Transition

The economies in transition, as classified by the UN, are Albania, Bulgaria, the Czech Republic, Hungary, Poland, Romania, Slovakia, and the countries of the former USSR (the Russian Federation, Ukraine, Georgia, Lithuania, Estonia, Latvia, Moldovia, Belarus, Armenia, Azerbaijan, Kazakhstan, Tajikistan, Uzbekistan, Kyrgyzstan, and Turkmenistan). Altogether, 394.5 million people, 7.2 percent of the world's population, live in the economies in transition. (The United Nations does not currently classify China as an economy in transition.)

In 1989, as these countries abandoned socialism and reentered the capitalist world market, the key social question was whether their average standards of living would gradually improve toward those of the First World or sink toward those of the Third World; or would there be different experiences for different sectors and classes of the populations, with some being launched toward First World prosperity and others relegated to Third World immiseration as new economic and class forces transformed and pulled apart the old order? By 1993 some answers to this question emerged.

Minimally, the transitions from socialism to capitalism in these countries required three fundamental changes: First, a shift from public to private ownership of a significant number of enterprises, resulting in the creation of a new class of entrepreneurial capitalists and the widening of class differences. Second, a shift from centralized state control and administration of prices to letting them be determined by market forces, resulting in immediate increases in prices for basic necessities which had been kept low. Third, in order for privately owned companies

TABLE 5–4 Economies in Transition, Regional Averages

	1989	1993
Infant mortality rate per 1,000	17.6	17.0
Life Expectancy at birth in years	70.7	70.5
Crude Death Rate per 1,000 population	11.4	12.4
Unemployment rate	0.1%	10.3%
Poverty Rate	16.5%	39.2%
Index of Real Income	100.0	74.9
Index of Income Inequality	100.0	106.0
Index of Crime Rate	100.0	168.6

Source: Calculated on the basis of information in UNICEF (1994b).

to compete in market conditions they had to have the authority to dismiss unprofitable workers, resulting in Eastern Europe's first postwar experience with significant unemployment. Thus, the predictable costs of the transition were increased inequality, higher costs of living, and allowing unemployment to develop.

By 1994, the first extensive United Nations study of the economies in transition (UNICEF, 1994b) documented the extent to which inequality, costs of living, and unemployment—the negative costs of capitalist development—had indeed increased (see Table 5-4). The study examined the experiences of the nine countries of Russia, the Ukraine, Albania, Bulgaria, the Czech Republic, Slovakia, Hungary, Poland, and Romania, which contained three-quarters of the total population for all of the countries involved in the transition to market economies. In these countries average unemployment rates jumped from far less than 1 percent in 1989 to over 10 percent by 1993. Meanwhile, as unemployment was rising, so too was the cost of living, as the average prices of food, rent, clothing, and other necessities rose significantly.

While the upper strata have benefited greatly by being able to garner high incomes and amass fortunes that were not possible during the communist era, the majorities have seen their average living conditions deteriorate dramatically. Per capita real income fell by a quarter. The most severely impacted saw their living conditions slide into poverty. If in 1989, an average of 16.5 percent of people were poor in the nine countries, by 1993 the rate had more than doubled to over 39 percent. If at the top, new millionaires were created while average incomes declined and poverty expanded at the bottom, it is not surprising that income inequality grew by an average of 6 percent in the region.

The generalized social deterioration has been accompanied by an explosion of criminal activity, with the crime rate for the region more than doubling between 1989 and 1993. During the same period the male murder rate increased by 79 percent.

One of the most disturbing impacts of the transition has been an increase in death rates. In the same way that the statistical association between rises in unemployment and death rates has been studied (see Chapter One), the association between the transition and rising death rates is now being examined. Between 1989 and 1993 the average crude death rate (deaths per thousand) for the nine countries jumped from 11.4 to 12.4. Cumulatively in that period 800,000 more people died than if the nine countries had maintained the same death rates as they had in 1989. These avoidable deaths represent the most severe consequences of the transition. Indeed, according to the report, "the mortality and health crisis burdening most Eastern European countries since 1989 is without precedent in the European peacetime history of this century."

So far, mortality rates have not risen for infants and children. The highest increases in mortality have been borne by males between the ages of twenty and fifty-nine for, according to Giovanni Andrea Cornia (UNICEF, 1994b, p. vi.), three transition-related reasons: "widespread impoverishment, erosion of preventive health services, sanitary infrastructure and medical services, and social stress." A surge in heart and circulatory diseases, stimulated by the stressfulness of the social adaptation crisis, accounts for about 80 percent of the excess deaths. There have also been a significant 25 percent increase in suicide rates. Cornia concludes that:

> Most of the additional mortality due to heart problems, suicide, homicide, alcohol psychosis and cirrhosis of the liver appears to be related to an explosive rise in social stress, a condition which arises when individuals have difficulty responding to new and unexpected situations. Greater poverty, unemployment, migration, divorce, separation, loss of relatives, lack of hope, loss of self-esteem, insecurity about and fear of the future, increase in criminal offenses, conflicts at work and in the family are the main sources of stress. This "social adaptation crisis" has been exacerbated by the collapse of the political, social and economic organizations which framed people's lives for 50 or more years—a collapse entailing loss of national pride, a widespread sensation of meaninglessness and loss of purpose. (UNICEF, 1994b, p. vi)

In 1989, the great promise of this transition was that it would unleash pent-up economic forces that would result in significant growth and eventual prosperity. But the light at the end of this transitional tunnel has grown more distant as the economies have had negative growth rates for most of the initial years of the transition, postponing any generalized realization of benefits for average citizens. Because of the economic and social deterioration in living conditions, leftist opposition parties with links to the former ruling communist parties have made major unexpected electoral comebacks in Bulgaria, Poland, Hungary, Ukraine, Lithuania, and Belarus.

Asian Socialist Societies

The United Nations maintains a separate classification for the four Asian countries—China, Vietnam, North Korea, and Mongolia—which have had a history of communist party rule and socialist economies. Nearly a quarter of the world's people live in these countries.

There are important differences between the countries though in terms of the extent to which each has either begun a transition to capitalism or adopted market reforms. Mongolia has made the most radical changes, to a large extent following the example of the former Soviet Union, to which it was closely aligned. In 1990, it gave up communist rule and initiated a transition to capitalism. Its experience with the transition has been largely similar to that of most of Eastern Europe, as reported above. Privatization and market reforms by 1993 resulted in a 20 percent drop in gross domestic product and a one-third decline in personal income (*The Economist*, November 26, 1994, p. 37). China and Vietnam, despite communist party governance and maintaining the socialist label, have both significantly opened their economies to market reforms and foreign private investments. In both, the former socialist models characterized by strict state ownership and central planning have been abandoned for new models which seek to create a kind of market socialism in which the economies can modernize and grow at faster paces. Whether the reforms can function within the context of original socialist goals or will prove to be simply steps toward the development of full-blown capitalism remains to be seen. North Korea remains largely immune to market reforms, maintaining the socialist model of strict state ownership and central planning that has guided its development since the 1950s.

Developing Societies

Developing societies—concentrated for the most part in Asia, Africa, and Latin America—contain within them 85 percent of the world's population. Between the poorest and relatively most prosperous there are more differences in average living conditions than among developed societies. The ratio between average incomes in Ireland, the relatively poorest of the developed countries, and Switzerland, the richest, is about one to three. In contrast, the ratio between average incomes in the low-income and upper-middle-income developing countries is about one to twelve. The difference in the Western Hemisphere, for example, between average living conditions in low-income Haiti and upper-middle-income Argentina is much greater than between those of the United States and Canada. Caution must therefore be exercised in drawing generalizations about developing countries. Nevertheless, it can be concluded that developing societies tend to have:

(i)   low gross national products per capita, average incomes, and accumulations of capital;
(ii)   in many cases, a history of having been a colony;
(iii) relatively high proportions of their labor forces still in agriculture;
(iv)   significant imports of finished goods and capital in the form of loans and investments; and reliance on the export of a limited number of raw materials and/or goods assembled in foreign-owned factories.

The typical developing country has a foreign-dominated economy, with its economic functioning being dependent on continual infusions of foreign investments, loans, and aid from developed countries, for which it pays a high price in profit repatriations, interest payments, and economic sovereignty. Their economies thus function at, and are integrated into, a lower level of the world economy and division of labor.

There is considerable dispute among social scientists regarding the historical origins of Third World inequality. Dependency theorists, such as Baran (1957), Frank (1969), Wallerstein (1974), and Amin (1980), hold that as the capitalist world economy developed, European countries seized control through conquest, colonialism, and other forms of domination of large parts of the economies of Asia, Africa, and Latin America. They forced Third World economies into molds which served their own development interests. The agriculture of Caribbean island countries, for example, was oriented toward production of sugar for export to the international market rather than all-round production for domestic needs. Modernization theorists, such as Rostow (1960), Hagan (1962), and Eisenstadt (1966), hold that the causes of Third World poverty and misery are primarily domestic, lying in precapitalist and preindustrial institutional structures which are antithetical to development needs. Still other social scientists blame rising population growth rates for continuing poverty in the developing countries (an argument that will be treated in detail in Chapter Eleven).

Overall, since 1970 there have been improvements in average living conditions in developing countries despite the existences of extreme poverty and starvation in some areas. Infant mortality rates for the first year of life, for example, fell between 1970 and 1992 from an average of one hundred to sixty-five per thousand live births, indicating significant average improvements in nutritional and public health standards. However, at the same time, the gap between the average living conditions in the developed and developing countries has been growing rather than declining. If in 1980 the 18 percent of the world's people who lived

in upper-income countries consumed 77 percent of total world income, by 1992 the proportion of the world's people living in the upper-income countries had declined to 15 percent, but they consumed a larger 79 percent of the total world income (World Bank, 1988, 1994). Hence, while absolute living conditions are improving on average in developing countries, the gap between them and those of the developed countries continues to widen.

Virtually all development theorists agree that agricultural efficiency is the primordial first step of development. The more technologically efficient the agriculture of a country, the more agricultural workers can be shifted to industrial and service production. The more developed a country, the relatively fewer the number of agricultural workers in its labor force and the lower the proportion that their product represents in the total economic product. Hence, the World Bank (1994, p. 166) reports that agricultural production accounts for only 3 percent of the total gross domestic products of all developed economies, compared to 29 percent for low-income economies, nearly ten times as high. Agricultural workers take up an even larger proportion of the labor forces of low-income countries, since agricultural products generally have lower market values than other products.

The more agricultural the technological level of a country, the more it must rely on agricultural exports to finance its imports and development projects. This is a problem, since the prices of agricultural commodities have tended to decline over time relative to those of other goods on the world market. Hence, countries dependent on agricultural exports are in a precarious position in the world market.

While the prices that food exports fetch on the world market have tended to decline relative to those of other commodities, those are often prices that are higher than what could be gained from domestic sales. Hence, many, especially large, landowners in developing countries have reoriented their production from domestic to more lucrative First World markets. In a number of cases this practice has caused shortages and corresponding price rises for food staples of the poor. In Brazil, large landowners shifted production from black beans, a diet staple of the poor, to soy beans which fetched a higher price on the international market. As the production and therefore supply of black beans decreased, their domestic price went up and out of the reach of many poor people. In Central America, landowners have turned crop land into pasture land on which to graze cattle, ultimately destined to feed the voracious appetite in the United States for fast-food hamburgers. Export-oriented agricultural practices since the 1960s have forced Mexico to import corn and beans, the traditional diet staples of the poor (see Barkin, 1990 and Philip L. Russell, 1994).

The problem of food exports is linked to the larger problem of reliance on raw materials versus finished product exports. In 1970, 72 percent of all exports from developing countries were in the form of agricultural, fuel, mineral, and other raw materials, whereas 73 percent of all exports from developed countries were in the form of finished industrial goods. As with food exports, over time the value of most other raw materials, with oil being a notable exception, has declined on the world market, while that of many finished goods has increased. Hence, many developing countries found the value of their exports decreasing at the same time that the costs of their imports were increasing. As a result a number have adopted development strategies of shifting away from reliance on raw material exports. By 1992, only 47 percent of developing country exports were in the form of raw materials, a sharp decline from the 72 percent recorded in 1970 (World Bank, 1994, p. 190). However, it still remains true that a large number of especially low-income developing countries remain reliant on a small number of raw material exports for the bulk of their export incomes. Raw materials make up the majority of the exports for twenty-eight out of the thirty-five low-income countries for which the World Bank has information.

As development strategies have inevitably led toward industrialization and away from reliance on raw material exports, many developing countries, such as India, Mexico, Brazil, and Argentina have in recent years substantially industrialized large parts of their economies. But this industrialization has not automatically resulted in closing the gap between First and Third World living standards. As developing countries have increased their rates of industrialization, the developed countries have increased their competitive advantages in the world market by controlling the production of high technology goods.

The effects, whether beneficial or harmful, of First World investments and loans to the developing countries have been the subjects of considerable debates. First World multinational corporations own and control large parts of the industrialized sectors that do exist in developing countries. While the multinational corporation provided the initial capital and technological expertise to set up the employment-providing activity, much of the profits are repatriated to the source country, precluding their use for the development benefit of the host country.

Foreign investment in industry has taken a number of different forms in the developing countries. In some cases it involves setting up a factory within the host country to avoid having to pay tariffs. Volkswagen, for example, set up a factory in Brazil in order to be able to sell its cars there at a competitive tariff-free price just as it and Japanese auto makers do in the United States. In other cases, it involves setting up a factory solely in order to take advantage of low-priced labor with the resulting goods being sold primarily on the world—as opposed to the developing country's—market.

In this latter respect, since the 1960s multinational corporations from the United States, Japan, and other developed countries have set up large numbers of assembly plants in Taiwan, South Korea, Mexico, Singapore, Haiti, and other developing countries. In a typical arrangement, components of a pair of blue jeans are designed and produced in the developed country. They are then shipped to the Third World factory for assembly. The final product is then exported back to the developed country for sale. The Mexican border cities as well as large parts of the Caribbean Basin and Southeast Asia are now major locations for these types of assembly plants.

Foreign investors, along with host Third World government officials and developers, maintain that these factories bring needed technology transfers, industrial development, and employment opportunities. Critics counter that they are only a new form of exploitation in a more highly developed international division of labor. They argue that these working classes are now producing products as well as profits that will be exported rather than serve national development needs.

In the Mexican border cities, such as Mexicali, Ciudad Juárez, and Matamoros, these types of assembly plants are called *maquiladoras* and they have displaced the tourism industry as the major sources of employment. Up until recently, over 80 percent of the *maquiladora* work forces were young women in their teens and twenties. As the *maquiladoras* have expanded in the 1990s they have added more male workers, but most still rely primarily on the labor of young women, who now make up about 60 percent of the work forces. *Maquiladora* managers believe that young women are more dexterous than men and therefore more suited to quick-paced assembly work. They also believe that they are more docile and thus less likely to cause labor problems.

Maquiladora industrialization has had a number of social consequences. On the positive side, it has produced economic growth in the border cities which has contributed to improvements in standards of living. But with employment opportunities more available for young women than men in the Mexican border cities, family roles have been severely disrupted. Women who had not been part of the paid labor force are now in it, while many men have had to remain at home unemployed. Tensions have grown within families, and the rate of male family desertion is high. Considerable numbers of children are now being brought up only by mothers who work full days in the *maquiladoras*. Adequate child care facilities are in chronically short supply. It is thus clear that *maquiladora* industrialization has been experienced as a mixed blessing in the border cities.

Since the 1970s, payments of interest on loans held by foreign banks, governments, and multilateral agencies (primarily the International Monetary Fund and the World Bank) have surpassed repatriation of profits from investments as the largest source of the foreign drain of potential Third World capital. For the most indebted of the developing countries, foreign debt service (principal and interest) payments represent a serious hemorrhaging of potential development capital. Mexico and Argentina, for example, in 1988 made payments on their foreign debts equal to 49.5 and 37.3 percent respectively of their total export earnings. Overall for the developing countries, foreign debt service was 20.6 percent of export earnings (World Bank, 1994, p. 206).

From the point of view of First World financial interests, the danger that lurks in the Third World debt crisis is that there will not be the wherewithal to keep up with payments, thereby causing interruptions in cash flows. From the point of view of developing countries, the heart of the crisis is that debt servicing payments are increasingly made at the expense of providing necessities for domestic populations as well as having funds available for investments in development.

A World Bank report (cited in Farnsworth, 1988) estimated that in 1988, as Third World living standards were declining sharply, the seventeen most indebted countries (which included Nigeria, the Philippines, and most of Latin America) paid back First World countries and lending agencies $31.1 billion more than they received in new loans and investments. The report indicated that the net loss resulting from debt servicing payments exceeding new loans had been increasing steadily for some time. The net loss of $31.1 billion in 1988 was triple the 1983 loss. For the developing countries as a whole, the report concluded, First World countries were taking out $18.2 billion more than they invested in new loans.

In a number of cases in the 1980s severely indebted countries reached the point where they did not have sufficient export earnings to maintain payments, resulting in crises. News of the Third World debt crisis in the 1980s was in and out of the newspapers, like a sore on the world economy that festered and receded alternatively but never fully healed. The International Monetary Fund (IMF), an organization to which most countries belong but which is largely controlled by the developed countries, managed the debt crisis on a country-by-country basis. The customary IMF resolution of a country's debt crisis was to require that it adopt an austerity plan that included lowering government spending and wages. The intended effect of each IMF-prescribed austerity plan was to lower costs of production of the country's exports and make them cheaper on the world market, thereby increasing demand for them and overall export earnings. Part of the increased earnings could then be used to resume payments on the country's debt. In return for adopting an austerity plan, the IMF gave the green light to other international lenders to resume short- and long-term loans. In the short run, cash flows resumed their circulations. But in the long run, new loans only added to the accumulating mountains of debt as well as mortgaging the future financial sovereignty of the country.

By 1988, it was clear that the mounting debt of many Third World countries was unpayable and that attempts to force payments through imposition of IMF austerity programs were provoking civil disorder. In February 1989, riots against the IMF austerity program for Venezuela resulted in three hundred deaths. U.S. Treasury Secretary Nicholas Brady then announced a new policy, known as the Brady Plan. First World lenders and multilateral agencies, including the IMF and the World Bank, would forgive part of the principal of loans in return for the country's adopting a more favorable climate for foreign investment and free trade. Specific agreements would be worked out on a country-by-country basis.

Between 1989 and 1992, largely as a result of the new policies associated with the Brady Plan, there has been some relief given to the

Third World debt problem. Overall, debt service payments from the developing countries declined by about 10 percent, giving some new breathing space for economic recoveries. There has been though a trade-off in that in return for the debt relief, the developing countries that have entered into Brady Plan arrangements have had to accept increased foreign economic domination. There is also no guarantee that debts will not mount again to critical levels.

An additional problem facing most developing countries is the tendency for their upper classes to claim unusually high proportions of national income for their own consumption. The standards of living of the Third World rich rival and sometimes surpass those of their First World counterparts. To maintain those styles and standards of living, they corner as much of the national income as they can, precluding the distribution of many necessities to the majority poor; and much of that income is spent out of the country on shopping trips to Europe and the United States, vacations, luxury imports, and foreign schooling for their children. The Third World rich hence attempt and largely succeed in living a lifestyle that is equivalent to that of their First World counterparts. But the cost of that lifestyle, especially the part that is spent outside of the country, weighs heavily on the country.

We can summarize the relationships between technological development, foreign economic domination, and living standards in the developing countries as follows. First, while Third World stages of technological development are low compared to those of First World countries, it is no longer accurate to simply state that Third World countries are agricultural, while First World countries are industrial. That simple dichotomy leads to the false conclusion that industrialization automatically increases living standards. Second, foreign First World interests through investments and loans significantly dominate much of developing economies and thereby siphon off profits and interest payments. Instead of contributing to domestic capital formation and growth, these profits and interest payments rebound to the benefit of the already stronger First World investor economies. Largely as a result of the first and second conditions, the living standards of developing countries remain low compared to those of developed countries.

New Problems

The sudden and dramatic collapse of the Second World following 1989 accelerated all of the tendencies toward capitalist development on a global scale. With socialist economic systems no longer existing as an alternative or threat, central governments have increasingly adopted free trade and privatization policies to reform and rationalize their economies according to capitalistic principles. There is no question that free trade policies such as the North American Free Trade Agreement (NAFTA) and the General Agreement on Tariffs and Taxes (GATT), by removing governmental attempts to regulate trade and investment, will lead to a significant rationalization and growth of the world economy.

But that growth could have significant negative as well as positive social consequences. On the positive side, the prices of consumer products will decrease. On the negative side, though, as already indicated above, the increasingly free circulation of capital will be at the expense of worker security. A further worrisome feature of the coming period will be the effect of economic growth on the environment. Increasing industrial production to feed a rapidly growing world economy could seriously deplete the earth's nonrenewable natural resources.

A more immediate problem accompanying the restructuring of the world order has been the outbreak of increased political violence. When the cold war suddenly and unexpectedly ended, symbolized most dramatically by the coming down of the wall separating West and East Berlin in 1989, there was an unleashing of optimism that world peace would result. In the United States, long burdened by the world's largest military budget, there was talk of a peace dividend, that is, that military spending could now be substantially reduced and the savings could be used to cut taxes or expand social services or both. Talk of the peace dividend though quickly vanished as a series of wars exploded in the formerly socialist and other areas. The end of the cold war was accompanied by an increase, rather than decrease, in the number of people killed and otherwise suffering harm from wars.

The cold war, for however much it rested on a balance of thermonuclear terror, provided a bipolar order to the world-system. Despite George Bush's quick announcement in 1991 of a new U.S.-led "new world order," it has become clear that in fact a vacuum exists that has allowed antagonisms to explode into savage wars. Hence, Sadako Ogata, the United Nations High Commissioner for Refugees, in commenting upon the 23 million refugees that wars produced in the middle part of this decade, commented:

> Right after the cold war we thought all the problems would be solved. We didn't realize that the cold war had another aspect to it—that the superpowers provided order or pressed order on their respective zones of influence. And so ethnic or religious or national conflicts, whether within the Communist bloc or the Western bloc, had little chance of exploding. So now, post-cold war, we are seeing the explosion of much more traditional, dormant, maybe pre-World War I kinds of ethnic conflict." (*New York Times*, August 8, 1994, p. A5)

Refugee camp, Rwanda, 1994

SUMMARY

Capitalist societies—market societies in which the dominant economic class dominates by virtue of owning the central means of production in industry, finances, and commerce—grew steadily from the sixteenth to the early twentieth century, by which time they existed in most parts of the world and were interlinked through investment and trading relations.

In the early twentieth century, socialist revolutions began to remove countries from the capitalist system. Socialist societies—planned societies in which the state owned the central means of production—at their height contained nearly one-third of the world's population.

The post–World War II world economy was conventionally divided into three overall types of societies: First World capitalist countries which had high levels of technological development and standards of living, Second World socialist countries which had middle levels of technological development and standards of living, and Third World capitalist and socialist countries which had low levels of technological development and standards of living. For most of the latter half of the twentieth century socioeconomic structures within the world economy thus lay on a continuum between capitalist and socialist. Those near the middle of that continuum could be best described as having mixed economies. But in societies with substantially mixed economies, the balance of economic control either tipped in the direction of state or private ownership, making them either predominantly socialist or predominantly capitalist.

There are times when more occurs that affects the course of world history in a single year than in the previous forty: 1989 was such a world historical year. That year saw the beginning of the dismantling of socialism in the Soviet Union and Eastern Europe and an acceleration of market reforms in China. If in the decades before 1989 the world was sharply divided between capitalist and socialist societies, after 1989 almost all of the world's societies could be called either capitalist or in the process of becoming capitalist. By the mid-1990s, even those countries where communist parties remained politically in power—most notably China, Cuba, and Vietnam—had adopted significant capitalist-style reforms.

The internal class character of capitalist countries is now reflected internationally in the world economy by sharp differences in average standards of living between developed and developing countries. Modernization and other theorists maintain that Third World living conditions will improve as those societies promote economic growth policies by integrating themselves more thoroughly into the world market and adopt institutional reforms patterned after what has worked in the developed countries. Critical development theorists counter that the developed countries promote and maintain exploitative trade and investment relations with the developing countries that slow their ability to develop and improve living conditions.

In addition to the traditional problems that afflict the poor countries, the world order after 1989 has seen the development of new problems, including a severe economic and social deterioration in the economies in transition, heightened forms of economic insecurity as economies are more thoroughly rationalized according to capitalist models, and explosions of ethnic and nationally based tensions into wars in the formerly socialist and other areas.

Key Terms and Concepts
(in order of presentation)

Capitalism	Development
Socialism	Labor Force
Infant mortality rate	Alienation

Three Worlds	Fordism
Modernization	Flexible accumulation
World-system	Foreign debt

Endnotes

1. The most cited sociological analysis that defends income inequality is by Davis and Moore (1945). They argued that societies needed highly educated professional skills. In order to motivate persons to attain them—which involved investing extra years of education during which incomes were deferred—societies had to offer as a reward the realistic prospect of ultimately receiving significantly higher than average incomes. For criticisms of Davis and Moore's analysis, see Tumin (1953) and Szymanski (1983).

2. There is a large body of literature, mainly in the Western countries, which maintains that the countries that identified themselves as socialist were not socialist at all. Trotskyist-influenced writers claimed that the Soviet Union was a state capitalist society in which workers were rendered powerless by bureaucratic domination. Others, such as Sweezy (1980) and Kagarlitsky (1988), hold that the Soviet Union was neither capitalist nor socialist but rather a different, as yet to be fully understood, postcapitalist class formation. Still others maintained that these societies did not conform to Marx's notion of socialism. All of the above types of criticisms shared a common dislike of how the self-identified socialist societies were organized and functioned. While more hostile critics argued that the societies were undesirable because of defects in Marxian theory itself, Western socialist-oriented critics sought to preserve the validity of Marxism itself while distancing themselves from how it had been applied. Quite obviously, these societies also had their defenders who argued that those formations were both desirable and reflected valid applications of Marxian theory.

3. Infant mortality rates—the number of children who die before their first birthday per thousand live births—and average life expectancies in years are the two central measures of health conditions in comparative development research. Infant mortality rates rise and fall according to public health conditions—such as availability of potable water and sanitation—and access to medical care. The more developed and prosperous the society, the more these are available.

4. That is, with the possible exception of Mexico where the ruling Partido Revolucionario Institucional (PRI) claimed victory in the 1988 elections and retained its sixty-year hold over governing power. However, many domestic and international observers maintained that the PRI resorted to massive vote-counting fraud in order to hold on to power.

5. The UN (1994, p. xii) cautions that the labels are "for statistical convenience only and do not necessarily express a judgment about the stage reached by a particular country or area in the development process." Given the shifting nature of the world economy since 1989, the UN also cautions that the classification labels for countries are under review and may change.

6. There is a large overlap between what the UN considers to be developed countries and what the World Bank considers to be high-income countries. However, it is not a complete overlap. South Africa, Greece, and Portugal fall within the developed but not the high-income classification, while

Saudi Arabia, Singapore, Hong Kong, Kuwait, and the United Arab Emirates fall within the high-income but not the developed classification. The latter countries have high average incomes, either because of oil revenues or for other reasons that economists consider insufficient to currently ensure long-term prosperity.

7. Labor forces, in most definitions, include all of those actively engaged in the production of goods or services. The size of a labor force is thus smaller than that of the total population of a society, since the latter includes children, retired persons, disabled persons, and others who are not engaged in production, as well as labor force members. There is controversy over the status of homemakers, overwhelmingly women, who are not currently included. They produce a service, but since their labor is not directly paid, they are not currently considered to be labor force members.

Chapter Six

Classical Sociological Theory

Three nineteenth- and early twentieth-century theorists—Karl Marx, Emile Durkheim, and Max Weber—established the most important parameters and controversies of classical macrosociological theory. They had different philosophical premises, methods for studying societies, and research interests. They had different perspectives regarding the character and future of capitalism as a way of structuring societies and ways of life; and they had different perspectives regarding the active socialist movements of their day and the desirability of the institutional changes that they advocated.

Marx concluded that conflicts of interest lay at the roots of capitalist societies, which he considered to be history's most sophisticated embodiments of class exploitation and alienation. He sought in theory as well as practice the complete revolutionary overthrow of capitalism and its institutions. Emile Durkheim was more inclined to stress the extent to which the institutions of contemporary societies functioned in such a manner as to produce relative social harmony. As a reformist, he believed in the continued existence of capitalist and class societies, but with modifications to make them function better. Max Weber (1864–1920) was a pessimistic realist who viewed societies as being dominated by powerful elites. He granted that capitalist societies were alienating and exploitative but could see no better alternative. In one way of viewing classical theory, Marx, Durkheim, and Weber thus arrived at different intellectual conclusions, founding respectively what are called today the conflict, functional, and elite approaches to social theory and sociology in general. But from another point of view, the foundations of divisions in social theory simply reflected the ideological struggle between capitalism and socialism and the consequent division of the technologically advanced countries into First and Second World societies. In one camp belonged the works of Durkheim and Weber; in the other those of Marx.

MARXIAN THEORY

Socialist ideas and movements spread in Europe in reaction to the early nineteenth-century industrial factory system. Grimy factory districts, grueling sixteen-hour workdays, low pay, high industrial accident rates, and employment of child labor produced widespread revulsion. Capitalism as a system came under close moral scrutiny. Some urged reforms, such as limiting the length of the workday, increasing rates of pay, and abolishing the use of child labor. Others went further, concluding that the capitalist system as a whole needed to be replaced by a socialist one of equality and common ownership of factories, mines, banks, and other workplaces. Marx and his collaborator, Frederick Engels, were the greatest exponents of the latter course of action. Through their relentless and meticulous critique of the capitalist present they constructed the theoretical bases for a socialist future.

The Dialectics of History

Materialism and dialectics were the key premises of Marx's and Engels' approach to social understanding. As materialists, they believed that human, not providential, actions were responsible for determining the fates of societies and courses of history.[1] As dialectical thinkers, they believed that reality was always in a process of change. They sought through their materialist and dialectical approach to uncover the human causes of social and historical change.

According to dialectical logic, which Marx and Engels inherited from G.W.F. Hegel (1770–1831), all processes of change have three component parts or stages—their theses, antitheses, and syntheses. The thesis is the beginning stage of development. Since nothing remains permanently the same, antithetical conditions arise which make the continued existence of the original thesis stage as is impossible. The antithetical conditions force a change in the thesis, resulting in the synthesis stage of development. But dialectical change does not happen once and for all. It keeps going on as chains of development, each link of which has its own separate thesis, antithesis, and synthesis "moments." Each synthesis is simultaneously the thesis of a new round of dialectical development.

Put differently, dialectical logic assumes that change develops as a result of resolving contradictions. Contradictions are problems. What causes change is the existence of contradictions which need to be resolved. Humans continually resolve the contradictions or problems of their existences. The tasks of science are to identify those contradictions and work on their resolutions.

Marx and Engels believed that social and historical development followed this kind of general dialectical pattern. Communal societies with primitive technologies were the thesis of world history, class societies the antithesis, and a future high-technology-based communism would be its synthesis. The task of Marxist social scientists was to accurately portray and actively participate in the changes that resulted in the progress of history toward its communist-egalitarian future and synthesis. For the capitalist present, the task was to reveal how the system worked. In particular, it was to uncover the economic, class, and political dynamics of capitalist societies so that the working class—the agents of socialist change—would be conscious of both their historical mission and the obstacles that they faced. Marx and Engels thus consciously saw their roles as being those of revolutionaries whose theoretical and scholarly work had revolutionary ends. They did not see themselves as academics producing scholarship for scholarship's sake.

While Marx and Engels as dialectical thinkers saw all of their work as occurring within the broad context of the unfolding of world history which they sought to understand, they concentrated their energies most on analyzing the capitalist present. Future socialism would come about, in their view, not by utopian designs and wishful thinking, but rather because unresolvable contradictions would develop within the capitalist system which could only be resolved by a complete socialist transformation. Their task was therefore to analyze how the capitalist system functioned and to identify its unresolvable contradictions.

To give the devil his due, Marx and Engels clearly noted that capitalistic societies had been history's most technologically innovative and materially productive. But there had continued to be great human costs. Capitalist societies produced great wealth through exploiting labor under alienating conditions.

Value Theory and Exploitation

Marx powerfully argued that exploitation was the lever of capitalist accumulation. According to his labor theory of value—the key premise of Marxian economic theory—all economic value in capitalist societies results from the labor of those who directly work on products.[2] Stock owners, speculators, financiers, and other members of the capitalist class control but do not produce value. Workers produce more value each working day than the amount of value which capitalists invest in their wages and other costs of production. Marx (1867) called this extra sum produced by workers *surplus value.* Hence, workers produce but do not receive surplus value. Rather, capitalists exploit workers by expropriating the surplus value that they have produced.

Out of surplus value comes profit. Part of profits are distributed as incomes to capitalists and their families. The other part is set aside to form new capital. The origin of capital thus is surplus value produced by workers. Capitalists pump surplus value out of workers which they appropriate and turn into profits and new capital, and use to continually control workers.[3]

Alienation and Labor

Marx (1844) saw alienation as being the necessary complement of exploitation. By *alienation* he meant that the worker was objectively removed from control over the capitalist-owned means of production and resulting products. Ownership of the means of production gave the capitalists the power to set the conditions of labor. The worker hence worked on someone else's product, under conditions designed by others, and in the interests of others. As a result, his or her job was performed under objectively alienating conditions.

Marx viewed labor in the abstract positively. That is, labor represented the synthesis of specifically human activity. Laborers creatively thought out resolutions to contradictions of existence and then effected them through work. Creative labor hence was a specifically human activity in a double sense. First, humans were the only animals to have the capacity for creative thought. They could labor consciously. Second, through exercise of their creative capacities in their labor they developed themselves. But wherever their conditions of labor were objectively alienated, as they were for large parts of the labor forces in capitalist societies, they lost this potential for their work to be a humanly fulfilling experience.

Marx's theory of labor alienation under capitalist conditions was a part of his more general theory of alienation, which he saw as occurring in all class societies. According to him, both creative labor and human solidarity were necessary conditions for human fulfillment, either one of which could be alienated. Creative labor is precluded for large parts of the labor forces when they do not own the means of production. Human solidarity is precluded in all societies based upon divisions of class interests, that is, all types of class-based societies, not just capitalism.

Class Conflict and Revolution

Capitalists and workers, in the Marxist understanding, are thus the fundamental classes in capitalist societies, and their interests are antagonistic. Marx (1865, p. 64) noted that "if wages fall, profits will rise; and if wages rise, profits will fall." But more importantly, according to him, capitalists had an interest in maintaining the system that had profited them so much, while workers had a historic interest in ending their exploitation. In Marx's and Engels' view, capitalist governments, like all governments, existed ultimately to maintain the prevailing economic system and protect the political interests of its dominant class, despite whatever democratic pretensions they may exhibit. Marx and Engels (1848, p. 110) thus concluded in a famous formulation that "the executive of the modern State is but a committee for managing the common affairs of the whole bourgeoisie."

Marx and Engels also considered ideology to be an important underpinning of the capitalist system. In an early writing they maintained that the ideas of the ruling classes tended to be ruling ideas:

> The ideas of the ruling class are in every epoch the ruling ideas: i.e., the class which is the ruling *material* force of society is at the same time its ruling *intellectual* force. The class which has the means of material production at its disposal, consequently also controls the means of mental production, so that the ideas of those who lack the means of mental production are on the whole subject to it. The ruling ideas are nothing more than the ideal expression of the dominant material relations, the dominant material relations grasped as ideas; hence of the relations which make the one class the ruling one, therefore, the ideas of its dominance. (Marx and Engels, 1846, p. 67)

Put simply, according to the Marxian view, the economically dominant class is able to make its own ideas and perspectives "ruling ideas" through its ownership or control of "means of mental production" such as newspapers, television stations, publishing houses, and educational institutions. In that sense, the economically dominant class has the most power to make its ideas ruling ideas. But its power is not absolute. Nonruling classes have different experiences and social perspectives. They, hence, can develop ideas of their own, especially concerning social questions. Logically, the different experiences of each class foster different consciousnesses. Marx and Engels were especially concerned with the development of working-class or proletarian-class consciousness, which they saw as a revolutionary force. They optimistically assumed that eventually the working class would gain a class consciousness of its historical interests and struggle to end capitalist domination. In its place they would establish a socialist society through common public ownership of at least the major productive, financial, and commercial institutions. The goals of socialism would be to progressively end class exploitation and institute egalitarian solidarity.

Leninist Theory

If Marx and Engels were the towering figures of nineteenth-century Marxism, V.I. Lenin (1870–1924) was the comparable figure for the twentieth century. As architect of the 1917 Bolshevik Revolution, he more than any other single individual was responsible for setting the century's subsequent course. The Bolshevik Revolution originated the cleavage between First and Second World countries. If it had not occurred, the course of twentieth-century history, including the character of the present period, would have been substantially different.

In addition to Lenin's world historical importance as the practical leader of an epochal revolution, he was a theorist whose ideas and analyses defined the Marxist-Leninist approach to revolutionary as well as to what became "actually existing" socialism, an approach which for the major part of the century was the dominant social theory of the Second World countries and influenced such Third World revolutionaries as Mao Zedong, Ho Chi Minh, and Fidel Castro. Although one of its leading tenets, the one-party state, has now been abandoned by many of its former adherents, other tenets of Marxism-Leninism continue to be influential in socialist thinking.

Like Marx and Engels, Lenin's writings were wide ranging, producing social theories in a number of areas. The centerpieces of that work were theories of imperialism, revolution, and the state. All three are component parts of what today is known as Marxism-Leninism, which for decades was the dominant school of social science as well as ideology in the Second World countries.

Lenin's (1916) theory of imperialism represented an updating of Marx's and Engels' analyses of capitalism. Marx had constructed a theory of the inner logic of the capitalist mode of production. Lenin, building upon that analysis, noted that by the early twentieth century, two developments—monopolization of ownership and internationalization of investments—within the leading capitalist countries had added new dimensions to the system. Marx and Engels had noted those as incipient tendencies in the nineteenth century. By the early twentieth century, the time of Lenin, those tendencies had matured into prominent characteristics of the capitalist system whose full analysis was unavoidable. Lenin defined imperialism as:

> capitalism at that stage of development at which the dominance of monopolies and finance capital is established; in which the export of capital has acquired pronounced importance; in which the division of the world among the international trusts has begun, in which the division of all territories of

the globe among the biggest capitalist powers has been completed. (Lenin, 1916, p. 737).

Within the leading capitalist countries—Great Britain, the United States, Germany, France, and Japan—fierce competition between corporations for shares of markets had resulted in winners who enlarged their shares and losers who were driven out of business. Smaller numbers of corporations now controlled larger shares of their respective markets, giving them near-monopoly powers. Monopoly powers allowed these corporations to realize superprofits. But not all of the excess capital that they thereby accumulated could be reinvested profitably in their own countries. They had to find outlets for it in colonial and semi-colonial areas controlled by their countries. Following the development of the monopoly stage of capitalism in the last quarter of the nineteenth century, there was a mad scramble by the great powers to increase colonial possessions and semi-colonial spheres of influence. By 1900, all five of the great powers had substantially increased their colonial possessions and enlarged their economic influence in formally independent Third World countries. For example, Lenin (1916, p. 726) cited Supan who calculated that between 1876 and 1900 the proportion of African territory colonized by the European powers jumped from 10.8 to an astounding 90.4 percent. In language which strikingly foretold contemporary issues of Third World development, Lenin (1916, p. 734) characterized as semi-colonial "the diverse forms of dependent countries which, politically, are formally independent, but in fact, are enmeshed in the net of financial and diplomatic dependence."

Monopoly corporations expanded their foreign investments, gaining control over mines, plantations, and factories within colonial territories and semi-colonial spheres of influence. These favored investments turned out to be even more profitable than investments within their own countries, stimulating further investments and economic domination of Third World countries by the great powers.

All of the great powers thus scrambled to expand their colonial possessions during the transition from competitive capitalism to monopoly capitalism and imperialism. In Asia, Great Britain had India, the world's second most populated country. France had Indochina. (The origins of the Vietnam War go back to this French colonial period.) The United States defeated Spain in the 1898 Spanish-American War and took Puerto Rico and the Philippines as colonies. According to Lenin's (1916, p. 730) figures, by 1914, over one-third of the world's people were living in colonies.

Lenin predicted that two types of wars would characterize the twentieth century. The great powers would fight among themselves as each attempted to expand at each other's expense colonial possessions and semi-colonial spheres of influence. At the same time, colonized Third World countries would seek independence through wars of national liberation. Lenin characterized World War I as a war of the first type in which the great powers were fighting over the redivision of economic control of world territories. Wars of the second type, that is, of national liberation, broke out especially following World War II in Algeria, Indochina, Mozambique, Angola, and other Third World colonies.

Lenin advocated that workers in First World countries oppose militarist policies that led to wars of the first type. His clear advocacy of colonized countries having the right to self-determination (political independence) won a following for himself and his party among such revolutionaries in the colonized countries as Vietnam's Ho Chi Minh.

Lenin believed that a part of the relative prosperity of First World countries resulted from repatriation of superprofits derived from foreign investments in the colonial and dependent countries. A part of those superprofits underwrote the incomes of the best-paid sectors of the working class, producing political conservatism and acquiescence to imperialist policies among them. Lenin's solution to this dilemma was for First World revolutionary parties to organize sectors deeper within the working class who did not have a material stake in the continuation of the imperialist system.

Lenin's theory of revolution in Russia was earlier developed in such pragmatically titled writings as "Where to Begin" and *What Is to Be Done* (1902). Capitalism had developed relatively late in Russian history. Even at the beginning of the twentieth century, precapitalist economic and social conditions prevailed in large parts of the country. Urban workers—the base of what Marx and Engels had assumed would be a revolutionary proletariat—were a small minority. The economy was still mostly ruralized with semi-feudal landlord and peasant classes. Unlike in the Western European countries, there was little hint of democratic development within the state. The state retained the autocratic character of centuries-old Czarism.

In one way of thinking, Russia was an unlikely candidate for the type of socialist revolution envisioned by Marx and Engels. It was economically and politically backward. In one of Marx's (1859) original conceptions, socialist revolutions would take place after all of the developing potentials of capitalism had been exhausted. That was hardly the case in turn-of-the-century Russia. But in another way of thinking, the Russian situation was potentially revolutionary. It was a part of the capitalist world. It was clearly ripe for change. The slowly dying body of czarism was surrounded by many would-be successors. In the struggle for postczarist power, Marxists had as much chance as anyone.

Lenin, as did many, foresaw the eventual disintegration of czarism, and he created a strategy of preparation for that event. The revolutionary vanguard party was the key instrument of that strategy. In an early debate and resultant split with social democrats, Lenin (1902) argued the need for a vanguard rather than mass party as the vehicle of socialist strategy. A mass party is open, above ground, loosely organized, and seeks to gain as many members as possible from the public. Lenin argued that such a party could not succeed in actually carrying out a revolution against czarism or the socialist transformation of Russian society. Rather, he argued, a tightly organized and disciplined party of professional revolutionaries with highly developed Marxist principles of ideological unity was needed.

Lenin's theory of the vanguard party proceeded from the observation that most revolutions did not fully command the support of more than a minority of the population. The American Revolution, for example, was fully supported by only about one-third of the population. One-third was against it, favoring continued colonial status, and the remaining third did not take a position. The same had been true of the French Revolution. Lenin believed as a kind of historical truism that as periods of potential revolution approached—in Marxian language, as dialectical contradictions began to ripen—populations stratified into vanguard sections who saw and desired revolutionary change, reactionary and backward sectors who wanted to maintain the status quo, and middle sectors who vacillated or did not take positions. The concept of the vanguard political party, which would be made up of self-conscious revolutionaries recruited from the vanguard sections of the population, flowed from that observation.

Such a political party would be made up of full-time, tightly organized revolutionaries. While not appealing for mass membership, it did appeal for mass support among those oppressed classes of the population—workers and peasants—that it believed had an objective interest in revolutionary change. Party members would be drawn from two sources: the oppressed classes—in whose interests the revolution would be carried out—and supporters from other classes. Workers and peasants stood to gain the most from a revolution. Capitalists and landlords had the most to lose. Small-business owners—the petty bourgeoisie—would be in the middle, gaining some advantages from a radical change and losing others. Clipping the wings of the strong competition from big businesses would be to their advantage. But a socialist state would also follow policies which would curtail their freedom to market goods to their best advantage. The overall revolutionary potential of the different classes thus stratified according to their economic interests. Also, within each class there would be class-conscious individuals, whose class stand would be directly based on their class's objective interests, and others, who would either be neutral toward a revolution or take the position of a class other than their own.

In many ways Lenin's strategy was based on merging the radical intelligentsia from middle- and upper-class origins, who saw the necessity of a revolutionary transformation, with the working and other oppressed classes—especially the peasantry—which would be the vehicles for that transformation. Lenin's strategy for merging radical intellectuals with the working and other oppressed classes was consistent with an important observation made earlier by Marx and Engels:

> In times when the class struggle nears the decisive hour, the process of dissolution going on within the ruling class, in fact within the whole range of old society, assumes such a violent, glaring character, that a small section of the ruling class cuts itself adrift, and joins the revolutionary class. (Marx and Engels, 1848, p. 117).

Lenin envisioned revolutions as occurring in two stages. In the first, the old regime was defeated. During this stage, broad unity could be amassed around the single goal and perceived necessity of ending the old form of government. The defects of old regimes—such as oppressiveness, corruption, and foreign domination—were usually glaring. Once the old regime was defeated, the revolutionary process would enter into its second stage, that of defining and constructing a new type of government. During this stage there would be inevitable differences among the forces who had brought down the old regime. The ensuing struggle for power would narrow the basis of unity.

A revolutionary party, in Lenin's reasoning, had to be conscious of the different conditions prevailing in the two stages. Its tactic in the first stage was to detonate the revolutionary process by appealing to broad unity around such goals as independence for a colony, ending dictatorship or military rule, and getting rid of corruption. (The famous slogan of the first stage of the Russian Revolution was "land, peace, and bread," which responded to peasant landlessness, the war weariness of the Russian people as World War I dragged on, and famine conditions resulting from the war.) The goals would be based on the directly prevailing conditions. The party would not prominently put forth in its mass agitation the goal of socialism. Once the old regime had been defeated, the party would then move to a higher level of struggle in which its goal would be the construction of socialism.

Lenin's theory of the two-stage revolution dovetailed with his analysis of class positions and stands cited above. In the first stage, elements from all classes, not just workers and peasants, would unite around broad goals of ending the discredited regime. The core of unity would narrow in the second stage to those who had revolutionary socialist working- and peasant-class stands.

Lenin advocated organizing the revolutionary party according to democratic centralist principles. The party was to be democratic in the sense that all the incumbents of leading committees and offices were to be elected by members. It was centralist in the sense that it was organized as a strict hierarchy with the decisions of higher bodies binding on lower ones. Thus in a democratic centralist organization, a base member votes for leaders who represent her or him in higher decision-making bodies. In general though, there is no direct election of the highest leaders by all of the members. These are elected by high-level bodies, which in turn have been elected to represent lower-level members. In the interests of effectiveness, decisions once made have to be carried out and publicly supported by all members, even those who were in disagreement.

Lenin (1917, 1918) maintained, as had Marx (1875) before him, that the new socialist state had to take the form of a revolutionary dictatorship of the proletariat. By that he meant that it had to represent exclusively the class interests of the working class and its allies. The class interests of capitalists and landlords would not be represented. Furthermore, the working class, through its vanguard party, had to have a firm hold on state power in order to survive. Counterrevolutions, led by ruling classes driven out of power and supported by foreign powers, were virtually inevitable after every radical revolution. The Leninist model of democratic centralist party organization thus was carried through to the construction of the Soviet state after the triumph of the Bolshevik Revolution and successful defense of its power during the 1918–1920 civil war and attempt at counterrevolution.

Societal unity, in Lenin's reasoning, would be a necessary condition for constructing the new socialist order. As factional fighting within a revolutionary party would divert energy away from the revolutionary tasks at hand, competing political parties within a new socialist society would bottle up the energy needed for carrying out radical economic and social transformations. Hence the model of democratic centralism within the Bolshevik Party became also the model for the political structuring of the one-party centralized Bolshevik state. Leninists argued that by promoting unity rather than political divisiveness, one-party systems advanced the socialist goal of social solidarity. They also justified one-party systems with the argument that workers and other oppressed classes had one overall class interest—attaining social justice through ending exploitation—which could be most efficiently advanced by a single unified revolutionary political party. On the other hand, creation of highly centralized control through one-party states has long been viewed by many as inherently undemocratic.

Leninist social theories have had relatively little influence in Western social science, where they were either ignored or treated simply as being part of the causes of fundamental defects in socialist-organized countries. Their influence of course was the opposite in the Second World countries, where they were taken very seriously as the dominant approach to the basic questions of social science and socialist constructions.

The 1989–1990 events in Eastern Europe and the former Soviet Union swept away the one-party states originally advocated by Marxist-Leninists. But other key tenets of Marxist-Leninist theory—particularly those regarding imperialism and revolution—continue to have social science significance. In Third World countries especially, Lenin's theories of imperialism and revolution continue to circulate widely.

Marx and Modern Sociology

Marx and Engels' social theories have influenced contemporary sociology in a number of manners, two of which stand out in particular. First, Marx and Engels' radical critique of capitalism with its revolutionary implications set off a furious ideological struggle which continues to rage across all of the social sciences. Their overall social theories remain the standard from which all socialist alternatives proceed. At the same time, they are the targets of all ideological defenses of capitalism. Neither side of this debate, which has continued with rivers of ink as well as blood for over a century, has been able to definitively prove its case. Each has proved its case to its own satisfaction, but not to that of the other side. History may well be the ultimate and only possible judge of whether Marx and Engels were fundamentally right or wrong. In any event, they achieved world historical importance for formulating the debate over the origins, character, and future of capitalist societies.

Second, Marx and Engels' class theories and hypotheses have had a special influence within sociology. Their class definitions continue to be adhered to by their followers. As capitalist societies develop, Marxian-influenced sociologists attempt to chart the internal development and changes within the working class (for example, the growing proportion of white-collar workers), study the internal development of the capitalist class, chart the decline of small businesses, and interpret the meaning of the growing importance of employed professionals and managers (often referred to as a new middle class), and portray the overall dimensions of the class system as it develops. Marx and Engels' hypothesis that eventually the working class would develop a class consciousness of their historical class interests continues to intrigue social theorists and be a question for social research.

EMILE DURKHEIM

Emile Durkheim's approach to sociology embodied strong elements of positivism and functionalism. He inherited the positivism from Comte, the mid-nineteenth-century founder of sociology, and shared with the early anthropological theorists of his day an organic and functionalist approach to the study of societies.

Positivism and Functionalism

Positivists, as well as contemporary neopositivists, believe that sociology can and should adopt natural science methods to study societies objectively. Social sciences, in their view, should follow the basic natural science procedures and techniques—classification and measurement of matter, determination of cause and effect relations among variables, and experimentation to test hypotheses. Contemporary neopositivism also emphasizes that sociology should deliver nonpolitical and value-free analyses. Positivism and neopositivism have had considerable influence in the development of sociology, but not without controversy.[4]

Functionalism is an approach to the study of societies which is rooted in the organic analogy that there are a large number of parallels between the functioning of a human organism, with its brain, central nervous system, cells, muscles, and heart, and that of a society, with its ideas, classes, division of labor, and culture. The relations between the parts of society are thought to be similar to those between the organs of a human body. As the human body is an organism in which the whole is greater than the sum of its parts, societies can be viewed as social organisms in which their wholes are greater than the sums of their parts. If societies, like human bodies, are viewed as functioning organically, then each subpart must have a function—that is, a role—in contributing to the survival of the entire organism.

Functionalism, the offshoot of the organic analogy, incorporates two overall principles: First, societies are viewed as systems in which the whole is greater than the sum of its parts. The task of the social theorist is to determine the systemic features of the society. Second, each institution, structure, or other subpart of a society is to be described in terms of its function in contributing to the maintenance and development of the overall social system.

Durkheim's functionalism greatly influenced anthropological theory and studies. Anthropologists, such as A.R. Radcliffe-Brown (1881–1955) and Bronislaw Malinowski (1884–1942), approached non-European and usually preliterate societies as social organisms to be understood unto themselves. Instead of applying ethnocentric European ideas as to how a society ought to be constituted, they attempted to freshly determine in each case how it actually functioned by analyzing the role that each of its social parts—such as its culture, belief systems, religion, and kinship institutions—played in establishing and maintaining overall social order.

The Division of Labor in Society

Like Marx earlier and Weber later, Durkheim developed his approach to the study of society in an early writing, *The Division of Labor in Society* (1893), which had been his dissertation at the

Sorbonne.[5] The principle purpose of that study was to "determine the function of the division of labor" (p. 45). The results were a far-reaching and influential interpretation of historical development in general and modern capitalist societies in particular as they were entering the mature phases of their development at the end of the nineteenth and early decades of the twentieth centuries.

Durkheim saw the development of the division of labor—both in terms of increased specialization of tasks and class hierarchies—as the motor force of history. Early societies had simple divisions of labor. More modern societies functioned with highly complex divisions of labor. He thus portrayed two sharply different types of societies according to whether their internal divisions of labor were simple or complex.

The division of labor of past societies was, according to his analysis, simple because the degree of economic specialization was as yet undeveloped. Most peasant households performed similar subsistence-oriented tasks. They produced most of what they consumed. Very few, if any, consumer necessities were gained from trade with others. There was little objective interdependence between households. Most were relatively self-sufficient. Each household and village was an economy unto itself. These households and villages were linked together as similar segments to form larger, more geographically encompassing societies.

Commonly held deep religious and other ideas provided the cohesion of those societies. While each household or segment was an isolate, in the sense that it produced alone nearly all of what it consumed, it shared deeply held worldviews with other households. The most compelling example of this was the ideological force that medieval Catholicism exerted over peasant households in feudal Europe. It produced the veneer of ideological cohesion that overlay the economically fragmented feudal societies.

Durkheim concluded that the ideological conformity of earlier societies was the product of what he called a common collective conscience which dominated the thinking of individuals. By common conscience he (1893, p. 79) meant "the totality of beliefs and sentiments common to average citizens of the same society." The contents of most of what people thought were held in common with other members of the society. These commonly held beliefs formed systems of thinking which were powerful frames of reference through which individuals largely interpreted their experiences. As "determinate systems," they followed semi-autonomous logics of their own. Each individual's consciousness was a composite containing two parts: one formed through the internalization of the beliefs within this common conscience of society and one part formed from purely personal beliefs. The beliefs of any particular individual thus reflected both the commonly held beliefs of her or his society and her or his own beliefs.

In premodern societies, the common conscience was an overwhelming force molding personal consciousnesses with little room being left for purely personal beliefs. The monopolistic religious and ideological power of Catholicism over the mental life of medieval European feudalism would be a clear example. So too would be the deeply held religious beliefs of the Aztecs. In such traditional societies there was little room for individualism and nonconformity. The function of the powerful common conscience in these societies was, according to Durkheim, to provide cohesion and social order to a society that was otherwise scattered or segmented into largely self-sufficient autonomous estates, villages, and rural households.

There was little room for ideological or other types of nonconformity in traditional segmental societies. Since ideological conformity was a critical pillar of societal structure and stability, it had to be maintained and reinforced. Ideological and normative nonconformity threatened the very existence of the society. For that reason, according to Durkheim, law tended to be highly repressive. The state meted out excessively cruel punishments to those who stepped outside of legal and normative boundaries, as if to recapture the social balance that depended so heavily on complete conformity. Often punishments were carried out publicly with hangings in the plaza or other forms of execution preceded by lengthy torture and bodily mutilation to reaffirm the conformism of the majority and warn would-be nonconformists.

Modern societies are, according to Durkheim's theory, structured very differently. There is an extensive economic division of labor such that very few people or households remain that are wholly self-sufficient. Objective economic interdependence provides the most important basis of the cohesion of modern social orders. In answer to his original research question, Durkheim concluded that the function of the division of labor in modern societies was to provide the basis for social order by making each person dependent on all others. Interdependence within the modern division of labor, according to Durkheim, replaced ideological conformity as the foundation of social cohesion and order.

In modern societies, according to him, the common part of individual consciousnesses has been greatly reduced. There is no longer as great a need for powerful ideological or religious institutions to provide social cohesion because people are now more objectively interdependent owing to the growth of complex divisions of labor. Each household and unit of production is tied to others through nets of interdependency which provide the basis for social cohesion and order. With the decline of both the power of and the need for common consciences, individualism and nonconformity correspondingly increased.

Put differently, societies vary according to whether they contain a single unitary dominating belief system or a number of competing ones—whether, like in medieval Europe, one institutionalized belief system, Catholicism, almost completely embraces and engulfs the terrain, or whether, as in contemporary Western countries, a number of belief systems run as different thought currents through social life.

The importance of Durkheim's concept of the common conscience is the attention that it focused on common belief systems as entities to be studied as, in his words, social facts which play important roles in the fabric of social life. While he argued that the power of common belief systems had greatly declined in modern societies, he by no means concluded that they had vanished. Rather, they had fragmented. Instead of one dominating belief system, there was a multiplicity arising from different sources. Durkheim believed that the fragmentation of the common conscience in modern societies created difficulties for maintaining social order. He advocated reestablishing a common conscience, but one based on secular principles relevant to the needs of complex modern divisions of labor.

Durkheim's concept of the common conscience thus drew attention to the analysis of common belief systems and the roles that they have played in the development of history and the functioning of societies. Belief systems, as focuses of sociological research, require identification in terms of their contents, social origins, and roles. In past world history religions were the most important belief systems. Generally, the further back history is traced, the more powerful their social roles appear.

Durkheim's general theory thus interpreted history as moving from societies with simple divisions of labor and strong common consciences to modern societies with complex divisions of labor and weak Common consciences. Objective interdependence replaced ideological conformity as the basis of social order. What he called organic solidarity based upon interdependence replaced mechanical solidarity based upon ideological sameness.

Modern societies with complex divisions of labor though are not without problems. For their division of labor to function optimally, Durkheim believed that a number of reforms needed to be enacted.

Modern societies faced serious structural problems in that two of their critical functions were either not being fulfilled or were only being fulfilled partially. First, the division of labor was objectively interdependent, but it was not self-regulating. It needed to be managed rationally if it were to function smoothly. Second, the decline of religion had left an ideological vacuum which needed to be filled.

One of Durkheim's great social insights was that as a result of these and other structural problems, modern societies suffered from a condition that he called *anomie*. Human beings, according to the premises of his theory, needed reasonably well-defined structures within which to function. They needed to know what to expect from their routine interactions with others, whether in family, work, or other environments. When predictable social intercourse was not present or when that to which the person had been accustomed collapsed, stress-inducing social disorientation—the anomic condition—resulted. The tradition-bound social life of premodern societies had been, in that respect, superior to that of modern societies. It had been less anomic than that of modern societies which were constantly undergoing technological and social changes. Anomie was like, in his words, a constant wind that blew across modern societies causing uneasiness and, in extremes, suicide-inducing anxiety.

The modern state was, according to Durkheim's analysis, the appropriate agency to redress these structural problems. The state would plan and regulate through its taxation, credit, and other policies the economic division of labor. To replace the ideological vacuum left by the fragmentation and decline of religious institutions, it would socialize young people through public education into dominant social, political, and economic norms and values. As a result of both, anomie would be minimized, for a well-regulated society would be a less anomic society.

Durkheim's advocacy of an enlarged economic and ideological role for the state was in line with turn-of-the-century liberal thinking. Capitalist economies, in the modern liberal view, required governmental investment and regulation if they were to function properly. The ideal capitalist economy would be one in which the state fine-tuned the relationships between market-oriented production and consumer demands through laws, taxes, regulatory agencies, and control of the credit system.

One of the problems of modern societies, which Durkheim sought to remedy through state action, was the chaotic and inefficient ways in which labor forces were trained and rewarded. Inept progeny of rich tycoons took over companies while intelligent children of workers went uneducated. Modern societies allocated their collective labor forces inefficiently, wasting talented but poor people in humble positions and suffering from the inept sons of the privileged in powerful positions. To remedy this problem, Durkheim advocated using public schooling to sift and winnow children according to their native abilities, educationally prepare them according to their potential—what later became known as tracking—and see that they ended up in jobs that paid accordingly.[6]

Ideally, according to Durkheim, it would be possible through state planning to coordinate four hierarchies: ability, education, occupational position, and income. That is, one should be educated according to one's ability and then receive an appropriate job and income. Low-ability students would be educated only up to a minimally necessary point and then receive unskilled jobs with low incomes. High-ability students would receive higher educations appropriate to professional and managerial positions that would pay accordingly.

Contemporary sociologists have long noted that these hierarchies are in fact often not coordinated, leading to problems of morale and inefficiency. Highly educated teachers, for example, often are paid less than less-educated managers. Today sociologists use the concept of status inconsistency to refer to situations when people have inconsistent positions on the hierarchies of educational achievement, occupational position, and income.

Durkheim's model modern society was one in which the state oversaw an organically integrated and smoothly functioning capitalist economy with a class division of labor. Society should be constituted, according to Durkheim's (1893, p. 377) bluntly worded formula, "in such a way that social inequalities exactly express natural inequalities." Durkheim thus advocated a kind of meritocracy in which one's position and rewards in life would be determined by one's abilities. He did not advocate social equality, since he assumed that people should receive greater or lesser incomes according to their abilities and contributions to society.

Ultimately, in Durkheim's view, capitalist and class societies could incorporate social justice so long as their reward systems reflected actual differences in ability and function in contributing to the general welfare. As they stood, they were for the most part just, though in need of some reform to eliminate the effects of inherited privileges and disadvantages on the filling of upper-class and working-class positions respectively. Exploitation, by the logic of this explanation, only existed in the extremes of capitalist societies. By the logic of his analysis, he would have interpreted as exploited those workers paid below the minimum wage or high-intelligence workers who did not have the opportunity to educationally prepare for higher-level positions. But for the most part, people were paid according to their abilities and consequent contributions to society, and therefore not exploited.

Durkheim's theoretical justification for maintaining social inequality was in many ways symptomatic of both liberal and middle-class thinking. It was liberal in the sense that it advocated aggressive use of the state to reform problems in the functioning of capitalist societies. It was middle class in the sense that it advocated a meritocracy in which the middle-class educated professional classes would gain more power and income at the expense of both uneducated workers and undeserving upper-class inheritors.

Suicide

Durkheim's theory of suicide, briefly described in Chapter One, remains a classic in sociology. The shockingly titled *Suicide* was published in 1897, four years after *The Division of Labor in Society*, and there is a clear theoretical continuity between the two works. As in the former work, Durkheim identified individualism and anomie as endemic features of modern societies which, if unchecked, would aggravate a number of social problems, including suicide.

He offered a sociological explanation for the causes of suicide, when most considered a psychological explanation to be more appropriate. His was thus a theory of the specifically social factors involved in the causation of that most seeming individual of acts, the taking of one's own life.

Durkheim identified four types of suicide—egoistic, altruistic, anomic, and fatalistic—according to their social causes. The last though remained undeveloped in the theory. Under egoistic suicides he included suicides that resulted from excesses of individualism, which he had earlier discussed in *The Division of Labor in Society* as a problematic feature of modern societies. Excesses of individualism could be considered to exist when persons were insufficiently integrated morally into surrounding communities, including religions, groups, and families. By moral integration it is meant that the norms of the group are internalized by members. When moral integration is not strong, the group has little moral influence over the private and personal actions of its members, including the decision to take one's own life. Even if the community has a strong moral opposition to suicide, the member will feel free to act independently. This was thus his explanation for why Protestants had higher rates of suicide than did Catholics. While both religions equally condemned suicide as an option, the moral prohibition had a less binding effect on Protestants, since their churches encouraged free inquiry—resulting in a kind of intellectual individualism—while Catholicism was predicated on the member's acceptance and internalization of the church's strict moral authority.

Durkheim also used the concept of egoistic suicide to explain why people with different family and educational backgrounds had different suicide rates. A single person is more likely than a married person to commit suicide because he or she lives alone rather than as an integrated member of a family. Married persons with children are less likely to commit suicide than those without because the larger the family group, the greater its moral influence over individual members. The higher the formal education of a person the greater the propensity for suicide, because education encourages free intellectual and moral inquiry. In the same respect, men committed suicide more often than women because they were more educated.

If egoistic suicide resulted from social ties being too loose, altruistic suicide was the opposite, resulting from the ties being overly strong. In egoistic suicide, the person places her or his own desires above those of the community. In altruistic suicide, the person places the community's needs above her or his own. Examples of such suicides include Japan's Kamikaze pilots during World War II who intentionally crashed their planes into enemy ships, elderly Eskimos who took their lives when they could no longer produce so as not to endanger the survival of the community, and military heroes who take actions for the greater good, but which will most certainly result in their own destruction.

One could interpret the mass suicides at Masada in Roman times, and Jonestown, Guyana in 1979, as related to but not exactly the same as altruistic suicide. At Masada in 66 A.D., Roman forces were about to overtake the mountain fortress of Jewish rebels numbering just under 1,000. Rather than submit, the rebels committed mass suicide. At Jonestown, a Protestant congregation in self-imposed exile from the United States was facing increasing scrutiny from outside authorities. Believing that the authorities were about to destroy their community, over nine hundred people then committed suicide together, most by drinking poison. In both cases, the suicides demonstrated the primacies of community identities over individualism and are thus related to Durkheim's category of altruistic suicides. But in altruistic suicide proper, the suicide occurs in order to ensure the survival of other members of the community, whereas in the examples of mass suicides cited, whole communities marched together in solidarity across the divide separating life and death.

The anomic conditions of modern societies which bred insecurity and instability were a further cause influencing suicide rates. Durkheim thus viewed rapid economic changes, whether for the better or worse, as destabilizing the social situations to which people had adapted and become accustomed. These destabilizations resulted in the anomic condition which provoked stress, anxiety, and, in the extreme, suicidal behavior.

Durkheim and Modern Sociology

Durkheim's theories, or at least thinking that is similar, continue to be highly influential in contemporary Western sociology and social thought in general. The state's economic and social role in guiding and attempting to stabilize the development of Western societies, as advocated by him, has grown enormously. Contemporary public schooling in the Western countries functions largely as an agency of ideological socialization. Through tracking of students according to supposed abilities, it begins the process of social ranking—or more often, and contrary to what Durkheim would have hoped for, simply mirrors the previously existing social ranking of students' family backgrounds. Education is viewed as the means for students from lower-class backgrounds who have ability to get ahead. His notion that people ought to be socially ranked according to their merit as opposed to family backgrounds has general liberal appeal. Durkheim can be properly interpreted as a thinker who both foretold and influenced these developments in both Western societies and their social ideologies.

Durkheim's dichotomy of simple and complex societies, in addition to referring to past and present societies, can also be interpreted as referring to the dichotomy between the European societies of his day and their colonies in Asia, Africa, and Latin America. As such, it represented a late nineteenth-century theory of the differences between First and Third World societies. European societies had complex organic divisions of labor, while traditional Asian, African, and Latin American societies had simple mechanical divisions. This interpretation has made the theory relevant to modern attempts to understand Third World underdevelopment. Many contemporary theorists now associate the development of complex divisions of labor with development and modernization.[7]

Durkheim's concept of anomie continues to be especially influential in contemporary analyses of alienation and social stress. It has been applied in a variety of different settings, including studies of the stressfulness of divorce on children and former partners, unemployment on workers, and uncertain employment prospects on graduating students.

His theory of suicide remains the starting point for all contemporary theoretical discussions of the topic. Modern researchers continue to subject Durkheim's statistical and theoretical reasoning regarding the social causes of suicide to intense scrutiny. A number, such as Pope (1976) and Stark and Bainbridge (1982) have argued that the differences between Protestant and Catholic suicide rates that Durkheim found reflected more the socioeconomic differences between the two groups than the natures of their respective communities. Much of the difference between Protestant and Catholic suicide rates vanished when the two groups were compared within the same class levels, that is, upper-class Protestants with upper-class Catholics, middle-class Protestants with middle-class Catholics, etc. Girard (1993), on the basis of a study of suicide rates in forty-nine countries, questions Durkheim's more general explanation that the strength of a person's social ties protects against suicide. On the other hand, Simpson and Conklin (1989) found on the basis of a cross-national study that Islamic rates of suicide were low, even when socioeconomic factors were considered, suggesting that in this case Durkheim's original thesis that a traditional religion that strongly bound individuals to a collective belief system had an independent effect on reducing the propensity to commit suicide. None of these modern researchers, however, regardless of their evaluations of Durkheim's particular conclusions, have questioned his general conclusion that there are social causes of suicide and thus that psychological explanations alone are insufficient.

MAX WEBER

Max Weber's work represents a second variation of classical First World social theories. Weber viewed capitalism critically as a system of domination in which human and cultural values were often victims of expediency. But at the same time he defended it as preferable to socialism. The critical theoretical analyses and insights of Weber into the character of capitalism often overlapped with those of Marx, despite the two having very different political values. It is not without justice that Weber has often been called the bourgeois Marx.

Comparative Research

Max Weber studied and worried about the meaning of life in the Western capitalist countries as they drifted inexorably toward increasingly efficient bureaucratic control. As more and more aspects of everyday life became rationally organized in the interests of remote elites, more substantive questions of freedom, spiritual meaning, and purpose receded into the background, producing a generalized cultural alienation.

Unlike Marxists who found hope in revolutionary socialism, or romanticists who found solace in mental flights into the past or later existentialists who created meaning out of the individual stance in the face of adversity, Weber judged the human condition to be hopelessly bound for even more difficult times. There was no light at the end of the tunnel. His life ended as European fascism emerged from the rubble of World War I.

What made life in the West all the more puzzling was that it was both very rational in one sense and deeply irrational in another. Madness, as in nuclear war and death squads, can be rationally organized. In many ways Weber's interpretations paralleled those of his contemporary Franz Kafka whose novels portrayed men trapped in bureaucratic nightmares. What for Kafka was a theme worked out in literary form and content for Weber became the structure for a complete philosophical stance and research method.

To fully comprehend Western society, Weber attempted to locate its origins in a confluence of historical events of which the Protestant Reformation was of unique importance, to define the logic of its institutions, and to predict its fate. His studies ranged over continents as well as back into the far reaches of history. He studied the histories, religions, economies, and other institutions of China, the Middle East, and

India, as well as those of the Western countries, producing volumes of work which continue to intrigue specialists. All of this was done to shed light by way of contrast on what the unique factors were which made for the development of what he (1905) called "this sober bourgeois capitalism" in the West. He employed a comparative method on a truly global and grand historical scale. Because of the way he thought and the encyclopedic nature of what he knew, his mind constantly jumped cross-culturally and historically as he compared his materials.

Max Weber is often described as the last of the great universal theorists of sociology. World history was the backdrop for his portrayal of a large variety of Eastern and Western social formations. Religion, law, economics, music, princes, and armies contend and interrelate across pages of detailed attempts to portray how various societies formed and held together.

Weber's quest, however, was not systematic. His interests sent him in one direction—the study of commerce, for example—and then another, that of ancient society, and only later did he attempt at all to put them together in an overall framework. Reading Weber chronologically is to read successively seemingly unrelated lines of inquiry: commerce, law, rural areas, ancient societies, methods, the origins of Western capitalism, economy and society, religions of the East, and politics. While general themes run through the work, there is no overall systematization that Weber was able to accomplish. Unlike a Durkheim or Marx who found clear albeit different logics to history, Weber shied away from finding any such key. Rather, history and societies were a grand variety of different puzzles or constellations, each of which must be interpreted in its own right, and only then related to general trends.

The Protestant Ethic and the Spirit of Capitalism

Like Durkheim and Marx earlier, the general themes of Weber's life work were announced in an early writing, *The Protestant Ethic and the Spirit of Capitalism* (1905). In that study, he concluded that it was no accident that Protestantism and capitalism developed during roughly the same period in Europe. His general thesis was that the mentality promoted by early Protestantism was more in tune with the necessities of capitalist development than that which had been associated with medieval Catholicism. The rise of Protestantism had broken the ideological monopoly of Catholicism, which had had many doctrines and practices antithetical to the needs of capitalist development.

Medieval Catholicism had, for example, prohibited charging interest for loans—which it called usury—as immoral. Money, in the medieval Catholic view, was like a tool. If a person had a tool that was not being used, and a neighbor wanted to borrow it, then morality dictated that it be simply loaned without thought of requiring a payment. In the same way, if a person had extra money that another needed to borrow, he or she should simply loan it without expectation of being repaid a sum higher than the original. The Catholic prohibition on charging interest precluded development of capitalist banking. Early Protestantism took a different view, finding no moral difficulty with the charging of interest.

Medieval Catholicism viewed worldly pursuits of wealth and success as being at the expense of religious devotion. The church demanded that surplus time and funds be invested in noneconomic religious pursuits. To be fully devout, a man withdrew from the economic world and entered a monastery. The best investment of village surplus funds and time was in the construction of elaborate cathedrals. The village might well be poor, but their church would be grand. The retreat from economic activity to pursue religious devotion was also reflected in the large number of holy days that were celebrated in medieval Europe. As many as one hundred days a year were set aside for spiritual contemplation. The Catholic attitude toward worldly economic pursuits thus slowed capitalist development because the church absorbed time, and economic surpluses could not contribute to the accumulation of economic capital.

Protestantism took a different view of the relationship between religious devotion and economic pursuits. It considered hard work at economic success as not subtracting from devotion to God. Luther viewed economic work as a vocation. A person glorified God through hard work and success at his worldly vocation. One did not have to retreat from the economic world into a monastery in order to serve God directly. He could instead work hard at his business. Economic success, in Calvinist doctrine, was a sign of religious grace (that one was predestined to go to Heaven). Protestantism did not demand that communities invest all of their surplus time and funds in building enormous and finely crafted churches. Its churches were models of simplicity. If the grand cathedral had been the architectural symbol of Catholic-influenced feudalism, the no-nonsense factory would become that of Protestant-influenced capitalism. And as Protestantism gained in a region, the number of holy days celebrated declined. Business (from "busy-ness") days crowded out holidays (from "holy days").

Weber saw the effects of Protestantism on capitalist development within a larger cultural and historical context. Protestantism did not spring anew. It manifested a current of Western culture which, while submerged during Catholicism's feudal reign, had existed since at least the time of the Romans. The key characteristic of this thought current was a particular concept of rationality in which life activities were viewed in terms of goals which had rationally calculable means to their attainment. The key goal of a capitalist business, for example, is profit.

All aspects of the business including labor can be rationally analyzed and measured in terms of how they contribute to the central goal of making the profit. Double-entry bookkeeping was invented in the West as a way of keeping track of business expenses and revenues in order to calculate profit rates exactly.

The great irony and unintended consequence of Protestantism was that its leaders and followers had no idea that the effects of their efforts to glorify God would be to free up the ideological terrain for capitalist development which, once institutionally established, would relegate religion to distinctly secondary importance in daily life. Weber saw Protestantism as simply a temporary carrier of the Western concept of rationality. Later thinkers, such as Benjamin Franklin (who penned such capitalistic aphorisms as "a penny saved is a penny earned" and "time is money") inherited and carried on the rational ethic, but one that was shorn of religious trappings.

Much of Weber's later studies were devoted to examinations of non-Western cultures and religions in order to understand why capitalism had not developed as early in those areas as it had in Europe. In general, he believed that a set number of material and ideological conditions had to be in place for capitalism to develop. Many non-European regions had had all of the material prerequisites for capitalist development, but their religions and cultures were antithetical to its development. Without the ideological prerequisite—a general type of rationalist mentality that could function in a capitalistic context—there were not sufficient conditions for capitalist development to flourish.

Rationalization

The concept of rationality is often identified with the concepts of truth and validity. But one of the great insights of Max Weber was that what is perceived to be rational is culturally variable. What is rational within one cultural context is not necessarily so within another. In the West, a particular type of rationality increasingly took hold that was both different from those of other cultures and compatible with capitalist development.

Weber (1922) noted that all cultures implicitly or explicitly incorporated notions of "substantive rationality." That is, they defined life activities in terms of how consistent they were with the attainment of their cultural values. They judged an activity to be substantively rational if they believed that its pursuit or accomplishment would bring about the realization of a collectively held goal or value. Christian prayer was substantively rational, since it facilitated religious devotion, a Christian value. So too was Aztec human sacrifice, since within its cultural context, it was believed to facilitate the physical survival of Aztec society.

What determined whether something was rational in this sense was not whether it actually would lead to the accomplishment of what it was supposed to—there is no evidence that human sacrifice actually prolonged the physical survival of Aztec society—but rather whether it was culturally believed to be consistent with that accomplishment.

In addition to incorporating a strong cultural dimension, Weber's concept of substantive rationality was also essentially qualitative. Basing himself in the classical philosophical distinction and contradiction of quality and quantity, he saw activities as being consistent with goals and values as long as they were oriented toward their achievement, regardless of whether progress toward that achievement could be quantitatively calculated. A person could fast in hopes of attaining spiritual enlightenment without knowing exactly how long the fast would have to last or whether the enlightenment would necessarily come.

Where the West culturally turned the corner on rationality in Weber's judgment was in its increasing definition of it in terms of quantitative and calculable criteria, producing what he called "formal rationality." If substative rationality represented defining life activities in terms of goals whose attainment could not necessarily be exactly and quantitatively calculated, then the originally Western concept of formal rationality represented defining life activities in terms of goals whose attainment could be exactly and quantitatively calculated.

Some life activities are easily thought of in formally rational terms. The attainment of a business's central goal, profit, is eminently measurable as are the means to its attainment. But other goals are not, and here Weber's playing off substantive and formal rationality leads to critical as well as cultural insights. None of such central life goals as well-being, significance, and happiness can be exactly measured nor can means to their attainment be fully calculated. Yet they are goals which are no less important than those which are calculable. People can live longer quantitatively without having qualitatively better lives. Education can be thought of in substantively rational terms as enlightenment and development of the mind. There is no way to exactly measure how educated a person is, though it can be thought of in narrow, formally rational terms as the number of educational classes a person takes—but at much expense to its substantive meaning. As nearly everyone knows, hours spent in a classroom do not directly or even necessarily add up to proportionately more and more enlightenment and development of the mind. An even more absurd example would be to think of religious goals in terms of numbers of hours spent praying.

Substantive considerations are always more profound than formal ones in judging overall rationality. The more that rationality of life activities is seen in purely formal terms, the shallower and less complete the resulting mentality. The more capitalism and Western culture in general developed, according to Weber, the more formal and less substantive their notions of rationality became. The increasing sway of formal conceptions of rationality was hence, in Weber's estimation, the motor force of Western development.

Bureaucracies

Bureaucracies, in Weber's view, were the organizational manifestations of the ethos of formal rationality. They were impersonal large-scale organizations within which component parts were rationally organized as a means for attaining central goals. Increasingly, according to Weber (1922), working relationships within the West took place within bureaucratic contexts. As such, the bureaucratic form had become the dominant organizational context of economic life. Weber viewed it as both highly efficient and alienating. It was an efficient form for organizing and coordinating labor. It was alienating in the sense that its apotheosis of organizational goals was often at the expense of the goals and needs of the people who worked within it.

Bureaucracies were also highly effective forms of domination in two senses. In the first, they were like organizational machines that elites controlled and used to control the rest of society. In the second, workers within them were dominated by their managers. Beyond being forms of personal domination, bureaucracies were also forms of a type of impersonal domination. Because of their internal dynamics, bureaucracies took on lives of their own which were often beyond the control or intentions of their creators. Weber believed that bureaucratic domination was inescapable in the future of the West, whether capitalist or socialist.

Unlike Marx or Durkheim, Weber did not view the future optimistically. He saw increasing bureaucratic domination and the crushing of humane cultural values. He wrote on the eve of Germany's plunge into fascism when his worst fears came true. Bureaucratically organized death camps became the horrifying symbol of new realities. The allied defeat of Germany and the other fascist powers in World War II ended the worst manifestations of the developments that Weber feared, but it did not end the long-term development in itself. He undoubtedly would have seen bureaucratic domination, impersonality, and alienation continuing in the postwar institutions and drift of Western culture.

Though not optimistic on what the future held for the subjective life of the West, Weber was a great believer in scientific outlook and pursuit as an antidote—if not a resolution—for the increasing stifling of human creativity in bureaucratized societies. Science could not produce happiness, well-being, or even existential meaning for life, but Weber clung to the belief that it at least helped one in uncertain times. The pursuit of science—knowledge for its own sake—did not proceed for Weber with the positivistic self-assurance of a Comte or Durkheim that it would bring us that much closer to full knowledge about society. Weber's goals and claims were much humbler: science helped one to keep his or her bearings in a journey whose outcome was perhaps condemned from the beginning.

Weber, Modern Sociology, and Postmodernism

Max Weber exercised enormous influence over the development of twentieth-century sociology. His influence continues to be especially felt in the sociology of religion, studies of large-scale organizations, and studies of politics and the state (see Chapter Seven). In addition, Weber's general orientation to social thought continues to find resonance in contemporary times in two respects. First, Weber's advocacy of a detached and objective sociology as opposed to one engaged in social reform or revolution appeals to many. Second, his conclusion that the marches of rationalization and modernization would be at the expense of human and cultural values foresaw contemporary postmodernist thinking which since the 1970s, with expressions in such diverse areas as social theory, architecture, city planning, music, and painting, has critically challenged much of what has been done in the name of modernizing societies.

Marx and Durkheim can be considered to have been modernist theorists in the sense that they equated historical development with human progress. They were also modernist thinkers in the sense that their theories implied that societies needed to be revolutionized or at least reformed by removing anachronistic institutional features. Max Weber, on the other hand, saw historical societies as simply different cultural constellations to be understood in their own terms rather than ranked according to progress toward an ideal. Since Weber was completely agnostic about what the goals, if any, of history might be, he could not view history in terms of progress, much less unequivocally endorse wholesale modernization of institutional features. In this sense, Weber was among those thinkers who doubted whether the quality of life of modern societies was any better than that of past societies. If anything, Weber would have identified modernization with the formal rationalization of institutions about which he had deep misgivings.[8]

A half-century after Weber's death, in the early 1970s, postmodernism began as a thought movement in the First World countries and similarly challenged the identification of human progress with historical development and modernization. According to postmodernist theorists, both capitalist- and socialist-guided notions of development had resulted in the wholesale destruction of humanly valuable parts of societies and their replacement by alienating structures. When urban planners, for example, redesigned metropolitan areas so that traffic would flow more freely, they often ran expressways through the hearts of what had been vibrant neighborhoods. What appeared to be a rationalization and modernization of the metropolitan area was at the expense of existing human communities within it. Postmodernists in general have stressed the concepts of relativism, diversity, quality, and pluralism over what they have identified to be the modernist concepts of progress, standardization, rationalization, and universal truths. As such, and like Max Weber before them, postmodernist theorists have critically questioned both what constitutes human progress and whether it can or should be planned by societies acting collectively.

SUMMARY

Marxian theory and ideology have had a large impact on sociology, the social sciences in general, and the development of twentieth-century history. Marx, Engels, and other socialist theorists fundamentally challenged the bases and legitimacy of capitalist societies and their dominant classes. They threw down the gauntlet, setting off raging controversies, which will continue on into the future, over the fundamental question of whether humanity would be better served by continuing the capitalist form of organization or by replacing it with socialistically organized societies. From Marx and Engels came the overall materialist and dialectical theories of historical development, which posit the eventual supplanting of the capitalist stage of history by higher socialist and communist formations in which equality and social justice would reign, and theories regarding the economic, class, and political characteristics of capitalist societies.

Durkheim combined positivism and functionalism into a theory of the structures of past and modern societies. He developed a liberal reformist advocacy of state intervention to guide societal development, and a rationalization for the continuation of class inequality.

Weber can be considered to be a critical theorist of capitalist societies who neither celebrated nor wholly condemned their features. Unlike Marx or Durkheim, he was not optimistic about the abilities of men and women to guide the future development of their societies. He predicted a continuing drift of Western culture toward bureaucratic domination, impersonality, and alienation. In many ways, he was a Marx for the bourgeoisie. He critically and realistically examined the causes of capitalist development and the character of its present institutions without drawing revolutionary conclusions. In other ways he was a sociological Kafka, pessimistically portraying a society in which human

whether consciously or not, different theories or ideologies over how governance should proceed.

POWER STRUCTURES

There are three major competing approaches to the understanding of power in contemporary sociology: the pluralist, the elitist, and the class. The pluralist approach, which has roots in the theories of Emile Durkheim and functionalism, assumes that power in modern democratic societies neither is nor should be monopolized by any one individual, organization, or class. Rather, depending on the decision being made, different interest groups mobilize and exercise influence. Public decision making thus continually shifts between different interest groups and individuals in relatively modern and democratic societies. To the question, "Who rules?" pluralists respond, "It depends upon the issue. No one individual or group monopolizes all decision making because a plurality of interest groups have access, at least temporarily, to the exercise of power if they prevail in the competitive struggle." In one administration, lobbyists for business interests will have relatively great influence, in another, lobbyists for labor interests will have more influence. The pluralist approach thus is especially attuned to examining the competitive nature of political struggles in modern democratic societies. As such, the pluralist assumption that there is necessarily a real competitive basis to politics is not meant to be applied to premodern or nondemocratic societies.

Elitist theory, which has roots in a broad spectrum of rightist, even prefascist, nineteenth- and early twentieth-century theory associated with Vilfredo Pareto (1848–1923) and Gaetano Mosca (1858–1941), the work of Max Weber, and critical sociologists on the left, such as C. Wright Mills (1916–1962), assumes that all societies have elites and masses, with the former ruling over the latter. For elitist theorists, the existence of such elites is not so much a problem as a simple reality underlying all societies. History cyclically records the replacement of one elite by another. An elite can be overthrown by a revolutionary counter-elite, but both are elites nonetheless, regardless of the ideologies that they espouse. From an elitist theoretical perspective, the Bolshevik Revolution represented the Czarist elite being overthrown by a Leninist one, a rightist elite being replaced by a leftist one. Elitist theorists find it revealing to distinguish between those elites that allow a circulation of fresh blood into their ranks from the masses below and those that are closed to new members. The former, by co-opting talented members of the masses, are more successful at precluding the formation of counter-elites that will threaten their existence. Unlike pluralist theories, elitist theories are intended to be explanations of power in most historical types of societies.

Class-based theories of power, which follow most, but not exclusively, from the work of Karl Marx and Frederick Engels, assume that ultimate power in a society resides in control over its means of production, which include all of the factors that are necessary to produce goods and services—land, production sites, tools, and raw materials. Since no society can survive without production, those who control the way a society produces control the way it develops. In modern societies thus, power resides ultimately in the class that owns or controls industrial, financial, commercial, and other economic institutions. Those who own or control these factories, banks, major stores, and other means of production ultimately, either directly or indirectly, exercise control over other institutional areas.

While the pluralist, elitist, and class-based approaches represent distinct conclusions about how power functions, many sociologists who engage in empirical studies combine insights from more than one for their own understandings and orientations. It is not uncommon, for example, to view power in terms of both classes and elites or to acknowledge the existence of pluralistic struggles within levels of what is viewed in overall terms to be an essentially class-dominated power structure.

Contemporary studies of power structures have proceeded at both local and national levels. On local levels, some individuals are able to put into motion or approve decisions that will greatly affect the subsequent life of the town or city. They can, for example, mobilize capital to finance an urban renewal project or rearrange how public schooling will be carried out. On national levels, there are individuals who are in a position to decide such important questions as whether the country will go to war or whether interest rates will rise. In both cases, local or national, most ordinary citizens are not involved in the decision making despite being deeply affected by its results.

Both types of power structures—community and national—are subjects of research for a double purpose: to determine who the often hidden wielders of power are and to refine the understanding of how power functions in communities and societies.

There have been three traditional approaches to determining who exercises power in a community. The first, the decision-making approach, which is most closely associated with pluralist assumptions, studies how and by whom significant decisions are made. Decisions where competing interests clash can be studied to determine balances of power. For example, the decision to undergo urban renewal within a city brings out into the open a large number of competing interests. Depending on how urban renewal programs are planned, landowning interests stand to gain or lose significant amounts of money. A convention center will raise land values around it. At the same time, businesses and residents may be forced out to make way for the new building, causing them significant losses. In such projects, it is rare for there not to be both gainers and losers. It is a question of the relative powers of the competing interests as to which fate besets which.

Decision-making studies, however, have several important drawbacks. Decision-making powers may be delegated to loyal managers and agents. Those who make the decisions—for example, on city councils—may not be the ultimate holders of power. Also, there are many types of questions which never come up for decision making because it is not in the interests of the powerful. Studies of decision making thus may only give a partial glimpse of how power is wielded in a community or society.

A second approach to determining community power structures, the positional, relies on identifying the occupants of powerful positions. This is done by first identifying the economic, political, and social organizations through which power is wielded within the community. Then the actual individual occupants of those positions are identified and studied. Once individuals and positions are identified, it then becomes possible to determine how powerful organizations are interrelated. Powerful individuals tend to exercise power in more than one organizational context. Corporate leaders sit on several boards of directors. Top managers serve in voluntary organizations such as the United Way. Top bankers are members of university boards of trustees.

The positional approach has the empirical advantage of clearly identifying the actual occupants of powerful positions, who can then be sociologically studied as a group. It shares though the same disadvantage as the decision-making approach in that the occupants of formal positions of power may be subordinates of still more powerful individuals behind the scenes.

A third approach, the reputational, attempts to identify individuals who hold both formal and informal power. In this approach, individuals presumed to be knowledgeable about power in a community are surveyed. Each is asked to identify a set number of individuals who he or she thinks are the most powerful in the community. The lists are then compared and tabulated, with those individuals named on the most lists being considered the most powerful. Their occupational positions and other characteristics can then be studied. Most community power structure studies which have followed this approach have usually turned up lists of individual financial and corporate leaders whose names were mostly unrecognizable by the general public.

Studies of power on national levels represent simply more encompassing applications of community power structure approaches. By far, the most discussed and influential study of national power structures in modern sociology has been C. Wright Mills's *The Power Elite* (1956), which portrayed the United States. Following from a model of the institutional structures of modern societies developed earlier with Gerth (Gerth and Mills, 1953), Mills concluded that power in the United States resided in the commanding positions of three institutional hierarchies— the economic, military, and political. Those who controlled those institutional orders coalesced into a power elite that controlled the country as a whole. Mills examined the occupants of these positions—who included corporate owners and executives, the joint chiefs of staff of the military, and such key political figures as the president, vice president, members of the cabinet, key senators and congresspersons, and governors and mayors of major states and cities—and concluded that most of them came from elite social backgrounds. Most often they were educated at private prep schools and colleges. Most of the members of the power elite thus came from social backgrounds and socialization experiences that were distinctly different from those of the mass of ordinary citizens. He further found that the occupants of the commanding positions within each of the institutional orders where power resided—the corporate, military, and political—tended to move back and forth. A corporate executive, for example, would receive a cabinet appointment or a retired top military official would join a corporate board of executives.

Mills's portrayal of power in the United States as being monopolized by a small group was immediately questioned by pluralists, who contended that there was much more competition and circulation of different interest groups in the corridors of power. Marxian theorists (see Sweezey, 1956) questioned the seeming parity between corporate, military, and political bases of power that Mills's model assumed. They viewed corporate power as being paramount, with military and political power being derivatives. Nonetheless, Mills's work continues to be the modern classic in the area of national power studies, influencing subsequent work in the United States (see Domhoff, 1967, 1983) and other countries (see, for example, Porter, 1965).

THE STATE

The classic theorists of sociology—Durkheim, Marx, and Weber—all recognized the special importance of the state, that is, the governing power within societies, but their emphases were different. Durkheim, as described in Chapter Six, viewed the state positively as the institution ideally suited to regulate the functioning of modern societies and resolve many of their problems. Of the three classic theorists, he was the most attuned to the growing role of the state in modern societies.

In many respects the role of the state for the functioning of societies has grown greatly during the twentieth century, as Durkheim predicted and advocated. Two centuries ago there were relatively few public employees in any country. Then, the largest form of state or public employment was as soldiers. Today though, in all First World and most other societies, public employees make up increasing proportions of overall labor forces, which, in addition to soldiers, also include workers in education, legal systems, production, social services, and other areas. The state has become, as well as the institution through which societies are governed, a key part of the economic structure.

Marx and Weber placed greater emphasis on the state as an instrument of domination. Marx and Engels (see Engels, 1884) essentially categorized state forms according to the class interests that they protected. The slave state protected the class interests of slave owners. The feudal state protected the class interests of landlords. The capitalist state protects the class interests of capitalists. When the state does not function in the interests of the economically dominant class, there is a contradiction because economy and state are not integrated. In "The Communist Manifesto," Marx and Engels (1848) emphasized that the bourgeoisie had achieved economic dominance long before it gained political power. They believed that the contradiction between the bourgeoisie's economic hegemony and relative political powerlessness was the underlying cause of seventeenth-, eighteenth-, and nineteenth-century revolutions and civil wars in England and Europe. It took centuries for the bourgeoisie to break the grip that the economically declining feudal nobility continued to hold on state power. Only then could the bourgeoisie consolidate its economic dominance with political power. Only then could it complete its historical destiny and become a politically ruling as well as economically dominant class. In a famous formulation, Marx and Engels (1848) concluded that as a result of this development "the executive of the modern state is but a committee for managing the common affairs of the whole bourgeoisie." In other words, the capitalist class became a politically ruling as well as an economically dominant class. In a modern capitalist society, thus according to the Marxian understanding, the owners and managers of the major private industrial, financial, and commercial enterprises through a variety of means, including campaign contributions which are seen as investments, lobbying, and organization of public policy think tanks, control the general course of state decision making.

The theme of domination was also present in Weber's theory of the state, which has had enormous influence in contemporary political sociology and political science. He (1918) defined the state as "a human community that (successfully) claims the monopoly of the legitimate use of physical force within a given territory." While dominant classes dominate economically by virtue of control over means of production, states dominate politically by virtue of control over means of violence—weapons—and the men and women who wield them as soldiers and police. That is the heart of state power. No state can survive for long if it does not have ultimate control of the weapons and military forces that exist within its territory. The popularly elected Aristide government of Haiti (1990–1991) was vulnerable to overthrow precisely because it did not have control over its own military. Aristide controlled the state administrative apparatus, but he did not have control over the most essential ingredient of state power, the military. It was an elected government without real state power. Military force is thus a final trump card of every state in danger, and it has been played innumerable times in past and present crises. In 1968, the French government maneuvered tanks on the outskirts of Paris as a warning to striking students and workers. In 1989, the Chinese government used troops to violently suppress student demonstrators. The appearance of tanks and troops indicates that a political crisis has reached the boiling point. States weaken when they lose control over weapons and military forces within their territories. Military leaders can act independently of political leaders, as they did in Haiti, or independently armed forces can arise within their territories, as they have in all societies that have undergone armed revolutions.

Weber's definition both differed from and overlapped that of the Marxists. Its most important difference was that it did not categorize states according to the class interests that they served. Its most important similarity was its emphasis on military force being at the center of state power. Weber (1918) approvingly noted Leon Trotsky's statement that "every state is founded on force" and undoubtedly would have agreed with Mao Zedong that "political power grows out of the barrel of a gun."

But in Weber's conception, weapons and armies, while crucial to any state's existence, are not sufficient to guarantee its long-term stability. Governments also need to be perceived as legitimate by their citizens. To govern effectively, they need to have the consent of the governed, or at least a substantial proportion of them. No government can exist for long if it is viewed as illegitimate by a substantial segment of its population. Its command over guns will keep it in power for the short run, but it will have to change to accommodate the wishes of its population or it will be overthrown.

The concern with legitimacy is also evident in the prison writings of the Italian Marxist Antonio Gramsci (1891–1937).[1] According to Gramsci (1956), a rising class, such as the bourgeoisie or the proletariat, becomes a ruling class not solely through seizure of the state apparatus and coercively imposing its will over civil society. In addition, it estab-

Kathe Kollwitz, The Outbreak

lishes its moral, political, and cultural leadership—what he termed *hegemony*—over allied strata. That is, much like Lenin's theory of the two-stage revolution (see Chapter Six), Gramsci saw a great range of forces allied against an old order. Many classes and strata could unite over the goal of deposing an old corrupt or simply reactionary ruling class. But there would be far less unity over how the new order should be constructed. It is here that Gramsci argued that if the working class were to become a ruling class, it must first convince its potential allies that its vision of the new order was in their interest and attractive. This, Gramsci implied, was a process that occurred historically as the working class developed into a hegemonic class. It was not to be confused with temporary alliances, as in electoral campaigns. The beginning of the first stage would long predate the outbreak of a revolutionary crisis or imminent collapse of the old order. Hence, in contrast to some interpretations of Lenin's theory of the two-stage revolution and concept of the dictatorship of the proletariat, Gramsci saw the working class coming to power less through coercion than through democratically establishing its ideological, moral, and cultural leadership—in Weber's term, *legitimacy*—and uniting the majority of society.

All states attempt to produce and maintain legitimacy. They face legitimacy crises and weaken when substantial numbers of their citizens perceive them as corrupt, incompetent, oppressive, or dominated by foreign interests. It is not so much the legitimacy of particular government officials that is of issue. They can always be replaced. Legitimacy crises of these types can be handled within the governing system, as when Richard Nixon was obliged to resign the presidency of the United States after the Watergate scandal. Rather, the more serious type of legitimacy crisis is one of confidence in the governing system itself. Legitimacy crises of this type require radical institutional changes to be resolved.

For purposes of legitimacy, ideally nation, state, and territory coincide to form one integrated nation-state. In order to be perceived as legitimate, the state must be closely identified with the nation over which it rules. There are always underlying legitimacy problems when nations are ruled over by alien or foreign-identified state apparatuses. Contradictions between nation and state have been indeed the largest cause of wars in this century. Unresolved national issues continue to underlie armed conflicts in many parts of the world, including Northern Ireland, Israel, and Ethiopia.

Weber (1921) defined the nation as a "community of sentiment." People who share the same national origin feel a common bond which they do not share with people from other national backgrounds. Weber added as an almost defining characteristic that nations normally tend to produce their own states. If they are frustrated in that quest and must endure being dominated by a state with which they do not identify, instability results.

Colonialism was the clearest example of the contradiction between nation and state. In all colonial situations there are actual or potential legitimacy problems due to the contradiction between the different national identities of state rulers and the ruled, since colonizing powers form their own state apparatuses to administer their territories. France appointed French citizens to administer the governments of Algeria and Indochina in the nineteenth and twentieth centuries. For hundreds of years Great Britain used British citizens to govern India and a number of African colonies. Until 1952, the United States directly formed the government that administered Puerto Rico.

The same contradiction can emerge in neocolonial situations, where foreign powers indirectly dominate countries. If state officials are too closely identified with those interests, they can lose the confidence of their compatriots by being open to the charge of betraying the nation to

South Central Los Angeles, 1992

foreigners. In a different manner, contradictions between state and nation can besiege postcolonial countries. Most of the present boundaries separating African countries were established during the colonial period by France, Britain, Germany, and Portugal according to their interests and relative powers, rather than according to the logics of prenational tribal identities. Tribal areas and peoples were split by colonial boundaries, sowing the seeds of future problems.

LEGITIMATIONS OF POWER

Beyond the question of national identification, Max Weber concluded that there were different reasons why people accepted the authority of states to rule over them. Different states, in brief, could rest on different types of legitimacy. In his view, three different types of legitimacy—traditional, legal-rational, and charismatic—had played roles in history as foundations facilitating state governance. A fourth type, democratic, has since become especially evident.

Traditional

In states underpinned by traditional legitimacy, people obey out of long-standing habit. The governing system and authorities have been institutionally entrenched for so long that people take them for granted. Alternatives to status quo arrangements are unknown or inconceivable. In Weber's view, traditionalism accounted for the widespread public acceptance—either active or resigned—of most precapitalist state structures. Slow paces of social change in feudal and other precapitalist societies encouraged a conservative traditional worldview. Rulers could change through death or replacement, but the essential traditional structure of governance and obedience would remain unchanged. Traditionalism has also been a strong force in the twentieth century. It has underpinned state structures in China, Japan, and Ethiopia, among others. It continues to be an active force underpinning contemporary Middle Eastern monarchies.

Legal-Rational

Weber's description of legal-rational legitimacy was a logical extension of his theory of the growing dominance of formal rational modes of thought in modern societies (see Chapter Six). He counterposed legal-rational to traditional legitimacy as the form most suited to modern state structures. In this type of legitimacy, people obey because they believe that state rulers and rules have been chosen on the bases of reasonably devised constitutional procedures with which they agree. They presumably obey, not out of habit or ignorance of alternatives as in traditionalism, but rather out of reasoned acceptance of the rules of the game. Formal-rational systems vary according to whether or not state rulers are chosen democratically, with the democratic variety having developed as the most important contemporary form of legitimation of state power.

Charismatic

This is an historical wild card which often augers a period of significant change, for better or for worse. At various times and in various situations, truly exceptional leaders emerge. What makes them exceptional is that they are perceived by their followers as being uniquely gifted to lead. The charismatic leader has an aura about her or him which magnetically draws committed followers. The charismatic situation is characterized by a sense of immediacy and communion between leader and followers. Unlike traditional situations, where people obey out of long-standing unreflected habit, or the legal-rational situation, where they obey out of reasoned agreement with how the system works, people follow and obey the charismatic leader out of attraction to her or his magnetic personal qualities. The leader's perceived charisma may be a function of extraordinary public speaking skills or simply mode or style of being. It may as much be created by the wishes of followers as emanate from leadership qualities. Charismatic situations are often associated with periods of significant social changes, often upsetting traditionally or legal-rationally constituted state structures. Charismatic leaders can dispense with traditionally accepted or constitutionally based norms and directly appeal to their followers. "It is written, but I say to you." Charismatic leaders, such as V.I. Lenin, Adolf Hitler, Mao Zedong, Ho Chi Minh, Ayatollah Khomeini, and Fidel Castro, have clearly played instrumental roles in the shaping of the political history of the twentieth century.

DEMOCRACY

Democratic legitimation became a near-universal norm in world politics by the middle of the twentieth century, with most of today's world leaders claiming the right to rule on the basis that they were constitutionally selected to do so through formally democratic means. All of the leaders of the world's First World societies claim that they have been selected through democratic processes. So too did the leaders of the post–World War II socialist countries—though that was widely disputed. The same claim is made by the majority of Third World leaders. If democracy is met with near-universal approval, dictatorial rule—whether carried out by an individual, family, or group—is met with near-universal disapproval.

The road to democratic legitimation in world politics has been long. Before the twentieth century, very few societies had instituted formal processes for democratically selecting leaders. The dominant classes of most societies saw little need or felt little pressure to involve ordinary citizens in any way in governance. Once democratic selection processes began to be instituted, they often contained significant restrictions, such as restricting voting rights to property owners, males, or those who were literate. It has only been in this century that voting rights were extended to all adults in the First World countries.

But while democratic legitimation has become nearly universal, it would be a mistake to assume that the claim of democracy is the same as democracy itself, or that formal democracy necessarily constitutes substantive democracy in a given society. Democracy (from the Greek *demos* or "people," and *kratos* or "rule of") generically means "rule of the people." As such, the concept is counterposed to other types of rule, including monarchy (rule of the one), aristocracy (rule of the best), and oligarchy (rule of the few). But if democracy means rule of the people, to what extent do the people actually rule in any modern society?

The answer to that question depends upon how the notion of *rule* is defined. If rule means participation in the actual making of all decisions, then the people rule nowhere. If rule means participation in the selection of people who make decisions, then the people rule, at least indirectly or formally, in many societies. However, the extent to which the wishes of the people are represented in the decisions that are actually made varies greatly.

While the world contains a large number of societies that have formally democratic constitutions, there is no one universally approved form of formal democracy. Rather, the world's nominally democratic societies differ according to how they institute democratic participation, with the different systems having different consequences for the character of politics. In some systems, such as that of the United States, there is direct voter selection of the top leader. These vary according to whether there must be a run-off election if no candidate receives over 50 percent of the vote. For example, the Brazilian constitution requires that there be a run-off election in such conditions, while the U.S. Constitution does not. Thus, Bill Clinton could take the office of the presidency in the U.S. in 1993 despite having received only 41 percent of the vote in a three-way race. In other systems, which are in place in the majority of European countries, there is indirect selection, with voters selecting the members of a national parliament which in turn selects the top leader. In some systems, national parliaments are made up of representatives of single geographically defined districts, where the top vote-getter represents the district. In other systems, parliaments are made up of representatives of political parties, with each party being awarded representatives according to its proportion of the total vote. In some systems, representatives to the parliament vote strictly according to party guidelines, in other systems, they vote more independently.

Systems of formal democracy vary according to the number of political parties that substantively participate. The postwar socialist countries, which claimed to be formally democratic—the formal name of East Germany, for example, was the German Democratic Republic—invariably took the forms of one-party states. Their ruling communist parties were constitutionally guaranteed monopolies over the exercise of political power. Such other parties as there were led entirely token existences. Thus Article 6 of the Soviet Constitution stated:

> The leading and guiding force of Soviet society and the nucleus of its political system, of all state organizations and public organizations, is the Communist Party of the Soviet Union. The C.P.S.U. exists for the people and serves the people.

The Communist Party, armed with Marxism-Leninism, determines the general perspectives of the development of society and the course of the domestic and foreign policy of the U.S.S.R., directs the great constructive work of the Soviet people, and imparts a planned, systematic and theoretically substantiated character to their struggle for the victory of Communism.

Communists justified their monopoly over political power with the claim that they democratically represented the interests of the proletariat. This, according to their justification, represented substantive socialist democracy, since the proletariat was the majority.

A number of Third World countries have also had single dominating political parties and claimed to be formally democratic. Single-party Third World states have often emerged from revolutions, with revolutionary leadership either transforming its organization into a ruling party or reconstituting itself as such a party. Those developments have been especially apparent in countries where the ruling party claimed revolutionary nationalist legitimation in a revolutionary struggle against a colonial, foreign-dominated, or corrupt regime. Examples in this century can be found in the histories of Mexico after the 1910–17 revolution, Algeria after the 1962 defeat of French colonialism, and Iran after the 1979 overthrow of the Shah.

First World countries vary according to whether they have two or multiple parties. In general, two-party systems are favored in those countries where parliaments are made up of representatives from single districts. Multiple-party systems emerge in those countries where parliaments are made up proportionally of representatives of the parties that contend according to votes received. It is difficult for third parties to emerge in systems where there is single-member representation of districts because voters are reluctant to give their votes to candidates who are not perceived to have a chance of winning. In proportional representation systems, on the other hand, voters are more willing to give votes to minority parties, since those parties are guaranteed to be represented in the parliament even if they do not receive a majority of the votes. This latter form tends to favor more ideological pluralism in politics. The former, according to its advocates, favors the center of the political spectrum and more efficient decision making.

POLITICAL STABILITY

Political stability is a condition that varies greatly among the world's societies. Almost at any given time there are crises or potential crises, including civil wars, revolutions, and coup d'etats, that threaten the existences of at least some state apparatuses somewhere in the world.

State power and political stability rest, if we follow Max Weber's conceptualization, on the material foundation of control over the means of violence and the ideological foundation of command of legitimacy or consent. Few contemporary world political leaders or theorists would disagree. This conceptualization of state power lends itself to a useful typology (Figure 7-1), constructed from its two constituent variables of military control and legitimacy. A given state can be in control of both, one or the other, or neither of the variables. The typology thus yields four types of state situations which affect political stability: (1) military control with legitimacy (the most stable), (2) military control without legitimacy, (3) legitimacy without military control, and (4) neither military control nor legitimacy (the most unstable). For convenience, we will call them, respectively, secure states, military rule, endangered civilian rule, and crisis-prone situations.

For obvious reasons, type 1—military control with legitimacy—is the most stable political and state situation. The government has firm control over its military forces, and they are clearly superior to any other armed groups that might exist within its boundaries. Citizens view the state as governing with their consent. They may elect new officials to replace old ones whom they no longer support, but there is no perceived need to replace the whole political system. At the present time all First World and a number of other societies appear to fall into this category.

In type 2—military control without legitimacy—the state is in firm military control, but it governs without sufficient consent from the governed. State systems of this type may be able to last for long periods of time, as the Pinochet military government of Chile and the apartheid state system of South Africa demonstrated, but they face continuing obstacles to governing effectively. General Pinochet, who had governed

FIGURE 7-1 Typology of Political Stability

LEGITIMACY

M			Strong	Weak
I	C			
L	O	Strong	1 Secure state	2 Military rule
I	N			
T	T			
A	R	Weak	3 Endangered civilian government	4 Crisis
R	O			
Y	L			

since overthrowing the civilian socialist government of Salvador Allende in 1973, was obliged to hold an election for the presidency in 1990, which he lost to Patricio Alwin, a civilian. South Africa was finally obliged by internal and external pressure to institute universal suffrage in 1994. Universal suffrage, in and of itself, however, does not guarantee political stability.

In type 3—legitimacy without military control—the endangered civilian government enjoys sufficient popular support, but it either does not control its own military or its military is weaker than a competing force within the territory. The Aristide government in Haiti was an example of a popularly elected and supported government that did not control its own military. It was therefore vulnerable to being overthrown. The 1930s Spanish Republic was an example of a popularly supported government whose military forces proved to be weaker than those of the insurgent fascist general Francisco Franco.

For obvious reasons, type 4—neither military control nor legitimacy—is the most unstable, crisis-prone state situation. The state neither is popularly supported nor does it have control over military forces operating in its territory. It is a state in name alone. Lebanon has been the most well-known recent example of such a situation. The Lebanese government's military has had very little territorial control with most of the country having been divided up into fluid zones fought over by rival non-government militias.

It is thus an unescapable reality of contemporary world politics that military force and legitimacy are essential foundations of state power. The strength of both variables must be calculated in assessing the stability of any state apparatus.

POLITICS AND IDEOLOGY

If politics is about the struggle for power, there are different general ideologies to which men and women adhere, at least in those struggles that concern public or state power. These ideologies concern, first, how the struggle itself will be conducted—the politics of politics, so to speak—and, second, what will be done with state power if and when it is attained—the ideological goals proper. A third, and not inconsequential, issue concerns whether politics is carried out relatively honestly or corruptly, that is, whether successful political actors use the state power that they have attained to further their ideological goals or, first and foremost, as simple opportunities for personal profit. For our purposes here we will assume that politics is carried out honestly enough for there to be a relationship between background ideological goals and exercises of power.

The politics of politics concerns the institutional rules under which the competitive struggle for power is conducted. Here there have been two general approaches in world politics. The first—adhered to by conservative, liberal, and socialist parties—endorses political pluralism, that is, political systems in which a number of parties electorally compete to attain and maintain governing power. The second—which has been adhered to in this century by a number of otherwise ideologically distinct military, religious, fascist, revolutionary nationalist, and communist parties—endorses maintenance of state parties in which one party exclusively governs by being institutionally fused to the top of the governing apparatus.

A number of diverse ideological goals have motivated political action in world politics, but the central thrusts in the last century and a half can be characterized in left-right terms. The distinction between right- and left-wing politics originated in nineteenth-century European parliaments where supporters of the government sat on the right side and those of the opposition on the left. Rightism became associated with conservatism and defense of the status quo, while leftism became associated with opposition politics and advocacy of social change. Those vague political meanings carried over somewhat into twentieth-century usage. But more importantly, twentieth-century usages of the concepts of rightism and leftism have been more directly concerned with economic policies and class interests. Rightist parties have been associated with capitalist-style reforms and upper-class interests, and leftist parties with socialist-style reforms and working- and lower-class interests.

The five most significant political ideologies for most of the twentieth century, ranging from right to left, have been fascism, conservatism, liberalism, socialism, and communism. They have set the spectrum of secular politics. Other political ideologies, such as anarchism, have existed but have not had the same impact.

Fascism

Fascism represents extreme right-wing authoritarianism in the forms of movements to conquer state power or governments that rely on using highly repressive means to maintain order. There have been both First and Third World varieties of twentieth-century fascism.

Fascists have often come to power with the support of dominant capitalist classes, as in Germany and Italy, in order to protect their interests in a deteriorating economic or political situation. Economic depressions or the rising strength of lower-class movements and leftist parties have thus been economic and political conditions respectively which have provoked dominant classes to resort to using fascist means to maintain control.

Fascists believe that the masses are incapable of democratically governing themselves. Rather, they must be governed firmly if order is to prevail (Mannheim, 1936). Fascist governments have thus used state terrorism—assassination, torture, paramilitary death squads, concentration camps—to repress lower-class movements and left-wing opponents. Fascists envision a hierarchically structured organic society in which elites govern the willing masses cleansed of subversive elements. Pre-World War II German and Italian fascism was characterized by both charismatic leaders and mass support. But fascism need not have a mass base. The military government of General Augusto Pinochet, which overthrew the socialist government of Salvador Allende in Chile in 1973, was often described as fascistic despite lacking a mass base of support. The fascist ARENA party, which became the governing political party of El Salvador in 1989, is an in-between example. It has been able to attract the votes of a significant part of the population despite its leaders having been repeatedly linked to death squads which have been used to repress El Salvador's labor, peasant, and student organizations.

Conservatism

The basic thrust of contemporary conservative ideology is advocacy of free market capitalism. Private enterprise, according to conservatives, should be given full reign, with state economic regulation and interference kept to a necessary minimum. Except for defense spending, state budgets should be trimmed back. Social spending on education, health, and housing should be cut back. The market should be the ultimate economic regulator. If companies cannot survive market competition, they should go bankrupt. If individuals cannot earn enough income to avoid poverty, they should be poor. The market, according to conservative beliefs, is thus the best judge of economic quality and dispenser of social rewards and punishments. Conservatives therefore believe that class inequality functions positively. The market, not state redistributive policies, should determine how wide the gap will be between economic classes. The Thatcher and Major administrations in England and Reagan and Bush administrations in the United States have been the most prominent recent proponents of consistently conservative policies.

Liberalism

Liberals advocate state-regulated capitalism. They share with conservatives a general belief in the viability and desirability of private enterprise, market-based economies. But they believe that if capitalist tendencies are not regulated, economic and social crises will occur. Since the world depression of the 1930s, liberals have successfully advocated that states use controls over credit systems to regulate business cycles so that recessions do not slide into depressions. In the social sphere, liberals advocate that the state use its taxing powers to redistribute some income from the top to the bottom. Liberals believe that if the gap between class living conditions widens too far, social crises will break out which will threaten the stability of the whole system. In the United States, the dominant part of the Democratic Party advocates liberal economic and social policies.

Socialism

Nineteenth-century socialists originally advocated revolutionary change to produce economies with complete public ownership of the means of production. But by the early decades of the twentieth century, socialists or social democrats, as they are also called, increasingly endorsed evolutionary rather than revolutionary change. They believed that socialism would come about through elections of socialist governments which would gradually increase the state sector at the expense of the private. Socialists and social democrats today firmly endorse the notion of mixed economies with public and private sectors. Like liberals, they advocate use of the state to regulate the market and social relations. Unlike liberals, they are in favor of the state ownership of a number of key enterprises, which can include banks, mines, and manufacturing concerns. Socialists more aggressively advocate than do liberals state financing of extensive social programs, including free national health systems. Socialist and social democratic parties have been governing parties in England, France, West Germany, Italy, the Scaddinavian countries, Greece, Spain, and Portugal, among other countries.

Communism

Communist parties shared a core belief in the basic validity of Marxism and consequent commitments to working-class interests and socialist goals. They believed that the working class was the basic agency for socialist change and were in favor of a much more rapid construction of socialism than were socialist parties. Consequently, they advocated a greater extent of public ownership and state control over the economy than did socialists.

The Bolsheviks were the first major communist party in the twentieth century. Following the success of the 1917 revolution, communist parties rapidly organized in most other countries. They remained aligned to the Soviet Union through the 1940s. But since the end of World War II, Western and Third World communist parties progressively distanced themselves from the Soviets. Since the late 1930s, with the ending of the Third International which Lenin had formed, there has been no one international organization of world communist parties. The Sino-Soviet split, which surfaced in the early 1960s, was the final indication that world communism was no longer unified. From the late 1950s until the downfall of the socialist countries, beginning in 1989, there were considerable ideological and strategic differences in points of view between communist parties.

The Future of Political Ideology

The world historical year of 1989 symbolized a new era in world politics. The beginning of the collapses of most of the socialist countries that year capstoned a decade-old rightward shift in world politics, signaled most clearly by the conservative economic policies of the Reagan administration in the United States and the Thatcher government in the United Kingdom.

In the First World countries the rightward shift pulled Western liberals and socialists away from their original moorings. Socialist parties, such as those of Spain and France, embraced privatization of state-owned enterprises for which they themselves had advocated public ownership in previous decades. With the pendulum of state economic policy having swung so far to the right, statist solutions to capitalist problems, not to mention socialism itself, were increasingly edged out of political discourse in the Western countries.

In the Eastern countries, a number of former communists recast themselves as democratic socialists, while many others abruptly turned into their opposites and became capitalists. As reality inverted itself in the former socialist countries, a confusing inversion of the meanings of left and right emerged. Journalists increasingly described those advocating market reforms and privatization of state-owned industry as liberals and those defending public ownership as conservatives. And as tight communist ideological control over the old order crumbled, old suppressed nationalisms violently erupted into warfare in regions of what had been Yugoslavia and the Soviet Union. If the soldiers of the old Warsaw Pact countries were permanently poised to go to war over the ideological dispute that generated the cold war—a war that never came—those same soldiers after 1989 were more likely to be actually at war over one or another domestic ethnic-based conflict.

The 1980s also saw the ascendence of religious-based politics. The 1979 Iranian revolution brought to power Islamic fundamentalists who sought to infuse politics with their religious principles. Islamic fundamentalism now represents a serious force in nearly every Middle Eastern country, with Algeria and Egypt having been especially affected. In the United States, evangelical Protestantism—the Christian Right—became a political force, similarly seeking to reverse the secular separation of religion and the state.

These rapid shifts in world politics—the rightward move, the resurgence in nationalism, and the attack on secularism—have produced a kind of political anomie in the 1990s. The old structures governing ideological politics—especially the cold war contention between the superpowers—dissolved while new structures and their ideological reduxes had yet to fully take their places. A person in this decade thus cannot predict, with the same confidence as someone in the 1970s could, the course of world politics for the next decades.

Nevertheless, despite this present anomic nature of world politics, what can be predicted with confidence is that there will continue to be lefts and rights in politics. What will remain as the basic—but not exclusive—question of politics in the coming century, as it was in this one, is what the relationship should be between the state and civil society, between public and private interests, with leftists opting for the primacy of the former and rightists for that of the latter.

SUMMARY

All societies beyond the earliest have been marked by power as well as class differences, with power being exercised within a wide variety of private and public social settings. The functioning of particular institutions cannot be understood without an understanding of power differences between the actors within those institutions. Each institution, in brief, has its power structure, and these have been the subjects of sociological research.

The state is the ultimate arena of societal power. It is the unique institution within societies that can legally authorize the taking of lives, whether through military actions or, in those societies that maintain capital punishment, as a means of civil control. The classical theorists of macrosociology viewed the state as an institution of growing importance in the functioning of modern societies (Durkheim) and in the form of domination (Marx and Weber). Max Weber's definition of the state—that institution which has the monopoly over the control of the legitimate means of violence within a society—has been especially influential in the development of political sociology and political science understandings.

There have been various bases of legitimacy, that is, bases on which rulers have claimed the right to rule historically, and people have obeyed them. Weber outlined three: traditional, legal-rational, and charismatic. Democratic legitimation, a subtype of legal-rational legiti-

TABLE 8–1 *Titanic* Percent Survival Rate by Class of Ticket Held

	Men	Women	Children
First class	34.0	97.2	100.0
Second class	8.0	83.9	91.7
Third class	12.0	54.7	30.3

Sources: Lord (1955) and Davie (1987).

TABLE 8–2 Poverty and the Risks of War. Family Backgrounds of Wisconsin Soldiers Killed in Vietnam Compared to All Families.*

	Families of Casualties	All Families
Poor	27.2	14.9
Nonpoor	72.8	85.1
	100.0	100.0

*Note: Percent poor among the parents of Wisconsin servicemen killed in Vietnam through December 31, 1967 compared with the parents of male seniors in the Wisconsin high school class of 1957.

Source: Zeitlin, Lutterman, and Russell (1973).

contemporary social stratification and inequality: class, race and ethnicity, and gender. As a structural principle, class inequality runs through virtually all contemporary societies, with people occupying unequal positions of power and pay at work, living in unequal housing, wearing clothing of unequal quality, having unequal educational opportunities, and so forth. Class inequalities are most fundamentally based on economic structures, but they often are related to historically created racial and ethnic divisions. Blacks in the United States, for example, disproportionately occupy lower-class positions because of the history of racial discrimination that originated with slavery. Similarly, Southern and Eastern European immigrants to the United States disproportionately occupied lower-class positions because of ethnic discrimination. Crosscutting the inequalities wrought by class, race, and ethnicity are the social inequalities attached to the biologically given position of being a male or female within a society.

Investigating and determining how class, race and ethnicity, and gender inequalities—socially created inequalities that are associated with economic structures, historical developments, and biological differences—interrelate, often reenforcing each other, within societies is one of the principal challenges facing contemporary stratification research. Beneath this now commonplace trilogy of class, race, and gender are considerable theoretical issues, controversies, and debates. Marxian, nationalist, and feminist theorists place priority on, respectively, class, racial or ethnic, and gender issues. In extremes, these amount to ignoring the importances of the nonprioritized inequalities—the Marxist who sees only class struggle, the narrow nationalist who refuses to recognize class conflict or gender issues within the oppressed racial or ethnic group, the ultra-feminist who sees men as the enemy. But, more commonly, they represent different sensitivities and advocacies within contemporary critical attempts to grapple with social inequality.

ECONOMIC AND SOCIAL CLASSES

The concept of class (from *classify*) has a long and controversial history in sociological research. In general, we can distinguish two broad traditions within this research: one that concentrates on analyzing different *economic* classes—such as employers, workers, and small business owners—that make up the labor forces of societies, and the other that concentrates on analyzing different *social* classes—such as upper, middle, and lower classes—that live within communities and societies. What differentiates the two traditions are the settings—labor forces or communities—within which people are classified into classes. It follows that the two traditions offer complementary portraits of inequality at work and inequality in communities.

The first tradition, which has roots that go back to Max Weber and Karl Marx, relies on what can be called a relational concept of class, with economic classes being defined according to the different relationships that people have to the means of producing wealth in a society. Each type of economic system in world history beyond the earliest communal societies has contained a central means of producing wealth, the control of which has been monopolized by the most powerful economic class. In state societies, royal families and high officials controlled the state apparatus which allowed them to collect taxes from peasants. In slave societies, owners controlled slave labor which was the most important generator of economic surpluses and wealth. In feudal societies, landlords controlled the land, which allowed them to collect rent from peasants. In capitalist societies, capitalists own the means of production (capital) and employ workers from whose labor they garner profits. In the postwar socialist societies, managers and political officials controlled state-owned businesses that employed most of the labor forces. Outside of these primary class locations there have been other secondary class positions within economic divisions of labor. In slave societies, merchants existed alongside of masters and slaves, as they did in most feudal societies alongside of landlords and peasants. In capitalist societies, middle classes exist alongside of and between capitalists and workers.

The second tradition of class research, which has theoretical roots that go back most directly to the work of W. Lloyd Warner and Joseph Schumpeter, concentrates on how people experience and perceive social inequality within their communities. Social classes, within this tradition, tend to be defined according to the different levels of income and standards of living within which individuals and families live. Social classes thus are made up of people who share a common standard of living—rich, poor, or some position in between—within a society. There is also a tendency for people within the same social class to see themselves as social equals and as different from people in higher or lower classes.

Social class position is related to but not wholly deducible from economic class position. In general, incomes derived from economically dominant class positions support upper-class lifestyles, while incomes from economically dominated class positions support less prosperous social class lifestyles. But a particular economic class position can be associated with more than one possible level or class of social standard of living. A Main Street clothing merchant, who is economically a small business owner, can enjoy a proper middle-class standard of living. Down the street a shoeshine operator, who is economically also a small business owner, will be much more likely to have to endure only a lower social class standard of living.

In sum then, to this point, economic class position is determined by location within the economic division of labor. Social class position is determined by the level of income or relative standard of living within the society. Economic class terms have to do with relationships of work or production (masters, slaves, capitalists, workers, etc.), while social class terms generally have to do with consumption possibilities (rich, poor, upper, middle, lower, etc.).

The first step in developing a class profile for a particular society is to determine what economic and social classes exist and calculate their relative sizes. The next step is to determine how class stratification is influenced by and interrelated with other forms of stratification, such as racial, ethnic, and gender inequalities. Put differently, it is important to determine the correlates of economic and social classes, that is, to what extent racial, ethnic, gender, and other groupings are proportionately or disproportionately represented within each of the economic and social class categories. This profile can then serve as a basis for documenting causes and results of institutional forms of class, racial, ethnic, and gender discrimination.

In examining the recent and contemporary world, it is apparent that the class structures of developed societies differ from those of developing societies.

Developed Societies

The labor forces of developed capitalist societies generally have four economic classes: capitalists, the new middle class (employed professionals and managers), small-business owners, and workers. These reflect the economic division of labor of advanced industrial market societies. Capitalists (the bourgeoisie in classical language) own businesses that are large enough to have employees or workers. Capitalists thus function economically both as owners and employers. The capitalist class includes all of those individuals whose income is derived from the profits of large businesses. Such profits can be derived directly from ownership of a particular business or indirectly from investments spread over different stocks. Some members of the capitalist class directly work where their capital is invested. Others are *rentiers* who do not work, but instead live off dividends, interest payments, and capital gains. At most, capitalists account for 2 percent of the labor forces of First World societies.

The new middle class developed in the twentieth century with the growth of state and corporate bureaucracies, which created positions for employed professionals and middle-level managers. In the past, most professionals, such as doctors, lawyers, and architects, were owners of their own small businesses; likewise the vast majority of positions that required managerial skills were in small businesses. With the development of corporate and state bureaucracies and the parallel decline of small businesses, the location for exercise of professional and managerial skills shifted from self-employed to employed locations. This was often referred to by sociologists (see Mills, 1953, for example) as the shift from the old middle class of small-business owners to a new middle class of middle-level employees in large corporate and state bureaucracies. Employed middle-level professionals and managers now make up as much as 20 percent of the labor forces of First World societies.

The classical small-business owners class was composed of farmers (the largest sector), professionals, merchants, and artisans (self-employed skilled workers, such as carpenters and electricians). Like capitalists, small-business owners derive their income from business profits. But unlike capitalists, they are not fundamentally employers. At most, they employ a few auxiliary helpers, often family members. The small-business owner's most important employee is himself or herself. Small businesses continue on the margins of the corporate economy, employing now not more than 10 percent of the labor force, down from a high of 70 percent or more in the nineteenth century.

The working class is made up of all those below middle-level managers and professionals in the employed labor force. During the industrialization phase of capitalism, most workers were employed in factories.

But with the rising productivity of the industrial sector of the economy, it has been possible for increasing numbers of workers to be shifted away from factory employment and into offices, sales, and services. Workers of all types make up as much as 65 percent of developed capitalist labor forces, by far the largest share of any economic class.

Many people have income derived from both capital profits and the sale of their labor. It is the relative proportions of each that identify their substantive class position. A capitalist may work at a profession and have a public identity as such. But that may mask her or his real class identity. According to newspaper reports, the late Jacqueline Kennedy, widow of both a former president and a shipping magnate, earned a salary of $45,000 as an editor in 1990. She also had a fortune of $200 million which generated in that year at least $15 million of additional income. Put differently, at least 99.7 percent of her income was generated by the capital that she owned. In 1989, the former president of the United States, George Bush, and his wife, Barbara, had a combined income of $456,780. Forty-one percent of their income came from his $189,167 salary as president. The 59 percent balance came as returns from the ownership of capital (Associated Press dispatch in *The New York Times*, April 13, 1990, p.10). In 1993, President Bill Clinton and his wife, Hilary, had a combined income of $293,757. Most of their income came from his $189,167 salary. But another $42,284 came from capital gains, interest, and dividends (*The New York Times*, April 16, 1994, p. 8). Meanwhile, Vice President Al Gore and his wife, Tipper, had a combined income of $453,907, two-thirds of which came from business investments (Associated Press dispatch in *The Hartford Courant*, April 16, 1994, p. A6). It appears thus that while the Gores enjoy a capitalist base to their income, the Clintons are moving toward establishing such a base. On the other side of the ledger, workers, middle-class professionals, or small-business owners may divert a part of their savings into stock investments. Income from these investments, though, only accounts for a small fraction of their total income. Just as Jacqueline Kennedy's having a job does not make her a member of the working or middle class, a worker's minuscule stock holdings do not make her or him a capitalist.

Economic class categories reflect the structure of a society's economic division of labor. But, as mentioned, the ways in which people perceive their class existences do not necessarily directly reflect economic class categories. A college student from a middle-class family may take a summer job as a worker. Economically, he or she functions as a worker for that period of time, but socially he or she continues to identify with a middle-class social existence. Even where adults have settled into life-long economic class roles, they may not perceive of their class existences in those terms. Especially in First World societies, where consumerism has become an important way of life, what may be paramount in the minds of many is the standard of living or lifestyle that their incomes afford.

There are a number of ways of getting at how social class levels are perceived. W. Lloyd Warner (1949) pioneered much of social class research by simply asking samples of people within communities to name what they thought the town's classes were. From these interviews he was able to derive a six-class model: upper upper class (old wealth), lower upper class (*nouveau riche*), upper middle class (professionals, business owners), lower middle class (sales clerks, office workers), upper lower class (regularly employed workers), and lower lower class (the unemployed and poor).

For a number of years in the United States, researchers polled people, asking them with which of three broad social classes—upper, middle, or lower—they identified. Eighty percent or more usually answered, "middle class," which led to various conclusions that the United States was a middle-class country or that class divisions had nearly disappeared. Then Richard Centers (1949) modified the design of the questions, giving respondents four rather than three choices. They were now asked which of four social classes—upper, middle, working, or lower—they identified with. The results were that over 50 percent identified with the working class, a somewhat lower percentage with the middle class, and as in the original research, very small percentages with either the upper or lower class extremes, percentages of social class identification that have continued to hold in the United States. In a 1984 national survey (Center for Political Studies, cited in Gilbert and Kahl, 1987, p. 252) 50 percent of respondents identified themselves as working class and 47 percent as middle class.

While there are many different views today regarding the identity and number of social classes in developed countries, Centers's original conclusion that there were four—the upper class, the middle class, the working class, and the lower class—continues to resonate with the greatest acceptance among the general population and a large number of social scientists.

Joseph Schumpeter (1927), Paul Sweezy (1953), and others have importantly identified the characteristics of social class existence by noting that social classes are like communities in which one moves freely and comfortably among equals. Moving in social classes above or below one's own presents difficulties and is uncomfortable. Sweezy characterized a social class as a network of "freely intermarrying families." The patterns of social class existence are also evident in where people eat. Max Weber used the term "commensality," which refers to who one feels comfortable eating with. Quite clearly, restaurants have social class characters to them. Their prices act to restrict access to particular income levels. The prices reflect not only the quality of the food and its preparation but also the exclusivity of the clientele and atmosphere. One is reminded in this context of C. Wright Mills' (1956) observation that rich people never have to read the right hand columns of menus. Bars follow the same pattern. People like to drink with social equals, resulting in lower-, working-, middle-, and upper-class bars. Finally, most cities residentially reflect social class patterns, with observable upper-, middle-, working-, and lower-class neighborhoods and districts.

In addition to developing economic and social class profiles, stratification researchers have sought to quantitatively measure and statistically express a number of related issues. There is considerable research into the degree of relationships that exist between positions within stratification hierarchies and such varied characteristics as voting behavior, health, educational achievement, and entertainment habits. As alluded to in the beginning of the chapter, social class position affects survival. Spruit (1982) extensively reviewed studies of the relationships between social class and mortality and morbidity (sickness) and found invariably that the lower the social class the higher the rates of both. The issue of social mobility commands much research attention. To what extent is class position inherited and passed on intergenerationally within family lines, and to what extent is there opportunity for people to rise above their class origins? The concerns of this research follow from the original circulation of elites proposition (see Chapter Seven) that closed class systems are vulnerable in the long run to stagnation and the rise of revolutionary challenges from below if they continue to frustrate the aspirations of talent from humble origins.

Developing Societies

Since virtually all developing societies now have capitalist market economies, their economic class divisions of labor resemble to a degree those of developed societies with roles for capitalists, workers, small-business owners, and a new middle class of employed professionals and managers. But the relative sizes of these classes are different, and there may also be sizeable peasant classes in the countrysides.

The relative distribution of the labor force between the two economic middle classes—small-business owners and the new middle class of employed managers and professionals—resembles that which existed in First World societies a number of decades ago before corporate and state bureaucracies developed as major employing entities. There are more small-business owners than employed managers and professionals. Third World cities, and even the countryside, abound with commodity enterprises. Vendors push carts hawking everything from food to apparel. Other merchants compete for buyers in open-air markets. Craft workers' shops line whole streets and districts. While some of these small-business owners are indeed socially as well as economically middle class, most in fact live socially at working- or lower-class levels. They form a kind of *lumpen* (from the German "rag") bourgeoisie. If Third World societies do follow the general stages of development which have already occurred in First World societies, it can be expected that in time large businesses will squeeze most of these micro-businesses out of the market.

Third World peasants, in the economic meaning of the term, are small farmers who, along with household members, consume most of what they produce. They are fundamentally outside of the market economy. They may take surpluses and sell them on market days, and they may purchase some commodities, but most of what they produce they consume themselves, and most of what they consume comes from their own products. In a number of Third World societies there are still substantial classes of people who live in this manner.

Use of the term *peasant* in a Third World context can be confusing because it is employed in both an economic and a social sense, which are different. In its Third World social connotation, the term simply means the rural poor, who include the types of noncommodity producing farmers just cited, commodity-producing farmers (who, economically, are a rural small-business class), and landless rural laborers (who, economically, form the rural working class). In most cases, the three rural economic classes of peasants, small-business farmers, and workers merge socially in the sense that they share similar standards of living and consider themselves to be social equals. They form a single peasant social class despite being drawn from three different economic class positions.

Third World social scientists often use the haunting concept of *marginalized* to refer to people on the peripheries of national labor forces. These include landless peasants in the countryside, for whom there are no regular sources of employment, and urban dwellers, who have recently migrated from the countryside and similarly are unable to find steady employment. Together they make up the poverty-stricken social lower class.

The source of their immiseration lies in the economic transformation of Third World agriculture. Large landowners have increasingly monopolized ownership of land and, along with competition from low-price imported grains and other foodstuffs, squeezed small producers out of local markets. As food production in general has become more efficient economically in the sense that fewer laborers are needed to produce the same amounts, increasing numbers of rural workers have been released from that type of employment. The result of these and other trends is that Third World countrysides support proportionately less people than they did in past eras. As immiseration grows, people leave

Splendor and Misery, photo by Tina Modotti, Mexico, 1927

for the cities. But the urban economies are not so developed as to be able to absorb productively the large numbers of newly arriving impoverished peasants from the countryside. These "marginalized" people crowd into shanty towns that ring the larger cities, eking out existences as best they can.

Third World social scientists have also increasingly used the concept of the *popular classes* to refer to all of those who, in an absolute sense, share the fate of being poor. These include workers, small-business owners, and the marginalized. Together, the make up absolute majorities in most Third World societies.

What is striking about Third World social class structures, in comparison with those of First World countries, is their greater rigidity and inequality. Perhaps because many Third World societies retain significant feudal vestiges, at least in the area of their consciousness and ideology, the notion of significant class mobility is not seen, especially by the upper classes, as either a realistic possibility or necessarily desirable.

Postwar Socialist Societies

The postwar socialist countries developed class structures that were uniquely different from those of the developed capitalist countries. But as they began in 1989 to move away from strict state ownership and toward mixed economies, their class structures correspondingly shifted and began to approach those of capitalist countries. Nevertheless, the postwar socialist class structure remains worthy of examination as an important alternative experience.

Given the different nature of their economic systems, the postwar socialist countries had different structures of economic classes than did First World capitalist countries. There were no capitalist classes of any significance, since the major means of production were owned by the state rather than private individuals. Direction or management of socialist means of production rested in the hands of a class of political officials from the governing communist parties, and managers who functioned economically as a class in the sense that they performed a particular role in the division of labor of socialist production systems. Below them were middle-level managers and professionals, who were comparable to their counterparts in the Western countries. At the base of socialist societies were the majority working classes. On the margins of the economies small-business owners—farmers and shopkeepers, mainly— continued to exist.

There were thus clear economic role differences within socialist production systems, which were qualitative enough to be considered economic class differences. Indeed, it would be difficult at this point in history to conceive of any large-scale production system that could function without class differences between managers, workers, and intermediate ranks. Such class systems were a natural concomitant of the sizes and complexities of socialist production systems, within which large-scale bureaucratic organizations were the most typical locations for working relationships. The existence of such economic class differences, though, did not mean that the postwar socialist countries were unable to make progress toward their implied goals of abolishing class distinctions.

The ruling working-class ideology dignified in an almost ennobling sense the status of being a worker. Unlike in the developed capitalist countries where class mobility into middle- and upper-class positions is the mark of success, in the postwar socialist countries one was encouraged to feel proud of being a worker. Hence, however much there were functional differences between working- and middle-class occupations in production, these did not produce as much pronounced social class and status differences as they did in Western countries. In short, while economic class differences necessarily remained, social class differences narrowed considerably. The introduction of market reforms and privatization in Eastern Europe and the countries that once belonged to the old Soviet Union has had the inevitable effect of widening income differences and thereby social class differences.

DISTRIBUTIONS OF WEALTH AND INCOME

Distributions of wealth and income are important indicators of class equality and inequality within societies. There are two types of wealth. Personal wealth includes properties, such as homes, cars, and boats, that owners consume as private citizens. Capital wealth includes all properties, such as land, businesses, and stocks, from which owners derive incomes. Income includes everything that individuals receive from all sources: from wages, salaries, invested capital wealth, or indirectly from benefits available to all citizens (the so-called social wage), such as state-subsidized free or reduced-cost public education.

Two individuals can have equal amounts of income. But if the source of one's income is interest and dividend payments from invested capital wealth and the source of the other's is wages or salaries, the first has distinct advantages in terms of living conditions over the second. The first can devote her or his time to pursuits, such as politics, culture, or leisure, without having to worry about whether they pay an adequate income. The second must always keep a paying job. The first can always easily get a job if more income is desired. The second does not have the option of easily acquiring capital property to supplement the paycheck.

As we have seen above, in capitalist societies the richest individuals and families get the bulk of their incomes from the ownership of capital wealth (stocks, bonds, and real estate for the most part). Middle- and working-class people get the bulk of their income from wages or salaries. Put in more classic political economic terms, capitalist income comes from profits derived from the ownership of capital wealth, while the income of most other people comes from the sale of their labor. Distributions of wealth are invariably more unequal than are distributions of overall income because only small minorities of the populations own significant amounts of capital wealth.

Figures on distributions of overall income are publicly accessible for many countries. They indicate that income distributions are highly unequal in all countries. They tend to be significantly more unequal in developing than developed countries. On average, the richest 10 percent in developing countries receive 39 percent of all personal income, which greatly exceeds the 25 percent received by their developed countries counterparts (World Bank, 1994, p. 220).[1] Part of the reason for this pattern is that because of television and increased international travel, global standards have developed for upper- and middle-class lifestyles whose maintenance requires a larger proportion of national incomes in poor than in developed countries.

Figures on wealth and income distribution have political importance because the more there is an extreme polarization of income and wealth between upper and other classes, the less likely there will be political legitimacy and long-term social stability. They have economic importance because if the effective demand—income necessary to purchase commodities—of the majority of the population is too low, producers do not have markets and go out of business.

Governments have the power to alter the distribution of income. Progressive taxation and funding of social programs (the social wage) function in the direction of equalizing incomes. Lowering tax rates for

TABLE 8–3 Redistribution of Family Income Upward in the United States between 1980 and 1992

Percent of Total National Income Received by:	1980	1992
Poorest 20 percent	5.2	4.4
Second 20 percent	11.5	10.5
Third 20 percent	17.5	16.5
Fourth 20 percent	24.3	24.0
Richest 20 percent	41.5	44.6
Total	100.0	100.0
Richest 5 percent	15.3	17.6

Source: U.S. Bureau of the Census, 1994, p. 470.

the rich, such as capital gains taxes, and cutting back social programs have the opposite effects. In capitalist countries, conservatives and liberals differ over how much and in what direction state redistributive actions are necessary to maintain distributions of income within functional political and economic limits. Depending on who is in power, state policies affecting income distributions see-saw back and forth. The conservative Reagan and Bush administrations in the United States (1981–1993) pursued policies which resulted in a redistribution of income upward (see Table 8–3). The share of national income taken by the richest 5 percent of families increased by 15 percent, while that of the poorest 20 percent decreased by 65 percent.

There is great resistance among the Third World rich to use the state for reforms to either redistribute wealth (especially land) or overall income downward. Third World economies are generally not prosperous enough to allow upper classes to redistribute some of their income and wealth downward and still enjoy standards of living that are equivalent to those of their First World counterparts. As Weisskoff and Figueroa (1976, p. 75) observed, "in order for the top 5 percent [in Latin America] to sustain a standard of living established by the middle class in the industrial countries, it must mobilize a proportionately larger share of its own country's output."

Land redistribution has been the key demand of Third World peasants, a demand that the landowning oligarchies are unwilling to meet. Highly unequal distributions of land were at the root of rural problems in Guatemala, El Salvador, and Nicaragua, which exploded into revolutions and civil wars in the 1960s, 1970s, and 1980s.

Both leftist revolutionaries and counterinsurgency experts from First World countries agree that the maldistributions of land and income are root causes of most Third World revolutions. For that reason, both revolutionary movements and counterinsurgency programs advocate land reform and redistribution of income. Both the South Vietnamese National Liberation Front—the Viet Cong in newspaper accounts—and the U.S. Agency for International Development (AID) designed land reform programs for South Vietnam. In El Salvador, the U.S. AID designed and implemented a land reform program to counter the appeal to peasants of the insurgent Farabundo Marti National Liberation Front (FMLN). There are, though, key differences between land reform programs advocated by leftist revolutionaries and those designed and implemented as parts of First World counterinsurgency strategies to thwart revolutionary change in dependent Third World countries. Revolutionary programs generally target much more land for redistribution than those programs designed as parts of overall counterinsurgency strategies, and are therefore more objectionable to large landowners.

RACE AND ETHNICITY

Within multiracial societies, there can be a clear correspondence between racial characteristics and the likelihood of having particular economic and social class positions. The more racism—the ideology that there are superior and inferior races—is institutionally ingrained, the more likely that such correspondences will exist.

The origins of racism and racial tension within multiracial societies have been generally economic. Racism as an ideology usually develops to rationalize or justify exploitation or unfair economic treatment of one racial grouping by another. The enslavement of black Africans by whites of European descent is a particularly clear example. The labor needs of plantation economies in the Americas stimulated the African slave trade. Once blacks were in the Americas as slaves, a whole ideology of racism developed to rationalize and justify their unequal treatment.

The institutionalization of racism and racial tensions has, as is obvious, outlived the institution of slavery. Blacks in the United States are disproportionately more likely to be members of the economic working class, less likely to be capitalists or new middle class, and more likely to be in the social working and lower classes than are whites. Racism as an ideology is reproduced intergenerationally by its being both a cause and outcome of economic discrimination against blacks. It is a cause of discrimination for obvious reasons, and the result that it produces inferior living conditions for blacks reenforces the racist rationalization of innate inferiority.

The intimate relationship of class and race in many—but not all—societies exists despite the concept of race itself being largely rejected today by most physical anthropologists as an adequate scientific basis for classifying people. Physical anthropologists have generally given up trying to develop taxonomies or classification schemes of discrete races. Among those who made such attempts in the past, there was never agreement even on what the number of supposedly different races was. For sure, there are physical differences among people, with skin color variations between dark and light standing out the most, which can be called racial characteristics, but it makes little sense to try to trace those to distinct races, and it makes much less sense to allege the existence of innately superior and inferior races (for discussions, see Simpson and Yinger, 1985, Chapter 2, Miles, 1989, Chapter 1, and Reynolds and Lieberman, 1993).

Among groups that share the same so-called racial characteristics, there can be ethnic or cultural differences which correlate with the distributions of upper and lower positions in class structures. The concepts of nation, nationality, and national minority have been traditionally employed to describe peoples who share common ethnic characteristics which result in their developing distinct national identities—such as being French, Irish, English, or Russian. The most important characteristics of national identity are common language, land, culture, and history. The French, for example, have common characteristics of language, territory, culture, and historical experience that are different from those of the English. French people therefore feel a common identity among themselves that they do not feel with English people. National or ethnic minorities result when peoples either migrate from their home territory to another where another nationality dominates (the Chinese in the United States are an example), or they are indigenous to the territory, such as Native Americans, but another nationality or ethnic group dominates.

In multicultural societies one or more ethnic groups may disproportionately monopolize upper positions in the class structure and restrict access to them by ethnic minorities. Immigrant workers from Southern and Eastern Europe, for example, found themselves relegated to the economic and social lower positions in the United States at the end of the nineteenth and early decades of the twentieth centuries.

In multiracial and multicultural societies, where racial and ethnic prejudices exist and where the different racial and ethnic groupings generally only socialize within their own communities, a unitary economic class system may be accompanied by multiple social class systems. While the economic structure is integrated in the sense that there is one economy with its corresponding economic classes, the different racial and ethnic groupings who work alongside of each other may retreat at the end of the day into separate social existences within their own communities. If they lead separate social lives, do not see themselves as being on equal social terms with members of other racial or ethnic groups who share similar economic class positions, and do not intermarry with them, then they are in a separate social class despite sharing the same economic class. White and black workers, for example, can be in the same economic class but different social classes if they do not see and interact with each other as social equals.

CLASS AND RACE IN NORTH AMERICA

A comparative examination of the three countries of North America—the United States, Mexico, and Canada—reveals how class and racial dynamics can form in similar and different ways within neighboring societies.

The North American continent before the European conquest was home to a large number of indigenous societies which varied greatly between classless hunting and gathering bands and the Aztec Empire in which clear class differences existed between those who controlled the state apparatus, merchants, peasants, slaves, and others. The conquest, which took place in phases and in different parts of the continent for over three centuries, stopped further indigenous class development. As the Spanish and other European conquerors consolidated control of the various areas of the continent, they either interlocked their own class systems onto the already existing ones of the Indians, as in Mexico during the early period, or they simply constructed their own societies and class systems on a *tabula rasa*, so to speak, as in New England or on the U.S. and Canadian frontiers. In either case, Indian class systems for the most part soon vanished. The only indigenous class position that substantially survived the conquest and has survived almost to the present was that of the peasant, especially in Mexico, who continued to practice a form of subsistence-based horticulture regardless of who held power.

If in the pre-Columbian period, societies had varied according to their level of technological development and degree of social complexity, in the colonial period they varied according to which European power was the colonizer, with Spain, England, Holland, and France staking claims to different parts of the continent and to the dominant economic relations that each was institutionalizing.

Capitalism, feudalism, and slavery were the triangular poles that defined these colonial class structures. Since each power had its own institutions and was at a different level of capitalist development, what emerged during the colonial period to some degree reflected the differences between the European powers. Spain, the most economically backward of the powers, implanted class institutions that were most rooted in feudal traditions. To a lesser extent, France implanted semi-feudal class structures in New France. England's colonies were the most unencumbered by feudalistic institutions and thus able to develop capitalistically at the greatest speed. The Mexican class structure, which largely revolved around landlords and peasants, thus was closest to the feudal pole while New England's, which revolved around market-oriented farmers and merchants, was closest to the capitalist pole. At the same time, slavery, which revolved around the class positions of owners and slaves, was implanted with its center in the south of what would become the United States but also in parts of the areas that would become Mexico and Canada.

The Europeans implanted more than their economic and class institutions on North American soil. They also, most importantly, began world history's largest intermingling of racially different people since, in one way or another, the colonial and postcolonial drama threw together Africans and, to a much smaller extent, Asians as well as the European conquerors and the original indigenous inhabitants. Now four races and their mixed descendants would inhabit the continent. Never before in world history on such a scale had so many racially distinct people been brought together.

From the beginning of the colonial period there developed clear correlations between class and racial position—black slave and white slave owner, Indian peasant and white landlord, etc.—that were rationalized by the ideology of racial superiority and inferiority, that is, racism. The world's races began to merge in North America, but in different class roles. They integrated, but vertically, with Europeans being at the top, directing the colonial enterprises in which people of color played subordinate parts. Class and race continued to be correlates in the postcolonial period down to the present in North America, though not as strongly.

Quite clearly, capitalist development has been the guiding force of postconquest economic class development, with countries and regions varying according to how far they have come along its road. Capitalist development in general progressively results, as discussed above, in independent producers being expropriated from their means of production as capital accumulates and centralizes in the hands of large producers. Hence, economic class structures progressively shift from having large numbers of independent farmers and urban small-business owners to having large numbers of employees working within corporate and state bureaucracies. Put differently, capitalist development displaces the small-business owners class, sometimes called the old middle class, as it opens up new working-class and middle-class professional and managerial positions (the new middle class) within private corporations and state bureaucracies. The further developed a society's accumulation and concentration of capital, the more its labor force is made up of employees rather than independent members. This difference can be seen quite clearly today in the Mexican economic class structure vis-à-vis those of Canada and the United States. There is a proportionately lower concentration of capital in Mexico and consequently proportionately many more independent members in Mexico's labor force than in the other two countries.

The United States and Canada have developed quite similar postindustrial economic class structures that are, at the same time, very different from that of Mexico. In economic class terms, the most remarkable difference is that over 90 percent of the labor forces of the United States and Canada are made up of employees, while a full quarter of the Mexican labor force is self-employed. This century saw in both the U.S. and Canada a steady driving out of business of independent farmers and store keepers, and their—or their economic offspring's—repositioning as employees. For one generation, it was not atypical to have been born on a farm but end up managing an office. In class terms, as what was called the old middle class of small-business owners declined, growing corporate and government bureaucracies opened up new positions for middle-level managers and professionals (the new middle class). Of course, not every descendent of the former majority old middle class ended up in a new middle-class position. The ranks of the urban working class also swelled with farm recruits. The reason the economic class profile of Mexico is different thus is that the accumulation of capital in the sense of large business driving out small business has not proceeded as far. The Mexican countryside contains proportionately four or five times the numbers of farmers as does that of the U.S. or Canada. Similarly, Mexican cities contain proportionately about that many times the number of people who make their livings from ownership of small businesses as do either of the two other countries.

In a number of ways, the Mexican economic class profile resembles that of the United States or Canada about ninety years ago. It follows that the future will see a steady erosion of the position of Mexican small farmers and other business owners as private corporations increase their shares of the market. Some, as happened in the U.S. and Canada, will move into newly created middle-class managerial and professional positions; most, as is already happening, will swell the ranks of the urban working class.

If economic class development proceeds in an almost linear fashion toward the structures now shared in the U.S. and Canada—what the future holds for Mexico—social class history does not show so clear a progression. There are different ways in which social class configurations can develop around economic class structures. Thus the social class profiles of Canada and the United States are not as close as are their economic class profiles. Canada has followed more redistributive policies that favor the poor than has the United States, consequently, the size of its poor population is proportionately smaller. These are after-tax measures. In before-tax measures, the sizes of the populations are similar. In other words, if the relative size of the lower class—those people officially classified as poor in a society—was determined solely by what occurs in the marketplace, then the relative sizes of the Canadian and U.S. lower classes would be similar. But because Canada has more aggressively followed redistributive policies that favor the lower class than has the United States, the size of its lower class is significantly smaller.

In social class terms, the most outstanding difference between Mexico and its two continental neighbors is that its lower class of the poor makes up a much larger percentage of the profile. At least 40 percent of the Mexican population is poor according to one government study (PRONASOL, 1990). The real percentage is arguably higher since, according to the 1990 Census, one out of every two Mexicans within the country lives in housing without indoor plumbing. The Mexican poverty rate of over 40 percent at a minimum compares to about 14 in the United States and 9 in Canada. As a result of the disproportionately larger lower class, the Mexican middle class is disproportionately smaller, not exceeding 17 percent of the population, compared to about a quarter of the populations of the U.S. and Canada.

Today, the racial demographics of the three countries are strikingly different. Canada has proportionately the most whites, Mexico the most Indians, and the United States the most blacks. These contemporary figures follow logically from long-term historical developments. Canada had relatively little slavery in its history, hence its black population is minimal. It has been mostly a country made up of European immigrants who, as in the United States, have had periods of ethnic conflict. Canada's Indian population, while proportionately larger than that of the United States, is much smaller than that of Mexico.

Mexico, historically the location of the Aztec and other empires, had the densest Indian population before the conquest and continues to have the densest population today. Over 98 percent of the Mexican population exists somewhere on a racial continuum between the poles of white and Indian. Blacks and Asians exist in Mexico but to a much smaller degree than in the United States or Canada.

The United States is the most multiracial of the three countries, since there is significant representation of whites, blacks, and Asians, though it has proportionately the smallest Indian presence.

In all three countries there are substantial numbers of mixed-race persons. In Mexico, mestizos, who combine Indian and Spanish descent, make up nearly 80 percent of the population. In the United States, estimates of the proportion of blacks who also have European or Indian ancestors range between 60 and 90 percent (Davis, 1991). In Canada, the métis population combines Indian with French and English descent. In continental terms, mixed-race persons are the largest racial minority, however, they are culturally perceived very differently in the three countries. Mexico defines itself with pride as a mestizo society. Canada, though it has relatively few mixed-race persons, officially recognizes their existence, with the métis being the most outstanding example. The United States, however, with some exceptions in its history, has not identified mixed-race persons as such. They have been identified either as blacks in the case of mulattoes, or according to the majority part of their descent in the case of mestizos. There are though some indications that this cultural practice may be changing as the number of mixed-race persons who do not wish to negate or have negated part of their identity continues to grow in the United States.

Today, a half millennium after Europeans began their conquest over the indigenous societies of North America, whites continue to disproportionately occupy the top economic and social class positions in the United States, Canada, and Mexico; and in all three countries racism and racial tension continue to be serious social problems, though with differing manifestations.

GENDER

The most primordial division within the human species—between males and females—has been the subject of considerable stratification research for the past several decades, in large part stimulated by the 1960s revival of feminism.

In most societies, males have more power than females, exercising greater power in economic production, political decision making, and over the domestic households within which they live. The original condition of this gender stratification is often called *patriarchy*—"rule of the father" literally, but male domination in a more generalized sense. Its most brute expression is male domination being imposed by physical force, as in cases of rape and domestic violence. The concept of sexism is to gender inequality as the concept of racism is to racial inequality. Both represent attitudes that rationalize or justify the continuation of the inequality. These run the gamut from patronizing views of "the weaker sex" to raw misogynous prejudices.

Patriarchical domination has been institutionalized and integrated in different ways in state, slave, feudal, capitalist, and socialist societies. Its origins remain shrouded in controversy. As briefly described in Chapter Four, Frederick Engels (1884) believed that there was an original period in world history of equality between the sexes, but that once males began to accumulate private property and wealth, they consolidated their economic gains by imposing power over their households. Patriarchy thus, according to Engels, became institutionalized for all succeeding generations. Engels' explanation remains the leading hypothesis of the origins of patriarchy, but not without detractors who have either offered alternative explanations or found evidences of historical patterns that did not conform to the hypothesis. Nevertheless, there can be no doubt, whatever the origins, that male domination has been a salient feature of world history. The depth of the historical institutionalization of patriarchal attitudes is indicated by voting being initially restricted to males in most countries.

The relationship between patriarchy and capitalism has shifted over time. In the early stage of capitalist development, most economic production continued to be centered within households for household consumption. Very little of it was destined for market sale. Patriarchal relations reigned within these households, mainly farm economies, but it would be difficult to argue that male labor produced more value than female labor, since very little of either had a market value attached to it. Both were valuable not in the market sense but in the sense of their usefulness to the survival needs of the household. Both genders worked hard at producing these survival necessities, which included food, clothing, housing, and child care and raising. There was thus a gender division of labor within production, but it was not necessarily an unequal one. At the same time though, men were still the ultimate repositories of societal power. Thus, in colonial America, for example, only men could own property, vote, or give testimony in court (Ryan, 1979).

As capitalism developed, especially during the nineteenth century, a new stage emerged in which an increasing gender-related division opened between labor expended in the household for household use and labor expended in the outside market economy for wages or profits. Male labor began to be increasingly concentrated in the market economy where it was valued in market terms, while female labor continued to be expended mainly within the household economy where the type of value it produced, no matter how necessary or useful, was considered to be of secondary importance. This led Frederick Engels (1884, p. 158) to argue that "the emancipation of women and their equality with men are impossible . . . so long as women are excluded from socially productive work and restricted to housework, which is private." Engels' implication was twofold. First, women had to enter the paid labor force where market value was created; and, second, it would be possible to achieve, or at least begin to achieve, women's equality under capitalist conditions.

In the contemporary stage though the issue is no longer entry of women into the labor forces. That has already substantially happened. Women make up about 41 percent of the labor force of the United States and 35 percent of that of the total world economy today (World Bank, 1994, p. 219). Rather, the issues are achievement of equality within labor forces and necessary off-the-job social services and support.

The participation rate of women in the U.S. and other labor forces grew in part because of the revival of feminism, which argued that for gender equality to occur, women would have to achieve positions of equality within paid labor forces. So long as their labor was performed exclusively within households, it was unpaid and did not generate economic power and equality, as also had been noted by Engels. However much though that feminist considerations spurred many women to seek jobs outside of the house, economic necessity was an undoubtedly more important stimulant. Up through the 1950s in the United States, it was possible for most middle- and working-class families to live moderately well on the basis of one income. But that is no longer possible for most families. It now takes two incomes to maintain most middle- and working-class standards of living. Whatever the relative weighing of the causes, the two-wage-earner family is now a firm social reality in many countries.

In the United States, women have not only increasingly moved into the labor force, but they have also begun to increase their representation in its middle class managerial and professional strata. The advance has been of such magnitude that today there are proportionately more women than men in those occupations—in 1992, 33.4 percent of full-time, year-round women workers were in professional or managerial occupations, compared to 29.3 percent of males (U.S. Bureau of the Census, 1993b, p. 152). The impressiveness of that occupational advance though is tempered by its being concentrated largely in those occupations, such as teaching and nursing, that have traditionally been open to women and the reality that overall professional and managerial women workers receive only 70 percent of what males receive. Gender wage differentials continue to exist at all occupational levels, as indicated by Table 8–4.

As many women have voluntarily or involuntarily assumed responsibility for attaining household incomes, the extent to which men have been willing to correspondingly increase their responsibility for performing necessary domestic labor—child rearing, food preparation, cleaning,

TABLE 8–4 Gender Income Inequality. Median Earnings of Year-round Full-time Workers

	Men	Women	Ratio: Women to Men
Managers	$42,509	$29,816	0.70
Professionals	$44,015	$31,261	0.71
Technicians	$33,010	$24,055	0.73
Sales	$31,346	$17,924	0.57
Clerical	$27,186	$20,321	0.75
Service	$20,606	$12,931	0.63
Farm	$14,897	$10,079	0.68
Craft	$28,923	$19,045	0.66
Laborers	$23,005	$15,772	0.69
Military	$22,569	n/a	
All workers	$30,358	$21,440	0.71

Source: U.S. Bureau of the Census (1993b, table 32, p. 152).

etc.—has varied. Many working women, thus, must endure a double shift—one in the paid labor force and one at home without help. Arlie Hochschild (1989, p. 3) surveyed the estimates of a number of researchers during the 1960s and 1970s of how long men and women in the United States worked when paid work, housework, and child care were added together. She averaged their estimates and came to the conclusion that women worked approximately 15 hours more a week than men. For the 1980s, according to her research, the gap between the lengths of the respective workweeks had narrowed little if any.

In addition to women from two-wage-earner households, a growing proportion of women workers are the sole supports of their own households. Rising rates of divorce, births out of wedlock, and women who choose to remain single have increased the numbers of female-headed households in many countries. In past historical periods, when traditional family households predominated, it could be assumed that there were as many women as men in each of the lower, working, middle, and upper social class categories. There were as many wives and daughters as there were husbands and sons in each of the households. Women enjoyed or were denied social class privileges, not on the basis of their gender, but on the basis of the household in which they were lucky or unlucky enough to be born or end up married into. But as more women-headed households have developed in the last few decades, income discrimination against women in the labor force, the failure of fathers to financially support their children, and the inadequacy of governmental income support programs has resulted in their being disproportionately below or just above poverty.

By the early 1980s, writers, activists, and social scientists began to note what they called an increasing feminization of poverty. Females today make up 51 percent of the population in the United States but 57 percent of the poor. The disproportion is greater if the adult poor alone are considered, which is a more important comparison, since it is adults who must attain the incomes that support families. Women make up 52 percent of adults but 62 percent of the adult poor. Altogether, women and their children make up over three-quarters of the population classified as poor in the United States.

While it is thus true that women are more likely to be poor than men, among women there are clear racial differences in terms of the likelihood of being poor. As Figure 8–1 indicates, in the United States 32 percent of black and 27 percent of Latina women are poor, which far exceed the 12 percent of white women.[2] Since the poor population constitutes the lower social class, poverty figures such as these are indicators of the extent to which class, race, and gender intersect.

172

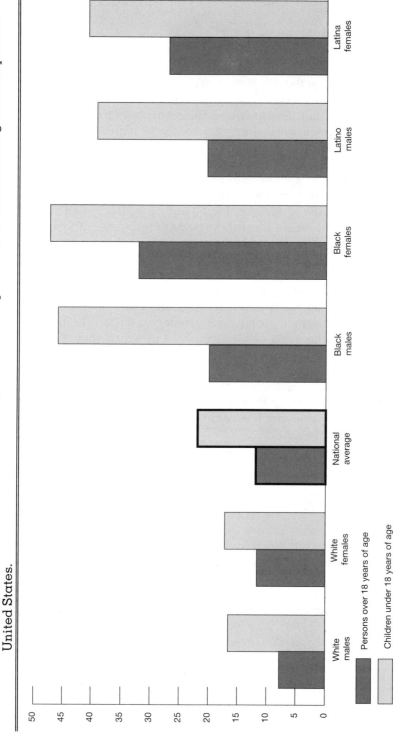

FIGURE 8–1 Intersections of Class, Race, and Gender, as Indicated by Percents of Persons Living in Poverty in the United States.

Source: Calculated from U.S. Bureau of the Census (1993, table 5, p. 10).

SUMMARY

Economic and social class research initially involves social mapping. Its tasks are to develop descriptive profiles of how people are vertically distributed within societies.

Economic classes are based on fundamental roles within economic systems. Each type of economic system or structure (slavery, feudalism, capitalism, socialism, etc.) has its own set of particular class roles which must be fulfilled. Definition of the different economic class positions follows from the nature of how the economic system functions. Economic classes therefore are based on the roles that people play in the production systems of societies.

Social classes are groups of people who share the same standard of living and perceive themselves as social equals within societies. Whereas economic classes are composed of people who share the same role in production, social classes are composed of people who share the same level of consumption. Economic class position is usually the largest determinant of social class level, but it is not an exclusive determinant. A small-business owner, for example, can be a member of the middle, working, or lower social class, depending on the income afforded by the business. Social class terms thus embody the notion of relative placement within the overall social hierarchy, as in the terms upper class, middle class, and lower class. There are also potentially confusing class terms, such as working class and peasantry, which have different meanings, depending on whether they are used in an economic or social sense.

Developed capitalist countries generally have four economic classes—capitalist, new middle class, small-business owners, and workers—and the greatest social science consensus is that they have four social classes—upper, middle, working, and lower.

Third World economic class structures resemble those of the developed countries to the extent that they have positions for capitalists, workers, a new middle class, and small-business owners. In addition, many also continue to have a role for an economic peasantry. The social distance between the social upper and lower classes of developing societies is significantly greater than that which exists in developed countries.

The postwar socialist countries also had a hierarchy of economic class positions. But there were no positions for capitalists. Instead, the highest economic class position was occupied by top political officials and managers. As in the capitalist countries, there were economic class positions for workers, small-business owners, and new middle-class middle-level managers and professionals. However, the social class structure of the postwar socialist countries was less unequal than that of the developed capitalist countries. Their egalitarian ideology and lack of opportunities to accumulate private capital wealth diminished social class differences and made them less inheritable.

Economic and social class hierarchies can intersect with and be importantly influenced by racial and ethnic stratification. In multiracial societies, there is often a high correlation between racial characteristics and class position. The same type of correlation can be observed in many multiethnic societies. In these respects, in each of the three societies of North America—the United States, Mexico, and Canada—there have been both historically and in the present significant correlations between class and race.

Economic and social class inequality also correlates in important ways with gender inequality. Women are more likely than men to occupy low-paying positions in the labor force. Their subordinate position and discrimination within the economic labor force has had increasingly adverse social consequences as the proportion of women-headed households has grown.

Key Terms and Concepts
(in order of presentation)

Economic class

Social class

Economic classes: capitalist,
   new middle, small-business
   owners, working, peasant

Social classes: upper, middle,
   working, lower, peasant

Personal and capital wealth

Distribution of income

Race

Racism

Ethnicity

Patriarchy

Endnotes

1. Before 1989, the least unequal income differences were in the socialist countries. In Poland and Hungary, for example, the top 10 percent received about 21 percent of the national income, compared to 25 percent for their First World and 39 percent for their Third World counterparts respectively (World Bank, 1994, p. 220). Thus, in most cases, there was a greater difference in the pattern of the distributions of income between developed and Third World capitalist countries than there was between developed capitalist and socialist countries. Capitalist restoration in the formerly socialist countries, as mentioned, has inevitably led to a widening of wealth and income differences, changes that are still unfolding. It is still too early to tell whether the widening of income differences will stop at the distribution pattern that now exists in the developed countries or go on to approximate the much greater inequality that exists in most developing countries.

sense that their actions are not wholly reducible to the wills of individuals within them. Much is done in the name of particular organizations rather than particular individuals. As structures, formal organizations can outlive their particular human creators. Members can pass into and out of organizational roles while the organization itself remains.

Sociologists thus see societies as being composed of distributions of organizations as well as other groups. In order to grasp how a city or a country functions, its key organizations must be identified and analyzed. To a large extent the character of a society depends on the character of those organizations, which can be structures for dominating or for facilitating freely cooperative and democratic endeavors.

ORGANIZATIONAL FUNCTIONING

In analyzing an organization, sociologists distinguish between how it functions internally, in terms of the performances and interactions of its members and various departments and units, and how it functions as a whole in relation to other organizations or individuals under given economic, political, legal, and other conditions. One type of sociological study might, for example, analyze problems of low morale and productivity within a particular corporation; another might analyze the influence exerted by a particular lobbying organization on legislators. In either case what is at issue is how effectively the organization functions in terms of its goals.

Analyses of the internal functioning of organizations focus first upon structures of interaction. Every organization of any size has a formal division of labor. Members perform different specialized roles that carry with them different levels of authority and power. Such structures can either facilitate or hinder accomplishment of organizational goals. What may have been an appropriate structure at one point in time may no longer be so if other conditions have changed. If such structural deficiencies are found, then the need for reorganization is indicated.

But analysis of how an organization is formally structured is usually not sufficient to fully reveal how it actually functions. Sociologists have found that most large-scale organizations have significant informal structures of interaction that exist alongside of their formal structures. Jobs overlap. People bend rules. Some individuals accumulate through personal relations far more power and influence than that indicated by their formal titles. In short, informal arrangements supplement formal arrangements in organizations. They may supplement them in ways that enhance overall organizational functioning and accomplishment of central goals, or they may contradict them in ways that lead to malfunctioning.

In analyzing particular organizations, sociologists thus distinguish formal and informal structures of interaction. By formal structure they mean the intentional way in which the organization's division of labor is defined, both in terms of specializations for the various job or other titles and in terms of structures of authority. By informal structure they mean regularly occuring and significant interaction patterns that have not been defined by formal rules.

For any organization to function well as a whole in terms of accomplishing its central goals, it must successfully navigate the waters of its external environment. Profit-making businesses, in addition to being mindful of competitors, need to be aware of changes in their markets and relevant public, legal, political, and other conditions. Nonprofit organizations as well are affected by outside conditions. Budgets of public agencies are controlled by legislatures which themselves are affected by shifting political conditions. In all cases, the survival of organizations depends on how well they are able to strategically adapt to or overcome external conditions.

TYPES OF ORGANIZATIONS

Organizations differ according to their sizes—whether they are large or small—and how they are controlled—whether ultimate power is democratically vested in their members as a whole or formally restricted to owners or managers. These differences, which are interrelated, have sociological consequences. Interrelating the variables of size and mode of control yields a typology (Figure 9–1) of four fundamental types of organizations: (1) small-scale, owner- or manager-controlled organizations, (2) small-scale, member-controlled organizations, (3) large-scale, owner- or manager-controlled organizations, and (4) large-scale, member-controlled

Figure 9–1 Typology of Organizations

		MODE OF CONTROL	
		Owner/Manager	Members
S	Small	1 Small Businesses	2 Cooperatives
I			
Z	Large	3 Bureaucracies	4 Membership Associations
E			

organizations. For convenience, we will call them respectively small businesses, cooperatives, bureaucracies, and membership associations.

Small Businesses

Small businesses, which are large enough to have employees besides the owners, are the clearest and most common examples of small-scale, owner/manager controlled organizations. The power to make all significant decisions, given the prerogatives of ownership in private property systems, rests exclusively with their owners. Employees are employed to carry out the wishes of the owners.

Medieval guild-organized shops were the prototypes of the modern small-scale, owner-controlled business. Master craftsmen in the medieval period had complete control over journeymen and apprentices that they employed. The small-scale, autocratic organization can also be interpreted as being patterned after the patriarchal family in which the father had exclusive power to rule over the women and children of the household. Most early small businesses were in fact operated out of households, with the father running the business as well as the family and with women and children being subordinates in both.

In small-scale, owner-controlled organizations, superiors and subordinates generally work close by each other. This led Durkheim (1893, p. 354), among others, to the conclusion that small-business working relations were less alienating than those of bureaucracies where the social and physical distances between employees and workers are much greater. But despite occupying the same physical spaces, in small businesses, owners and employees occupy fundamentally different roles. They may perform the same tasks, but one has ultimate power over the other. The superior has the power to set the terms of work and to hire or fire the other.

Working together in close quarters requires superiors and subordinates to develop a working relationship, of which the superior has the power to set the terms. He or she can adopt the modes of being a petty tyrant who bosses according to whim, a paternalist who treats employees as children with alternating doses of kindness and sternness, or that of an owner who treats employees as co-workers and otherwise equals. Subordinates in turn must either adapt to the terms of the relationship set by the owner or leave. If they adapt, it can be either willingly or only on the surface, with subordinates harboring a submerged spirit of resentment or rebellion.

For owners and employees alike in developed capitalist countries, working in small businesses carries a number of disadvantages. Small businesses generally have low profit margins and consequent low levels of income for owners, and pay and benefits (health, retirement, etc.) for employees. Owners generally have to work longer hours than middle-level corporation and state managers to attain the same levels of income. There are few if any intermediate positions between entry-level positions and that of the owner, limiting possibilities for employee career advancement. Employees of small businesses are less likely to be organized into unions, further limiting the levels of their pay and other financial compensations.

Cooperatives

There are many areas of social life where small groups of people combine to form organizations that they in principle at least jointly control. They make all decisions through consensus, majority votes, or other forms of membership control or consultation. They may have elected leaders or function without a separate leadership body.

There are many cooperative-type organizations that exist on an ad hoc basis alone. People organize themselves around a particular momentary issue. A group of neighbors comes together, for example, to put pressure on a city government to put a traffic light at a dangerous intersection. The organization ends with the attainment (or with the giving up on the attainment) of its founding objective. Or, once organized, the people may go on to pursue other common interests.

Other small-scale, democratic organizations have more permanent, long-term existences. A group of neighborhood business owners may come together to form an organization that meets regularly to discuss and act on common issues. Groups form to study the Bible, stock market investment strategies, or public issues. Softball players organize themselves into teams and leagues which reappear each summer.

Cooperative organizations exist so long as they fulfill a useful function and function in an acceptable manner in the eyes of their members. Their existences can also be encouraged or prohibited by governments. State authorities can facilitate formation of local cooperative organizations by making available public meeting places and providing other forms of aid. They can also restrict or drive underground local organizations of the population through legal, police, and other repressive measures.

Bureaucracies

There is a vague uneasiness felt by many people about the powers of bureaucratic organizations to pattern how they work and live. More and more people work within bureaucratic state or private organizations; and even if they own their own businesses, they have to deal with tax, legal, and regulatory bureaucracies. As citizens, each person comes in contact with educational and other governmental bureaucracies. No one is free from being affected by decisions made by and rules emanating from bureaucratic organizations. The image that many have in mind when they speak despairingly of bureaucrats is of tyrannical officials whose work lives and seeming pleasures are based in the enforcement of overly rigid and maddeningly petty rules. For many, the very idea of bureaucracies is repulsive. American populism has long taken aim at "Washington bureaucrats." Libertarians and anarchists recoil at the thought of bureaucratic controls over private citizens. Others associate bureaucracies more positively with modernity and efficiency.

In bureaucracies, ultimate rights over leadership selection and decision making are vested at the top. Base members or employees do not in principle have any formal right to be involved in those decisions. There is no assumption that members need to or have any right to participate in such decisions. Top bodies make the decisions for the organizations and lower-level members or employees are expected to abide by them. Private corporations are organized in that manner as are state administrative apparatuses.

The term *bureaucracy* (from the French "bureau," or "desk," and Greek "kratos," or "rule of") was first used in the nineteenth century to describe the administrative officials and their staffs of European governments. The business of government was divided up into bureaus or departments, such as finances, public works, education, and foreign affairs, with an official put in charge of each. The official in charge in turn had a staff of subordinate officials who oversaw the work of lower-level employees. In the nineteenth century the term *bureaucracy* was thus almost exclusively identified with the administrative apparatuses of governments. By the twentieth century though the term took on a more generalized meaning, becoming synonymous with any large-scale, management- or owner-controlled public or private organization.

Bureaucracies are not intended to be democratic organizations, since ultimate control within and of them rests at the top in the hands of managers, owners, or other overseers, and base employees do not have the right to choose their managers or have final say over policy. The more that key economic and political organizations have a hierarchical bureaucratic form in a society, therefore, the fewer the areas of direct democratic control that exist within that society.

Managers perform the key leadership roles in all private or public bureaucracies. They are responsible for coordinating and administering the factors of production from planning to budgets to production. While the functional importance of management has grown, it is important to note that the managers themselves do not hold ultimate power. Corporate managers are ultimately beholden to corporate owners. State managers are ultimately beholden to political authorities.

In the most neutral of senses, managers simply perform the function of efficiently coordinating the work of large-scale organizations. The true function of a manager is to make sure that an organization's product or service gets produced in the most efficient and effective manner possible. To do that, he or she must have command over the labor force that is involved in directly producing that product or service.

Top managers, it is often pointed out, rarely know how to actually make the organization's product. Rather, they know how to direct the people who do know how to make it. A top automobile executive is as unlikely to know all of the skills involved in assembling a car as the president of a university is to know how to teach all of the subjects. Between top managers and productive laborers there are often intermediate managerial layers. The larger the scale of the organization, the more likely that such new middle-class positions will exist.

Since most large-scale organizations have some features in common, top managers can often circulate between seemingly very different types of organizations. In the United States, top directors of public sector bureaucracies, such as the Departments of Defense, Interior, Education, and Housing, are often drawn from the top managerial ranks of the private corporate world. The career of former President Dwight D. Eisenhower was a classic in this respect. After leaving the military as a general and before being elected president, he was a member of a number of corporate boards of directors and briefly president of Columbia University.

The common features of all bureaucracies have given rise to attempts to develop common principles of management. Frederick Taylor, a turn-of-the-century American engineer who originated what is called the *scientific management approach*, was the pioneer in this quest. Taylor observed that there was a large gap between the actual and the potential productivity of workers. He called upon managers to hire experts to study the work process itself and devise methods to make it more efficient and thereby close the gap between actual and potential productivity. Taylor and his associates subjected work processes to intense scrutiny and then recommended changes in order to increase worker productivity. They developed the now famous time and motion studies. Using stop watches, they timed how long it took workers to complete tasks and studied the motions that they went through. On the bases of these observations they proposed faster ways to accomplish the same work tasks that involved fewer or shorter motions on the part of the worker.

One of Taylor's earliest successes was at a Pennsylvania steel mill. The mill was powered by coal which arrived intermittently by train. To get it unloaded, the managers had followed the practice of putting out a notice soliciting temporary day laborers with the requirement that they bring their own shovels. They then hired in order of application. Taylor observed this and concluded that it was an inefficient and unnecessarily costly arrangement. It was possible to get the coal unloaded faster with fewer men and therefore at less cost to the company. He made two recommendations which were based on the principles of his scientific management. First, managers should selectively hire according to appropriateness for the job rather than simply on the basis of order of application. To unload coal, a big, strong man is preferred to a smaller, weaker one. Second, management should supply the tools (the shovels in the coal unloading example) because they can make sure that they are the most appropriate and efficient for the task to be done. Taylor observed that many of the day laborers brought small shovels, which resulted in each of their shoveling motions being less productive as well as strenuous.

Taylor's advice for how to get coal unloaded may seem to have been no more than common sense and almost comical in retrospect, but it typified an approach that was to be highly influential in managerial circles and that would profoundly reshape the workplace. Before Taylor, managers had essentially been content to oversee production, leaving decisions about how to get the work done to workers themselves, so long as it was done. Taylor urged managers to wrest from workers control over the design of the work process. Managers and workers had different interests. The goal of management was to produce as high a profit as possible, and that required keeping labor costs down by streamlining the production process. Workers, on the other hand, were more interested in keeping the strenuousness of their jobs within tolerable limits.

Taylor also observed that the vital knowledge of how to perform many production processes was in the exclusive domain of skilled workers. The craft of steel making in the nineteenth century, for example, was held and passed on by experienced workers on the plant floors. Managers once again only knew how to hire people who knew how to do the work. They themselves did not know the production secrets. This left management vulnerable in a double sense. If the worker or workers who knew the craft secrets were to die or otherwise leave, production would have to halt until suitable replacements were found. Similarly, in periods of industrial strife such skilled workers had inordinate power to shut down production. Taylor, therefore, urged managers to gain control over the craft secrets. The major device for doing that was to co-opt the possessors of those secrets, in particular engineers, into their own ranks. Engineers in the nineteenth century had been more like skilled workers than professionals with university degrees. By elevating their status and pay, managers were able to shift their identity and loyalty from workers to the company.

Of the scientific management school that Taylor founded, Max Weber commented:

> With the help of appropriate methods of measurement, the optimum profitability of the individual worker is calculated like that of any material means of production. On the basis of this calculation, the American system of "scientific management" enjoys the greatest triumphs in the rational conditioning and training of work performances. (Weber, 1922, p. 213).

But these triumphs of scientific management exacted high human costs in Weber's judgement:

> The psychophysical apparatus of man is completely adjusted to the demands of the outer world, the tools, the machines—in short, to an individual's "function." The individual is shorn of his natural rhythm as determined by the structure of the organism; his psychophysical apparatus is attuned to a new rhythm through methodical specialization of separately functioning muscles. (Weber, 1922, p. 213).

Weber's view that the scientific management school operated on the basis of a machine model of the workplace is widely shared today. Taylor essentially viewed workers as mechanical parts to be fitted into a smoothly functioning machine. Their feelings and emotions, in short, their human qualities, were of little importance to him. What counted was that they got the job done in the shortest, most efficient, most profitable manner possible.

The pejorative term *Taylorism,* as used today, is associated with workplace alienation and managerial strategies to pump as much work as possible out of workers without regard for their human needs. Taylor's name continues to be accorded classic status in managerial studies literature, but largely as a foil for more contemporary theories. The great fallacy of Taylor, according to virtually all contemporary commentary, was that he did not give due regard to the human qualities of workers. By treating them as parts of a machine, he fostered as much alienation as efficiency, and in the long run, worker alienation undermined efficiency. After Taylor, managerial experts became more concerned with winning the worker's loyalty to the company and improving workplace morale. But, as Harry Braverman (1974) observed, while Taylor and his ideas are no longer openly esteemed in managerial literature, it is not because they have been abandoned. Rather they are now, for the most part, largely taken for granted. He set in motion a series of managerial reforms in the design of the workplace which are still in place. His ideas have been supplemented by schemes to win the worker's loyalty and increase morale, as well as his or her performance.

Charlie Chaplin, Modern Times, 1936

Membership Associations

Membership associations, as we are using the term, are large-scale organizations in which all members are vested with the formal right to participate in at least leadership selection and often major decision making. As such, they are counterposed to bureaucracies, which are large-scale organizations in which members have no vested democratic rights. Labor unions and political parties are examples of large-scale organizations that are often structured as membership associations.

The associational form, in principle, enables democratic participation in society in a double sense. First, it enables people with common interests to come together in organizations that are large and powerful enough to effectively promote those interests. Second, by being democratically constituted, associations enable people to participate in decision making and leadership selections that directly concern them. In a very real sense thus the growth of functioning associations and societal democratization go hand in hand.

An organization can be judged to be formally democratic when it has within its constitution adequate mechanisms (such as provisions for voting, referenda, and recall elections) for membership control. Nominally democratic organizations, though, have different types of formal provisions for membership participation in decision making, which can be comparatively judged in terms of degree and type of democratic participation by members that they allow (see Lembcke, 1988). However, just as sociologists have found that organizations contain informal as well as formal structures, they have found that the existence of formal democratic provisions is no guarantee that an organization actually functions democratically.

In any large-scale association, holders of top offices have innumerable advantages over rank-and-file members in terms of power to affect decisions. Robert Michels (1911), in a classic analysis, went so far as to argue that there is an "iron law of oligarchy" that operates in all large-scale organizations leading to undemocratic leadership domination, regardless of formal intentions or pretensions. According to Michels, substantive democratic control is impossible in any large-scale organization.

Michels may have overstated the case, but he did draw attention to the clear danger of leadership domination supplanting membership control of associations. It continues to be the case that associational functioning is always at least potentially problematic. To some degree, size does constrain the possibilities for direct democratic control over any type of organization. The larger the organization, the less likely that it is possible for all members to be directly involved in the making of all decisions. There can be a tension or contradiction between democracy and efficiency in an organization. A large-scale organization would be paralyzed if it required that all decisions be made by consensus. It would also be considerably slowed down if it required that there be membership votes on all decisions. At best, therefore, members of large-scale associations can only periodically vote on leaders and policy. In the meantime, daily decision making must be delegated to elected representatives who presumably act on behalf of and in the interests of their constituents. The democracy that exists in any given association is thus always a matter of degree.

Mixed Types

Many organizations overlap rather than fit clearly into one or another of the above categories. Organizations can combine both associational and bureaucratic features. A labor union may be organized so that members, but not clerical staff, democratically participate in the selection of leaders. That is, the relationship between union leaders and members is associational, but the relationship between leaders and direct clerical staff is bureaucratic. For that reason, clerical workers for unions are often members of and represented by different unions. A university may be organized so that faculty democratically control most of their departmental decision making but have no formal right to participate in the selection of their top administrators and boards of trustees. The relationship between top administrators and faculty is thus partly associational and partly bureaucratic. Meanwhile, the relationship between top administrators and clerical and maintenance staff is fully bureaucratic.

SUMMARY

As societies develop, human beings increasingly interrelate within organizational contexts. By identifying key economic, political, and other types of organizations, sociologists are able to grasp an important dimension of how societies function. They study how organizations function in terms of other organizations and society at large, and they study how organizations function internally in terms of member participation, performances (in economic organizations especially), and interrelationships.

In the study of how organizations function internally, sociologists distinguish between formal and informal structures of interrelationships. By formal structures they mean the intentional ways in which organizational divisions of labor are defined—formal definitions of work expected, level of authority, etc. By informal structures they mean ways that members are interrelated that are not specified by formal provisions. Knowledge of these latter informal modes of conduct is often essential for understanding overall organizational functioning.

Four different types of organizations—small businesses, cooperatives, bureaucracies, and associations—can be distinguished according to the variables of size (small scale or large scale) and mode of control (owner/manager or member). Small-business-type organizations are dominated by their owners. Cooperatives are small-scale organizations which are in principle democratically controlled by their members. Bureaucracies are large-scale organizations in which the right of control rests formally with top managers or owners. Membership associations are large-scale organizations which in principle are democratically controlled by their members.

Because of their sizes and therefore power, bureaucracies and membership associations are the most socially significant types of contemporary organizations that sociologists study. They are in some ways the twin poles of contemporary organizational life—one, an intentional top-down structure, and the other, a nominally democratic form. In the study of bureaucracies, sociologists often focus on managers and how they perform their roles. In the study of associations, sociologists often focus on the extent to which substantive democratic control and participation by members exist.

Key Terms and Concepts
(in order of presentation)

Formal organization	Bureaucracy
Formal structure	Scientific management
Informal structure	Taylorism
Small business	Membership association
Cooperative	Iron law of oligarchy

Chapter Ten

The Family

There is a tendency to see contemporary family life as a haven from the tensions of the economic world. There, warmth and affection await people weary from the cold calculus of economic life. Indeed, sociologists consider families to be the principal primary groups within societies where interaction is personal, with individuals being treated as whole persons, unlike in society's multiple secondary group settings, like classrooms and workplaces, where interaction is more impersonal and individuals tend to be treated in terms of just their particular roles. But it is deceptive to see a great divide between family and economic life, for family life is greatly affected by what happens economically. The ability of a family to have enough to eat, decent shelter, and the other necessities for a comfortable existence within which warmth and affection can reign depends greatly on whether it has an adequate income. The relationship between family and economic life also runs the other way, with economies being dependent on the existence of family units or their institutional equivalents.

FAMILY, ECONOMY, AND SOCIETY

Family life has been a necessary condition of economic production. Families are production units themselves which function within the total production of societies, for economic production involves the reproduction of the species itself as well as the production of goods and services. People must make themselves as well as the means (that is, goods and services) to their survival. Reproduction of the species is the absolutely necessary complement to the production of goods and services. Neither type of production could exist without the other.

Within families the energy of present and future laborers is produced and maintained. Labor is expended within families so that their members who are in the labor force can eat, sleep, and be cured of illnesses. Without that labor they would not be able to return to work each day. Children, in cold economic language, are future workers who must be nourished, cultivated, and trained so that they can grow up to work. Families are like workshops—while schools are like factories—for the production of future laborers. Labor forces could not be replenished without the family labor that is performed in bringing up future workers.

Put in a broader social sense, the family historically has been the primary institution responsible for the physical, emotional, and moral development of children. Society's members are reproduced within families. It can thus be plausibly argued that child rearing has been the primary function of all types of families. For sure, families without children also have a functional importance for society. Adults within them receive necessary emotional and other forms of support. But in the most historical and objective of senses, the family's greatest importance to society rests in its mission of child rearing. Historically or in the present, no other institution has been as directly responsible for the welfare of children. Without enormous labor on the part of responsible adults within households, children and societies themselves could not survive.

Babies come into the world physically helpless, dependent upon household and family labor for their survival. They require that adults be constantly present to feed, clothe, clean, and cure them of illnesses. Babies can suffer death or life-long damage—especially in brain development—if they do not receive adequate food intakes. While medical specialists play a role in the physical development of infants, the primary, absolutely necessary role is played by family or household adults, a role that extends beyond infancy to the onset of adulthood.

Within family households children develop emotionally. They learn from and adapt to the mental life of the household. Early childhood and adolescence, according to most psychologists, are critical periods in emotional development. It follows that the more emotionally healthy the household, the more likely that children will grow up into emotionally stable adults. Conversely, the more mentally unhealthy and unstable the household environment, the more likely that the emotional development of children will be harmed. Emotional health, of course, is only influenced by—not totally dependent upon—family environments. Emotionally troubled persons can grow up in otherwise stable households, as mentally healthy adults can come from emotionally unstable homes.

Families and households are also the environments within which children develop morally. They acquire values and the fundamental sense of how to differentiate right from wrong. It is there that the super-ego—the part of the mind where judgments of right and wrong are made, according to Sigmund Freud—develops. Children are profoundly influenced by the explicit or implicit values of their households. There are strong possibilities that they will internalize those values and reproduce them in their own families as adults. But here, as with mental and emotional health, it is only possible to speak in terms of probabilities and tendencies. There is no certainty that children will necessarily follow the values of their families. They can also modify or completely rebel against them. Whatever the outcome though, the values spoken and practiced within the family household originate the moral development of children.

The family thus performs key economic and social functions. Economically it is a unit of labor for the production and maintenance of labor itself. Socially, it is the institution most directly responsible for the physical, emotional, and moral development of children.

FAMILY SOCIAL PROBLEMS

In an ideal world all children would be born into families where they would receive the best possible physical, emotional, and moral care. But this world is far from ideal. Contemporary family life is beset by a large number of problems which have detrimental consequences for children and, of course, adults too. Among them are poverty, divorce, alcoholism, violence, and absence of adequate child and health care.

Poverty

The most serious problem directly affecting the physical development of children is poverty, which is especially widespread in the Third World. In conditions of poverty, children are less likely to have adequate food intakes, which are necessary for healthy physical development. No matter how responsible their parents may be, children will suffer the physical consequences of inadequate food intakes if they are born into conditions of poverty which are not mitigated by government or charitable food distribution programs. Carlson and Wardlaw (cited in UNICEF, 1990) estimate that 150 million of the world's children suffer from serious malnutrition.

In addition to malnutrition, poverty causes other unhealthy living conditions for children. Diseases, which usually strike children the hardest, are more likely to start and spread where the poor live without plumbing for potable (safe drinking) water and toilets. When children of the poor are sick, they are less likely to have access to doctors and health facilities. Worldwide, the number-one killer of children is dehydration, which results from chronic diarrhea. It is easily cured by doctors and other trained personnel. But they are not available to many Third World poor children, whose deaths are as unnecessary as they are tragic. In Mexico alone 455 children under five years old die per day— over twice as many as would if Mexico had the same rate as that prevailing in the developed countries (based on UNICEF, 1990, Table 1, p. 76). Put differently, there are at least 230 avoidable deaths of children every day in Mexico.

In the United States, children are nearly twice as likely to be poor as the general population. In the 1990s, close to a quarter of all children under six years of age have lived in poor families, while the general poverty rate has stood at about 13.5 percent. According to a comprehensive report (National Center for Children in Poverty, 1990), childhood poverty carries high social as well as physical costs. "Early childhood experiences contribute to poor children's high rates of school failures, dropout, delinquency, early childbearing and adult poverty."

Divorce and Family Reorganization

The traditional nuclear family includes two biological parents and their children. However, worldwide very large numbers of children do not live within that form, living instead in single-parent, step-, or adoptive families. When the proportion of a society's children living within the traditional form of the family suddenly decreases sharply, a series of generally unplanned-for consequences arises. This has been nowhere more evident than in the United States where, between 1960 and 1990, the proportion of children under eighteen years of age in the United States living in families where both of their biological parents were present dropped precipitously from nine to six out of every ten (Norton and Miller, 1992). If present trends continue, only a minority of children in the near future will live in what had been considered culturally to be the normal family arrangement. As the two-biological-parent form of the family—in which the majority of children still live—has declined, the single-parent and stepfamily forms have increased in significance.

Rising divorce rates were the leading cause of the steep decline of the two-biological-parent form in the United States. Between 1960 and 1980, the divorce rate more than doubled so that by 1980, one out of every two marriages could be expected to end in divorce (Castro Martin and Bumpass, 1989). The United States is not unique in that respect.

TABLE 10–1 Children Under 18 Years of Age Living in Each Type of
Family by Race and Latino (Latin American) Origin in the
United States, 1990

	White	Black	Latino	Total
Percent:				
Two-biological-parent	66.7	25.7	55.3	60.6
Single-parent	20.0	60.2	32.2	26.0
Step	11.7	13.0	11.0	11.9
Adoptive	1.6	1.1	1.5	1.6
Total	100.0	100.0	100.0	100.1
Total number	49,467	9,105	6,695	61,118

Notes: Due to rounding, percentages may not total 100. Numbers in thousands.
Source: Calculated from Norton and Miller (1992, Tables M and N).

Across the First World countries divorce rates have doubled and tripled
since the mid-1960s (Furstenberg and Cherlin, 1991). In large part,
legal changes paved the way for the increase in divorce rates in the
United States. In the past, divorces could only be granted when serious
fault, such as infidelity, abandonment, or insanity, was found in one of
the partners. But beginning in California in 1969, states rapidly enacted
statutes so that a divorce could be granted on the simple basis of incom-
patibility. By 1985, all of the states had enacted such no-fault divorce
statutes.

There is considerable disagreement over what the rise in the
divorce rate reflects. Some argue that it reflects increasing unhappiness
in families. Others counter that family unhappiness may not have
increased. They contend that in the past, when divorce was legally difficult, couples stayed together unhappily or separated while remaining
legally married. There is also disagreement over whether the rise of
divorces is a good or bad development. Some argue that no-fault
divorces can strengthen the institution of marriage by allowing people to
get out of bad relationships and into sounder, longer-lasting marriages.
No-fault divorces also allow needed flexibility for people who are happier
with two or more short-term marital commitments than with one exclusive long-term commitment.

Others argue though that the rise in divorce rates has undermined
the capacity of families to fulfill critical social functions. In particular,
divorces are likely to be traumatic events for children, resulting in
destabilization of their upbringings. In the early 1970s, as divorce rates
began to rise, most professionals assumed that what was good for the
parents was good for the children. If the parents wanted to divorce that
would be in the long-term interests of the children since, it was

assumed, the old unhealthy, unhappy family would be dissolved and eventually better arrangements would be found. Children, it was further optimistically assumed, would suffer discomfort in the breakup, but after two to three years at the most they would adapt to their new living arrangements. Subsequent research (e.g., Wallerstein and Blakeslee, 1989), however, casts doubt on that sanguine assessment. Disproportionately high numbers of children of divorces were found to suffer long-term emotional consequences which continued to affect them as adults. Negative consequences include distrust of and difficulty in forming close and intimate relationships on their own as adults and failure to fulfill their own educational and career potentials. Certainly, there are also children, possibly the majority, who adapt very well to divorces and do not suffer negative psychological consequences. There are also, undoubtedly, children who positively benefit from divorces, especially when the original family situation was particularly bad. But, there is a growing consensus that early estimations of the effects of divorce on children were overly optimistic. Many children have great difficulty in adjusting to divorces, difficulties that can continue to plague them into adulthood.

Children are also likely to suffer financially from divorces. It is not uncommon for them to be plummeted into poverty. Most women continue to be awarded custody of children by the courts, but they as a whole earn less money than men. As a result, the living standard of children can fall after a divorce. Most court decisions attempt to compensate for the lower income by requiring that the divorced father make child support payments. But, unfortunately, half of all divorced fathers have not lived up to this obligation, especially after a year has passed (U.S. Bureau of the Census, 1991). As a result, the courts, U.S. Congress, and a number of state legislatures have had to develop special measures to enable the collection of child support payments from negligent fathers. These measures, however, have yet to fully resolve the problem. They often require that the mother initiate and pursue protracted legal actions, actions which many women, for a variety of reasons, are reluctant to do.

In part, due to the increasing realization of the negative impact that divorce can have on children, family therapists and marriage counselors began to shift the thrust of their advice in the 1980s (see Lear, 1988). In the 1970s, most stressed that what was important was that each partner in a marriage be able to fulfill personal needs. If either one or both could not do it in the present relationship, they should dissolve that relationship and live alone or find another more fulfilling one. In the 1980s, the advice shifted to trying to find out what was positive in the relationship and what was needed to overcome problems.

Whether because of divorce, death of a parent, or birth out of wedlock, increasing numbers of children in the United States now live in households where only one parent—almost always the mother—is present. In 1960, fewer than 10 percent of children under eighteen lived in single-parent households; by 1990, the proportion had leaped to 26 percent—more than one in every four children (Norton and Miller, 1992). In the case of blacks, the single-parent household has become the largest single form of the family for child raising. Some 60.2 percent of all black children under eighteen years of age live within single-parent households (see Table 10–1).

Single-parent families are more likely to be poor than are married-couple families, which include both two-biological-parent families and stepfamilies. Forty-two percent of children under eighteen years of age in 1992 in the United States who lived in single-parent households were poor compared to 8.4 percent who lived in married-couple households (U.S. Bureau of the Census, 1993, Table 4). For children under three, the contrast is even greater. Einbinder (1992) found that 61.5 percent of those who lived in single-parent households lived in conditions of poverty compared to 12.8 percent of children living in households headed by married couples. The strong correlation between the single-parent form and poverty led a number of analysts, most notably Moynihan (1965), to argue that high percentages of out-of-wedlock births and family instability, especially among blacks, were impeding declines in poverty and other social problems. Moynihan's conclusion touched off a fierce debate with his detractors arguing that institutional racism was a more important cause of black poverty than family patterns. Nevertheless, the correlation between the single-parent form and poverty exists for white as well as black families. Thus, of children under eighteen living in single-parent households in 1992, whites were 4.6 and blacks 3.6 times as likely to be poor as those living in married-couple households (U.S. Bureau of the Census, 1993, Table 4).

In addition to living within single-parent households, increasing numbers of children are living within stepfamilies. When a single parent marries or remarries or when a just-divorced parent remarries, new stepfamilies are created in which there is one biological and one stepparent. The stepfamily has become a new focus of family research for two reasons. First, the proportion of stepfamilies has grown dramatically with the increase in the divorce rate, making it now a major subtype of the family. Just under 12 percent of children under eighteen years of age in the United States live within stepfamilies. But many of those now living within two-biological-parent and single-parent families eventually will live within stepfamilies as currently married biological parents divorce and remarry and as single parents marry or remarry. Thus, according to one estimate cited in *The New York Times* (November 22, 1988, p. 20), "more than one-third of children born today will live in a stepfamily before age 18." Second, stepfamilies have unique problems which require study and understanding. Interaction between stepparents and children can be problematic. Stepparents do not have the same degree of cultural legitimacy as biological parents in the eyes of children and others, and there is much that suggests that the role of the stepparent continues to carry considerable social stigmatization. Many childhood stories, such as *Cinderella* and *Hanzel and Gretel*, portray stepparents as necessarily evil or wicked to children. Yet stepparents are expected to assume the same responsibilities as biological parents for children's welfare. As the number of stepfamilies has grown, there has been a growing realization that they are prone to unique types of tensions (Maddox, 1976; Furstenberg and Cherlin, 1991). In part, that is because stepfamilies, despite being increasingly common, are still stigmatized culturally and viewed as abnormal. At the same time, large numbers of stepfamilies function well, indicating that it is possible for children to thrive in them as well as in more traditional two-biological-parent families.

Alcoholism

If one or both parents in a household are alcoholic, children are likely to suffer from an unstable emotional environment. Families which contain active alcoholics within them are beset by large numbers of destabilizing problems. Excessive drinking by one or more parents impairs their ability to perform necessary work and household roles. They can lose their jobs, causing family income to plunge. They can lose their ability to parent, causing children to be set adrift in a sea of emotional chaos. The destabilizing effects of alcoholism on families is a significant international problem, with the exception of the Islamic countries where alcohol sales are prohibited. It is estimated (Berry and Boland, 1977, p. 52) that one in five households in the United States is affected by the alcoholism of a male adult. If the alcoholism of female adults is considered, then as high as one in four households contains at least one alcoholic adult.

Most professionals today view alcoholism as a disease—not a moral condition—with mental and possibly physical sources. Alcoholics have a deep-seated mental and possibly physical compulsion to drink that results in the impairment of their abilities to function physically or socially. No matter how much they may want to stop drinking, it is not easy. They must overcome an extraordinarily powerful compulsion. Alcoholism is thus a difficult problem to treat, both for the alcoholic who wants to recover and for family members who want to regain household stability. Yet it is not an impossible problem, since many alcoholics and their families have been successful. Though no one approach to treatment can claim perfect cure rates, treatment programs and community-based self-help groups such as Alcoholics Anonymous have often proved to be helpful.

Domestic Violence

In recent years, social research in many countries has documented alarmingly high rates of domestic violence. Far from being nests of tranquility, many families are caldrons of tension which boil over into emotional and physical violence. The victims of domestic violence are usually children and women who are physically weaker than parents and males respectively. Domestic violence also causes incalculable emotional damage to children who grow up either as its direct victims or who witness it between parents.

Gelles (1985) defined as abusive and violent domestic interaction "kicking, biting, punching, hitting or trying to hit with an object, beating, threatening with a gun or a knife, and using a gun or a knife." Based on data gathered from a national sample in the United States, he concluded that "3.8 percent of women living with men are abused each year" and that "child abuse involves 3.6 percent or 1.6 million children aged 3 to 17." This undoubtedly was a conservative estimate. It relied upon the truthfulness of respondents who were being questioned about a subject that, like alcoholism, many people are reticent to admit openly or discuss openly.

Parents may use physical force spontaneously against children out of uncontrolled frustration or rage. There is little disagreement that this constitutes child abuse. They may also use physical force as calculated punishment to control and discipline children. Here there is widespread disagreement regarding how much physical force can be legitimately used. Spankings are acceptable in many cultures, though not slaps, punches, or stronger measures. Other societies, such as Finland, consider spanks and any other form of striking children to be unacceptable and illegal. Finnish parents who lay a hand on their children for any reason, including spanking, can be arrested and fined.

More widespread than child abuse is the practice of men using physical force to dominate their wives and girlfriends. Intimate partners can become intimate enemies with love and violence becoming intertwined in pathological forms. Social research has conclusively documented widespread wife and girlfriend battering in the United States. One study (Stark and Flitcraft, 1988) concluded that women abused by their husbands or boyfriends accounted for one out of every five trauma admissions to hospital emergency rooms. In the 1970s, organized women's groups increased public awareness in the United States of the extent of violence against women within families. That campaign established the need for battered women's shelters, where women could flee and find refuge. Those shelters, which exist now in most areas of significant population sizes, are unfortunately almost always busy, reflecting the dismal underlying social reality of considerable family violence.

Domestic violence within couples seems to move in cycles. Tensions set off an argument which escalates into violence. A cooling-off period follows. The husband or boyfriend realizes what he has done, apologizes, and begs for forgiveness. Daily routines of work and family life resume until tensions trigger another violent episode. Studies of women who seek refuge in shelters show that many of them have endured years of periodic physical abuse before fleeing. They stayed in the relationships out of a combination of hope that things would somehow get better and feelings that they were trapped without economic alternatives to take care of themselves and their children.

Domestic violence exists in all economic and social classes, but the most serious form of it—murder—occurs disproportionately in lower social classes (Pelton, 1981). The harshness of lower-class living conditions may be responsible for breeding greater family as well as general violence. It follows that if harsh living conditions increase the likelihood that there will be violent tensions within families, it may be that family violence is even more widespread in a number of Third World countries, where levels of poverty and absolute immiseration are much higher than in the First World.

At the same time, in the United States, all social classes are exposed to the rampant violence portrayed on prime-time television. Violence is projected on television as a normal, indeed preferred, response by heroes and villains alike to conflicts. While lower-class life is in reality more violent than that of other classes, all classes to some extent live within the television-engendered vicarious climate of violence. Both forms of violence—real and vicarious—may create a climate that increases the likelihood that physical force will be resorted to in family disputes.

Child Care

When both parents work outside of the home—an increasing reality in many societies—alternative arrangements must be made for the care of young children. The rise of the two-wage-earner family with its consequences for child care is the result of a series of historical and economic transformations. Until relatively recently in history, most people in virtually all societies lived and worked on farms where the location of home and work in the same physical space facilitated the care of children. The developments of capitalism, factories, and urbanization increasingly separated the physical locations of home and work life. But there was little resulting problem in child care because the gender division from the farm was reproduced in the city: Men went off to work in the paid labor force while women labored at home taking care of households and children. However, now with greater numbers of women being forced to find paying jobs to make financial ends meet at home, it has become increasingly difficult to maintain this traditional division of labor. The mobilization of women's labor into paid labor forces has left young children without the possibility of being cared for by their mothers at home. By 1990, 47.5 percent of all children under three in the United States were being cared for during the workday in a child-care center or by someone other than their parents (Hofferth, et al., 1991).

A number of European and Scandinavian countries, such as France, Sweden, and Finland, which have experienced massive entrances of women into their paid labor forces, have developed comprehensive programs to cope with the resulting gaps in child care.

But most other countries, including the United States, have not. In these latter countries, working parents confront a patchwork of mostly less than satisfactory solutions that range from an informal economy of neighborhood mothers who take in other children during the day to high-quality but highly expensive preschools that cater to upper-middle- and upper-class families. Most workers in established child-care centers—especially those that most middle- and working-class parents can afford—receive relatively low wages. It has been said, not without justification, that in the United States a person can make more money taking care of animals than taking care of small children. As a result, there is a high turnover of the labor forces within these centers. Many take low-paying child-care jobs as stopgap measures until they can find better-paying positions. With there being little incentive for workers to develop experience and professional careers within child care, children are taught and taken care of by a constantly shifting group of adults. Most working parents thus find the quality and affordability of available child care to be inversely related: What they can afford is unsatisfactory, while what they would like for their children is beyond their financial reach.

Health Care

Families, among their varied responsibilities, are directly concerned with the health of their members. When young or adult members are very sick or suffer serious injuries, they must rely on the help of other household members. Similarly, it is the family unit that is responsible in most cases for absorbing any financial costs that result from sicknesses or injuries.

The original health care dilemma for a society and its families is that there are unequal needs in a double sense. First, sicknesses and injuries are not equally distributed. Sicknesses strike some groups more than others—older people and those with inherited or acquired medical conditions, for example. Injuries occur unexpectedly to otherwise healthy persons as when automobile- and sports-related accidents occur. Second, given inequality in the distribution of income, families have different abilities to pay for the resulting costs of sicknesses and injuries. With these unequal distributions of medical needs and family incomes, if access to health care services were completely determined by ability to pay, many families would have to go without.

Societies have successively resolved this dilemma by spreading the financial costs of illness and injuries among larger and larger groups. At first, families that were struck by sudden medical crises had to rely on financial help from relatives, neighbors, or other members of their communities. Occasionally in the nineteenth and early twentieth centuries, membership unions and immigrant organizations in the United States contributed regular payments to special funds that could be disbursed to pay medical bills. These were forerunners of private insurance policies which spread out the medically related financial risks of illnesses and injuries among a larger population base of premium-paying families and individuals. But the ability to afford insurance policies varies from family to family. Hence, while private insurance programs significantly improved access to health care, they were not sufficiently affordable to ensure universal access.

As a result, by the 1990s all of the developed countries, with the notable exception of the United States, had developed comprehensive government-sponsored health care programs to cover all of their citizens. By socializing, that is, spreading out and equalizing, the risks and costs of illnesses and injuries among all citizens, they essentially resorted to a socialist solution to a capitalist problem. Rather than having effective demand determine access to health care, as would occur under purely market conditions, they have made health care, like public education, a right to which all citizens are entitled.

The United States, for reasons that have most to do with its own historical and political development, has resisted the removal or minimization of market forces in the determination of access to health care. Most families have access to health care via private insurance programs; but a significant number, which included 19 percent of citizens in the mid-1990s, had no insurance at all. Most families receive medical insurance as an employer-supplied fringe benefit of the jobs of the breadwinner or breadwinners. Because medical insurance is very expensive in the United States, most families that are currently covered would not be able to afford it if it were not an employer-supplied benefit. Their access to health care can thus be lost should unemployment occur. To compound matters, there are significant differences in insurance programs, with some covering much more illness- and injury-related costs than others. As a result, families in the United States, unlike those in other developed countries, have had highly unequal access to health care.

FAMILY SOCIAL POLICY AND LEGISLATION

It is unlikely that there was ever a past golden age of family life in which all children were happily well taken care of by their parents. For much of the past there were undoubtedly significant numbers of family conflicts and children who suffered poor physical and emotional living conditions. One of the reasons why present conditions may appear much worse than those of the past is simply that more attention is being directed toward them. Contemporary social research and advocacy groups have played key roles in uncovering and publicizing family problems, such as child abuse and wife battering. It is thus always necessary to distinguish between the objective existence of a problem and the extent to which there is public awareness of it. Serious social problems can exist without drawing much public attention. Similarly, less serious problems can be the focuses of inordinate amounts of attention.

Nevertheless, there are a number of trends which have aggravated family problems. The rise of the two-wage-earner family has drained family labor time away from the care of children. Rising divorce rates have resulted in children having to emotionally adjust to new family living arrangements—an adjustment which has proved to be much more difficult than anticipated by professionals in the field when divorce rates began to rise in the early 1970s. Increasingly, numbers of poor and unmarried teenage women are giving birth to children, the stability of whose upbringing will be problematic.

Nearly all commentators agree that the family is under pressure. But they disagree about what, if anything, governments should do to relieve it. Conservatives in the United States argue that government programs have weakened the family by removing incentives for family units to be self-reliant. According to them, the more governments subsidize health care, child care, and other living costs, the more families lose their functional importances. Conservatives believe that family living conditions ought to be largely determined by how the family's breadwinner or breadwinners fare in the economic marketplace. The more money made, the more comfortable the family's living standard will be. Dependence of their family as well as their own living standards on direct income gives heads of households, according to conservative theory, extra incentives to work hard and produce which ultimately benefits society as a whole with a strong economy.

Liberal, social democratic, and socialist theories, in progressively greater degrees, maintain that state aid is necessary to support families. State-financed education, health insurance, child care, and other programs socialize and equalize the costs of bringing up children. They ensure that all children, regardless of family income, have access to vital services. If the distribution of such services were left up to what families could individually afford, large numbers of children would go without in varying degrees and family living conditions for the poor would approach absolute immiseration. If governments did not provide food and income subsidies, babies from poor families would not have enough to eat or access to health care, resulting in higher infant mortality rates. Working- and middle-class families are also importantly in need of state-subsidized programs. Public education, which benefits all classes, is greatly subsidized. Student loans and grants for college education are often state supported. There are federally backed housing loans. There are a number of state-supported crisis intervention and disaster programs which are available to all families in time of need. Employer- or government-financed paid leave from work for new parents, which exists in many developed countries, benefits all classes.

There are two additional reasons that advocates of government support for families cite. First, whatever the merits or defects of their parents, children cannot be held responsible for the living conditions into which they are born. Any doctrine of fairness would dictate that all children deserve equal access to health, education, and other necessities. Second, children are the future of societies. Those societies that do not invest in their upbringing will surely pay the consequences. If generations of poor children are brought up in squalid, alienating conditions, which lead them to drop out of school, there will be future social costs of increased crime, inadequately trained labor forces, and unplanned-for pregnancies, among other problems.

Whatever the future form of the family, children will always be present in societies. What is socially done to protect and promote their potential development will positively benefit the development of society itself. There are great social risks involved in leaving the fates of children completely up to chance or the financial abilities of individual families. In this respect, a comprehensive corporate-sponsored study of the conditions of under-three children in the United States concluded:

> In contrast to all the leading industrialized nations, the United States fails to give parents time to be with their newborns, it fails to ensure pre- and postnatal health care for mothers and infants, and it fails to provide adequate child care. The result is significant losses in the quality of its future workforce, citizenry, and parents. (Carnegie Task Force, 1994, p. 19)

The key question for public policy is whether society as a whole, through government action, will take more responsibility for the welfare of children. There is reason to believe that if it does not, it will have to pay for the economic and social consequences in the future.

SUMMARY

Families, or their institutional equivalents, today perform vital economic and social functions. Domestic labor, which is necessary for the continual economic functioning and reproduction of societies, is performed within families. Domestic labor maintains the capacity of the labor force to continue working and, through the care and upbringing of children, produces new laborers. The economic function of the family thus revolves around the maintenance of existing labor and production through reproduction and nurturing of new labor. There is much to suggest that the care of children is also the key social function of families. Families are the societal units most directly responsible for the physical, emotional, and moral development of children.

Contemporary families face a number of problems which undermine the performance of their economic and social functions. Some are old and enduring problems, and others are creations of new trends, such as the entrance of women into the paid labor force and the resulting rise of the two-wage-earner family. Those problems include poverty, divorce, the effects of alcoholism on family stability, violence, lack of quality, affordable child care, and unequal access to health care. The key question facing public policy is the extent to which governments should subsidize the costs of families with tax-funded programs in education, health care, child care, and other areas.

Key Terms and Concepts
(in order of presentation)

Family	Nuclear family
Single-parent family	Alcoholism
Stepfamily	Two-wage-earner family

Chapter Eleven

Population

Demography is the specialization within sociology that studies the sizes, distributions, and rates of change of populations. Demographers derive their basic data from censuses, vital statistics (of births, deaths, and marriages), and population sample surveys. Demographic information is basic to the description and analysis of any particular society and therefore widely used. Governments use population counts for determining the allocation of services. Businesses use them to determine potential markets. Social scientists use information on the internal distributions of populations as raw material for empirical studies. In one respect, demography is thus a fairly straightforward and technical specialization devoted to the noncontroversial tasks of making counts. But behind that appearance, as with all parts of the social sciences, rest a series of controversial issues.

MALTHUS AND OVERPOPULATION THEORIES

Among the most important and controversial issues that demographers address is whether the world and the countries within it are overpopulated. Theories that the world is headed for an overpopulation catastrophe can be traced back almost two hundred years to the 1798 publication of *An Essay on the Principle of Population* by the English clergyman and political economist Thomas Robert Malthus (1766–1834).

Malthus argued that population grew at a faster rate than the production of food and other necessities, resulting in the long-term tendency for absolute increases in starvation and other forms of human deprivation. He concluded that populations double every twenty-five years with increases in production of food and other necessities lagging behind. In Malthus's (1798, p. 86) famous formulation, "population, when unchecked, increases in geometric ratio. Subsistence increases only in an arithmetical ratio." Consequently over time, in Malthus's reasoning, the gap between population size and means of subsistence would grow at an accelerating rate:

> Taking the whole earth . . . and supposing the present population equal to a thousand millions, the human species would increase as the numbers 1, 2, 4, 8, 16, 32, 64, 128, 256, and subsistence as 1, 2, 3, 4, 5, 6, 7, 8, 9; in three centuries as 4096 to 13, and in two thousand years the difference would be almost incalculable (Malthus, 1798, p. 86).

Malthus's projection of an impending overpopulation apocalypse directly countered the central argument of both utopian reformers and the ideologists of the still-unfolding French Revolution, that humans had the capability to rationally perfect their societies. No matter what they did, according to Malthus's dire prediction, humans would face a bleak future of accumulating food shortages which would undercut any possibility of improving the quality of life. Malthus did not believe that there was any way to avoid this looming tragedy.

Malthus's hypothesis though was mostly based upon speculative reasoning, since in 1798 there was very little valid empirical information about contemporary or past population sizes. That type of information has become more available in the twentieth century, which has made it possible to test his central hypothesis that populations grow at a geometric rate, doubling every twenty-five years. Figure 11–1 represents how Malthus believed world population grew. Figure 11–2, based upon current estimates of how world population has actually grown (Table 11–1), shows that world population grew at a fairly low rate until the 1600s, the beginning of the modern era, when it began to accelerate sharply. It did not grow at a steady geometric ratio, as had been hypothesized by Malthus.

However, Figure 11–2 is partially misleading because it does not include data from the period prior to 8000 B.C. In an influential article, Deevey (1960) replotted the growth of world population using logarithms instead of numbers. This enabled him to construct axes that handled longer periods of time and more people. As Figure 11–3 shows, world population has grown neither at one steady geometric rate as predicted by Malthus nor in the manner suggested by Figure 11–2. Rather, it has grown in three distinct stages characterized by periods of surges and levelings off.

FIGURE 11–1 Population Growth as Hypothesized by Malthus

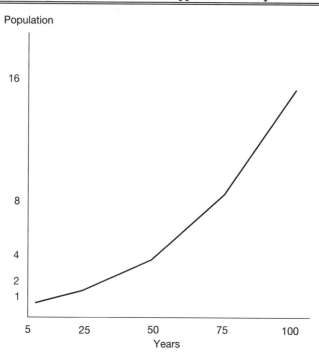

TABLE 11–1 Growth of the World's Population

Year	World Population (in millions)
23,000 B.C.	3.34
8000 B.C.	5.32
4000 B.C.	86.5
1 A.D.	133
1650	545
1750	728
1800	936
1900	1,610
1950	2,400
1990	5,101
1994	5,438

Sources: Deevey (1960); The World Bank (1990 and 1994).

FIGURE 11-2 World Population Growth in billions from 8000 B.C.
to Present

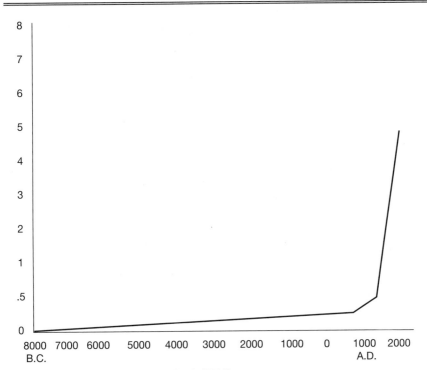

FIGURE 11-3 Logarithmic Growth of World Population from 23,000 B.C.
to Present

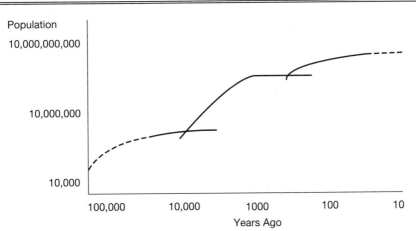

According to Deevey's general interpretation, each new stage was initiated by a technological advance that increased the amount of people who could be supported. The discovery and spread of horticulture and later agriculture initiated the second stage around 8000 B.C.; and the scientific-industrial revolution initiated the third stage around 1650. Deevey suggested that the current period of high population growth rates would eventually taper off as the maximum number of people who could be supported with industrial technologies was reached. That maximum would be, he estimated, at least several times as large as the current world population.

Deevey's and similar interpretations suggest that the great error of Malthus was that he had considered population growth rates as developing in isolation from economic and technological developments.

CONTEMPORARY WORLD POPULATION CONDITIONS

Despite Malthus's misconception of how populations grow, neo-Malthusians hold that it is still valid to see overly rapid population growth rates as outstripping resource bases (particularly food) and portending global disaster. Aldous Huxley once warned that overpopulation was the second greatest problem facing humanity (the threat of nuclear war being the first). It is widely assumed in the developed countries that overpopulation is one of the primary causes of Third World poverty.

Current discussions of population and possible overpopulation start with two observations. First, world population, which had been growing at a rapid rate, began to grow at an even faster rate after 1945, producing a surge within the surge generally associated with industrialism as shown by Deevey above. By the end of this decade, world population will be close to six billion compared to two billion four hundred thousand in 1950. Second, Third World populations are growing at much faster rates than those of developed countries (the reverse had been true before 1920).

Both of these observations can be interpreted according to the influential demographic transition theory, which is based upon the experience of First World population growth. According to it, population growth rates within particular countries go through three phases: an initial phase in which there are both high birth and death rates, resulting in population growing little or not at all; a period of declining death rates while birth rates remain unchanged, resulting in a surge in population growth; and a final period when birth rates decline, resulting in a leveling off of population growth rates. Put more succinctly, a demographic transition is "the process of change from high birth and death rates to low birth and death rates" (Kammeyer and Ginn, 1986, p. 254).

The developed countries have all completed this transition and currently have low population growth rates.[1]

The reason why both Third World and overall world population is
growing rapidly is because Third World countries are in the surge phases of their demographic transitions, surges that are sufficiently great to
accelerate overall world population growth rates. The surge in Third
World population growth rates was largely caused by the post–World
War II international diffusion of vaccines and other means of combating
infectious diseases. Dramatic reductions in death caused by infectious
diseases have resulted in more babies surviving infancy and more people growing to older ages. At the same time, birth rates have not
declined enough to offset decreases in death rates and move countries
into the leveling-off phase of the demographic transition. However, it is
most likely that by the first two decades of the next century the sizes of
annual increases in the world's population will peak (Livi-Bacci, 1992,
p. 202), inaugurating the beginning of the leveling-off phase of this lat-
est demographic transition phase in world history, as predicted by
Deevey above.

There are a number of reasons why Third World birth rates have
remained higher than those of developed countries. Developing countries have proportionately more people working in rural areas than do
developed countries, resulting in large families continuing to be economically functional, at least in the short run. Even those families that have
been forced by landlessness and rural poverty into moving to the mush-
rooming Third World urban centers find that children are productive at
early ages in cities within countries where child labor has not been
made illegal. As any visitor to a poor Third World city knows, many children work at selling newspapers and gum, washing windshields of cars,
doing odd jobs in workshops, and picking rags, among other occupations,
rather than attending school. In Third World countries privately funded
pensions and state-subsidized social security programs for retired workers are rare. Old people are supported by their families, which results in
an added incentive to have large families. Finally, in much of the Third
World, building a large family is as much a mark of prestige and success
as building a large fortune, especially when the latter is virtually impossible for the vast majority.

However, despite these obstacles, Third World birth rates have
been dramatically declining since the 1960s, when family-planning
information and contraceptive devices began to be spread in most parts
of the Third World. As a result, the proportion of couples in developing
countries who use contraception for birth control is now approaching
that of the First World; and the fertility rate for women has fallen dramatically between 1970 and 1992 from 5.6 to 3.3 children per mother
(World Bank, 1994, p. 213). Thus, though Third World birth rates

remain higher than those of developed countries, the gap has been closing rapidly.

It is abundantly clear that family planning, beyond its importance for lowering overall birth rates, has the effect of improving the prospects for a family's standard of living, especially in developing countries. The fewer the number of dependents in a household, the greater the per capita income of each. Parents can care for two or three children much better than they can ten.

The reality that relatively high population growth rates remain in most developing countries does not necessarily mean that they are absolutely overpopulated or that they must inevitably endure starvation and malnutrition. India, which is often pointed to as a greatly overpopulated country, has a lower population density (people per square kilometer) than Belgium, Japan, or the Netherlands, countries that are never considered to be overpopulated (The World Bank, 1994). Bangladesh, whose people suffer greatly from high rates of malnutrition, has one of the world's most lush food-growing areas.

These social facts indicate that Third World population growth rates or relatively large family sizes cannot be the sole explanation for why there is so much starvation and malnutrition. An alternative and more plausible explanation of Third World malnutrition is that it results primarily from the unequal distribution of the world's food resources. Each year more total food is produced in the world than total necessary consumption needs. It follows that if world food resources were more equitably distributed, malnutrition would diminish regardless of rates of population growth.

The misperception that overpopulation is the root cause of Third World poverty is unfortunately continually fed by First World media images, which constantly focus on crowds and crowded conditions for story backdrops. Television features about poverty in Mexico continually reinforce the image that the country is overpopulated by focusing on crowded shanty neighborhoods. The image would be different if the camera focused on vast stretches of uninhabited land owned by the rich or controlled by First-World-based agribusiness corporations.

This media practice results in stereotyping and exemplifies what sociologists refer to as the distinction between reality and the perception of reality. Perceptions of reality do not necessarily have to be produced according to what the actual underlying reality is.

In studying such phenomena, it is always necessary to keep in mind why perceptions can vary from realities. The perception that overpopulation is the root of Third World problems in large part serves First World and Third World elite ideological needs. Blaming the appallingly miserable living conditions which prevail for the majority of people in Third World countries on overpopulation shifts the focus from how

TABLE 11–2 Overpopulation: Perception and Reality—Some Examples

	Population Density (people per square kilometer)
Perceived as overpopulated:	
Mexico	43
India	269
Not perceived as overpopulated:	
Belgium	323
Japan	329
Netherlands	411

Source: The World Bank (1994) data.

resources and products are distributed within the world economy, which disproportionately benefit developed countries and the Third World rich at the expenses of Third World majorities. The not-so-hidden message of the overpopulation argument is that the poor cause their own poverty by having too many babies, a message which amounts to what sociologists call blaming the victim.

It can thus be safely concluded that overpopulation is not the underlying cause of Third World misery. While there continue to be families that have more children than they can adequately support, some areas may be overcrowded, and high population growth rates may slow economic development, there is no evidence that Third World countries are absolutely overpopulated in the sense of having more people than could be supported with an equitable system of resource and product distribution.

POPULATION CONTROL AND DEVELOPMENT

Since the 1950s, there has been a growing controversy regarding population control programs designed to lower Third World birth rates. Population control advocates argue that Third World growth rates undermine development in those countries in the short run and world stability in the long run. They believe that there is a need to actively lower Third World birth rates in order to lower overall population growth rates.

Up until the middle 1960s, the United States government largely avoided involvement in population control programs. The issue of government-encouraged birth control was politically controversial, given the Catholic church's historical opposition. Advocacy of population control programs for Third World countries was largely in private hands, with the Rockefeller Foundation and other private concerns taking the lead. By 1965, though, the Johnson administration had become convinced that the U.S. government had to underwrite population control efforts in the Third World. On June 25, 1965, President Johnson told the United Nations General Assembly that "$5 invested in birth control is worth $100 invested in economic growth" (cited in Barclay, Enright, and Reynolds, 1970, p. 2). The government replaced private foundations as the leading funder of such Third World population control programs as educational campaigns and birth control clinics. By the late 1960s, the United States Congress increasingly attached to bills authorizing foreign aid to particular Third World countries the requirement that they have population control programs (Mass, 1976, p. 58).[2]

But behind the well-meaning belief that cutting population growth rates would benefit the Third World poor were political fears and concerns which verged on racism. Politically, in a time when the Vietnam War, which pitted a First World power against a communist-led insurgency, was still raging, many believed that overpopulation caused poverty, and that poverty bred communism. The not-so-subtle racial fear was that Third World nonwhite people were increasing much faster than First World whites. One 1969 newspaper ad advocating population control (cited in Barclay, Enright, and Reynolds, 1970, p. 7) bluntly stated, "The ever mounting tidal wave of humanity now challenges us to control it, or be submerged along with all our civilized values."

The intersection of racist motives and population control goes back to the late-nineteenth-century upper-class eugenics movement in the United States. Eugenics was founded on the belief that countries ought to practice selective breeding of their populations in order to maximize strong over weak genetic traits. Not surprisingly, in the climate of those times, strong traits were associated with whites from Northern and Western European backgrounds, while weak traits were associated with nonwhites and Southern and Eastern Europeans. The eugenicists advocated national quotas on immigration (to maximize entry of peoples with "strong" traits) and sterilization of the mentally incapacitated. By the 1930s and 1940s, eugenicism died out in the United States, largely in reaction to Nazi practices which had been founded on similar beliefs in the genetic superiority of particular races and peoples. But many of the people who had been leading eugenicists transformed their concerns into the more broadly conceived concern for Third World population control to avoid worldwide overpopulation (Barclay, Enright, and Reynolds, 1970).

In the 1960s' rush to cut Third World birth rates, many abuses occurred. Poverty in Puerto Rico was blamed on overpopulation, and Puerto Rican women were urged by a well-financed campaign to reduce the number of their pregnancies. Doctors advocated that women undergo sterilization as the ultimate solution to birth control. By 1965, 35 percent of the women of childbearing age in Puerto Rico had been sterilized. Two-thirds of them were still in their twenties when the operation was performed (Mass, 1976, p. 95). In some countries, men were offered portable radios or cash if they would have vasectomies. In the domestic United States, nonwhites (blacks, Latinos, and Indians) were also subjected to a barrage of appeals to limit their birth rates.

NATIONAL POPULATION POLICIES

Governments can either have intentional or laissez-faire population policies. They can either seek to intentionally plan growth rates, or they can avoid involvement and leave the course of growth rates up to fate. Racist and political motives aside, there are legitimate reasons why countries can adopt policies which seek to intentionally decrease or increase their population sizes. Third World countries may conclude that the pace of population increase is dysfunctional for their development needs and seek to slow it. Other countries may conclude that their population bases are either not growing fast enough or are actually decreasing, and seek to stimulate population growth. The United States in the nineteenth and early twentieth centuries pursued policies to attract people to the country. A number of Eastern European and Scandinavian countries today deem themselves to be underpopulated and have policies aimed at increasing the number of people within their borders. The majority of countries in the world though do not have intentional population policies. Either they take the laissez-faire attitude of allowing growth rates to develop as they will, or they are in the preliminary stages of developing population policies.

Three variables—birth rates, death rates, and migration patterns—determine population growth rates and therefore form the areas available for national population planning. Birth rates can be stimulated by offering incentives to parents, such as tax breaks, paid leave, and other social benefits. Birth rates can be lowered in the most benign way by making birth control information and low-cost or free contraceptive devices available. Repressive approaches to lowering birth rates can impose a variety of types of penalties to discourage pregnancies. China, for example, began in 1980 a strict program to limit families to one child. Among the negative sanctions used was to deny the right of free education to a third-born child (Peters and Larkin, 1983, p. 183).

Only the most draconian national population policy would intentionally attempt to increase death rates in order to lower population growth rates. However, First World inaction toward famines and other death-causing disasters in the Third World has sometimes been justified on the basis of the argument that such disasters are not wholly bad, since they serve to decrease population sizes (for a critique, see Baran, 1957, pp. 237–248). In a more positive light, all national public health programs have the effect of decreasing infant and general mortality rates, and therefore serve to stimulate the growth of population. The withholding of such programs would have the opposite effect, whether intended or not.

National governments can either encourage or discourage migration into their countries as a means of affecting population growth rates. As mentioned, the United States filled up what was largely a sparsely populated country by allowing almost unlimited immigration up until the early twentieth century. (The Chinese were excluded after 1882—the beginning of racialist-oriented national quota systems.) The U.S. borders were only closed to large-scale immigration after the Immigration Act of 1921. Australia and New Zealand are countries today that are trying to increase their population sizes by encouraging immigration, though they are highly selective in who they actually admit.

MIGRATION AND URBANIZATION

People migrate within and between societies. In both cases, their decisions are affected by a series of what demographers call push and pull factors. Definite conditions, such as economic deterioration, famine, or war, influence decisions to leave one location—to push people out. Other conditions, such as perceived economic opportunities, greater prosperity, or peace, can attract or pull people to other locations. Any particular migration pattern can thus be analyzed in terms of its push and pull causes.

Economic misery and warfare are the primary push factors that today account for legal and illegal migration from Third World to developed countries. The latter economies in turn pull Third World migrants by their relative prosperity and often the availability of low-wage jobs. The latter economies have also been magnets for people from socialist and formerly socialist countries. The international direction of both legal and illegal labor migration is thus from relatively poor to relatively prosperous economies. People left the postwar socialist and continue to leave Third World countries for perceived better living conditions in Western Europe and the United States. The effects of such migration on Third World development are mixed. On the one hand, lack of land and jobs drives peasants and workers to search abroad for income opportunities. They often send money back to their families who remain at home. These remittances can be a considerable source of income to the national economy. On the other hand, professionals such as doctors and engineers leave not because they cannot find work, but because they can make more money in developed countries. Third World governments have often subsidized their educations with grants to study internally or abroad, only to see them then leave the country or stay abroad permanently once the degree is obtained. This so-called brain drain from the Third World has obvious negative consequences for development. The postwar socialist governments faced the same dilemma and responded with a repressive policy of forbidding out-migration by trained labor force members.

Within societies, people have responded similarly to deteriorating economic conditions by moving to other areas where opportunities are perceived to be better. By far, the greatest type of internal migration in the modern era in almost all parts of the world has been from rural to urban areas, producing the long-range trend of urbanization. Increasing agricultural productivity made it possible for smaller numbers of farmers and rural laborers to produce enough to feed growing city populations. As agriculture became more capital intensive, small farmers and rural laborers have found themselves unable to compete under the new conditions and forced off the land and into expanding urban occupations.

The shift of people from rural to urban areas, however, has seldom been a smooth process in which people simply changed types of jobs and household locations. Rather, in actuality, it has been usually unplanned and accompanied by severe dislocations, leaving a wake of subsequent social problems. In most cases, people have been pushed off the land at a faster pace than the creation of new urban jobs, resulting in large-scale unemployment. Examples of massive unemployment and its corrolary problems brought about by deteriorating rural economic conditions that forced people off the land go back to fifteenth-century England and are rampant in the Third World today.

The rural to urban shift has long been noted by sociologists as producing its own set of social problems, including alienation, family breakdown, and criminality. When people move they not only leave one area and type of occupation for another, they also leave ways of life that provided accustomed forms of social stability. Families that for generations had been in the same rural area had developed elaborate social networks of support among relatives. Most children grew up interacting with—and being controlled by—extended families and deeply rooted local institutions such as churches. But moves to urban areas produced radical breaks with these institutions which had produced social stability, albeit in contexts of deteriorating economic conditions. In the absence of compensating new institutions, children become socially cut adrift. When the urban experience fails to provide the hoped-for economic improvement, the problem is compounded. It is often then that juvenile delinquency, gangs, and other forms of criminal behavior tend to increase in urban neighborhoods made up of new domestic or international immigrants. Thus, at one time or another, both black neighborhoods and those made up of immigrants have been perceived to be dangerous in U.S. cities. What both have in common is that they were made up of uprooted populations. Blacks were uprooted from rural southern communities in the first part of the century and immigrants were uprooted largely from peasant communities in Europe and Latin America. When the immigrant group is perceived to be racially different from the already established population—as were blacks and most Mexicans who moved into U.S. cities—then racism and racial antagonism can exacerbate the problems of the uprooted population.

Even more socially disruptive has been the migration propelled by warfare. Over the last two decades, local and regional wars, such as those in Central America, the continent of Africa, Afghanistan, and parts of the formerly socialist countries, have increasingly produced forced migrations of refugees to locations either within or outside the borders of their countries. The number of such displaced persons more than quadrupled since the 1970s, causing the United Nations High Commissioner for Refugees to report that now one out of every 114 persons in the world has been uprooted and forced to migrate for security reasons to another area (*The New York Times*, August 8, 1994, p. 1). In most cases, the host areas have been ill prepared to absorb the new immigrants, resulting in overcrowded refugee camps, inadequate supplying of food, and rampant disease.

SUMMARY

Demography is the quantitative or statistical study of population sizes, distributions, and growth rates. It uses censuses, vital statistics, and sample surveys to compile statistical information. That information forms empirical raw material for a wide variety of studies by social scientists, government planners, business researchers, and others.

Demographic information and demographers have been at the center of long-standing controversies regarding whether the world and particular societies within it were becoming overpopulated. Such fears originated almost two hundred years ago with the works of Thomas Robert Malthus, who argued that population growth rates were greatly outpacing growth in production of food and other means of sustaining people. Malthus's central hypothesis—that population grew at a geometric rate, while means of subsistence only grew at an arithmetic rate—has not been substantiated by modern demographic information about present and past societies. Rather than growing at a steadily accelerating geometric ratio, world population has grown in stages characterized by periods of surges initiated by great technological revolutions and periods of leveling off.

While Malthus was wrong in his understanding of how populations grew, his central concern—that the world was headed for overpopulation—has reemerged in the last few decades. The term *neo-Malthusianism* is often used to describe contemporary overpopulation theories. These theories center both on total world population growth in general and Third World growth in particular, which now exceeds that of the developed countries.

The theory of the demographic transition is one of the most useful approaches to understanding and analyzing differences between First and Third World population growth rates. According to this theory, all societies, at least in modern world history, have gone or are going through a transition characterized by the following stages: an initial stage in which high birth rates are offset by high death rates so that overall population growth remains low; a period when death rates decline while birth rates remain high which results in a surge in overall population growth; and a final period when birth rates decline to match death rates which produces a leveling off of overall population growth rates.

As developed countries have completed the cycle of their demographic transitions, their population growth rates have already leveled off. Much of the Third World, on the other hand, is now in the surge phases of demographic transitions, with high population growth rates. There is considerable concern among neo-Malthusian theorists that Third World growth rates are causing economic and political problems in those regions and, ultimately, pushing the entire world toward overpopulation.

But there are a number of problems with blaming Third World economic and political problems on high population growth rates. There is no evidence that the majority of those societies are actually overpopulated. Many of the countries most often cited as overpopulated actually have lower population densities than a number of developed countries that are never thought of as overpopulated. If the world's food supply were equitably distributed, there would be enough to sustain the world's population. Many of the problems blamed on overpopulation are in fact more directly caused by unequal distribution of resources and goods.

There is considerable evidence that racist motives have formed an important part of at least some population control efforts. The intersection of racism and population control goes back to the late nineteenth-century eugenics movement in the United States, which advocated selective breeding of the population in order to encourage the reproduction of "strong" genetic traits associated with Anglo-Saxon and Nordic peoples. Nonwhite Third World peoples have most often been the targets of population control programs which have been designed, funded, and administered by white First World peoples.

In the 1960s and 1970s, a number of First World countries and agencies became heavily involved in designing and administering population control programs for Third World countries. Such programs ranged from reasonably beneficial distribution of means of birth control to abusive sterilization of Third World women, which raised serious ethical and human rights questions, as well as provoking anger and nationalist resentment within the countries themselves.

Despite the abuses associated with a number of population control efforts, there are quite legitimate reasons for countries to develop national population policies. Such policies can, on the bases of their analyses of the situation, encourage or discourage further population growth. There are three primary variables which affect population growth rates—birth rates, death rates, and immigration rates. Depending on whether they seek to stimulate or decrease the rates at which their populations are growing, countries can institute policies which either encourage or discourage citizens from having larger families. Similarly, they can adopt policies which either encourage or restrict further immigration.

Migration within and between populations is a process that affects the distribution of people. Demographers analyze particular migration patterns in terms of push and pull factors. That is, they attempt to determine the causes for people's leaving one area and being attracted to another. There are economic and political push and pull factors—such as war, economic misery, and perceived economic opportunity—involved in legal and illegal international migration. Domestically, urbanization has been the long-range trend in most parts of the world as people have migrated from rural areas to cities.

Key Terms and Concepts
(in order of presentation)

Demography	Eugenics
Demographic transition	Push and pull factors
Population density	Urbanization

Endnotes

1. The year in which Malthus made his dire projection, 1798, was during the surge phase of the First World demographic transition. It appeared that population growth rates were soaring because they were. But what Malthus could not see was that they were destined to level off. For that reason, it is always hazardous to predict future population developments from present trends. Statements such as "if present rates of growth con-

tinue . . ." are always fraught with potential error. Future rates of growth will be greatly affected by factors that do not yet exist.

2. Ironically, the United States government, which was the leading advocate of population control programs in the Third World during the 1960s and 1970s, stopped forcefully advancing that position during the 1980s and early 1990s because of the ascendancy into the White House of conservative Republicans who were committed to outlawing abortions; and China, which had forcefully criticized Western programs to control population growth rates in the Third World during the 1960s, instituted the world's strictest population control program. Two of the major proponents in the international debate over population growth in the Third World thus essentially switched sides.

Chapter Twelve

Social Research

The purpose of social research is to produce valid understandings of how societies and their constituent parts develop and function. Researchers based in universities, government agencies, and private businesses investigate two types of problems: those that involve current public issues, such as drug abuse, homelessness, and family violence, and those that arise from intellectual issues within the general body of social science literature, such as the role of Protestantism in the development of early capitalism, the origins of racism, and the causes of class mobility. Research products appear as books, lecture presentations, articles, documentary films, public programs, and in other forms.

Understanding the general principles of social research is obviously essential preparation for careers which require its production. Those include college teaching and a variety of research-oriented positions attached to government agencies and private businesses.

Only a minority of sociology students, though, pursue careers which ever involve production of research. For them, the importance of understanding social research principles is to be able to be critical consumers who can, as professionals and citizens, intelligently evaluate research claims. Teachers and social agency professionals need to be able to make sense of and evaluate studies which relate to their work problems. Citizens should take an interest in and be able to understand the importance and limitations of social science studies reported in the general press such as preelection surveys and studies of the long-term effects of divorce on children.

Social research develops through definitions of problems, reviews of appropriate literature, selections of research designs for the collection of pertinent information or data, and analyses of the problems with the aid of the newly collected information. Accomplishment of these tasks does not necessarily proceed in strict chronological order—researchers often, for example, redefine their problems according to the information that they have collected. Sociological theory is involved in all stages of research development. The theoretical premises of researchers, consciously or unconsciously, influence types of problems selected, literature consulted, research designs chosen, and analyses and interpretations of results. Ethical issues can also be deeply involved in any of the stages of research.

DEFINING RESEARCH PROBLEMS

There is an inexhaustible supply of possible research problems. In addition to areas that have never been researched, old research topics and results are constantly being reexamined and challenged. As societies develop, they constantly reinterpret their pasts, make projections about their futures, and have to deal with the social problems of their presents.

There are a number of ways to identify contemporary research problems. Quality daily newspapers are the best, though not infallible, sources for gaining quick overviews of the ranges of contemporary social problems which have become social issues. They spotlight instances of contemporary social problems (drug-related murders, wars, corruption trials, family violence episodes, prison riots, famine-related deaths, etc.) and cover the related perceptions of commentators and political figures. Journals and books are the best sources for gaining familiarity with other general problems such as the causes of Third World underdevelopment, the consequences of different population growth rates, and the origins of discrimination. Government agencies and private foundations also advertise for research proposals for particular types of problems whose investigation they are willing to fund.

REVIEW OF THE LITERATURE

Once the problem has been identified and defined, relevant existing research and commentary must be located in libraries in order to find out what is already known or at issue.

Finding background information in libraries is somewhat of a science itself.[1] The first step is to define the problem in such a way that it conforms to the classification systems used by libraries. This is done initially by scaling down the general topic or research problem to a key word or two such as: alienation, prison behavior, French politics, drug addiction, and so on. With the key words at hand, three types of publications can then be searched: reference works (encyclopedias and dictionaries), books from the general collection, and periodicals and journals.

Encyclopedias and specialized dictionaries are good resources for getting introductory, general, and often up-to-date overviews of topics. They also often contain bibliographic information for further reading.

Card catalogues (or computerized equivalents) contain complete files of library collections of books. They are usually separated into two parts. One section contains a card for every one of the library's book collection alphabetized in order according to both title and author. The other contains a card for every one of the nonfiction books in the collection alphabetized in order according to subject, making it possible to look up all of the holdings that the library has for a particular subject such as slavery or alcoholism. If there is no subject heading for the topic of interest, chances are that there may be a different subject heading that contains closely related material. The *Library of Congress Subject Headings*, which cross-references all subject headings contained in card catalogues, can be useful in this case.

Articles contained in journals, magazines, and newspapers are not listed in card catalogues. For those, libraries keep indexes (such as *Social Science Citation Index*, *The New York Times Index*) which usually categorize articles topically. A useful index is the *Essay and General Literature Index*, which accesses articles contained in edited collections. Another is the *Public Affairs Information Services*, which lists pamphlets and government reports as well as selected journal and newspaper articles. Libraries also have collections of abstracts (such as *Abstracts in Anthropology* and *Sociological Abstracts*) which list articles by subject areas and in addition contain a paragraph or more describing the article.

Many libraries today also have computer access to data banks which contain listings of articles and books. These can be accessed through key words—for example, slave revolts in nineteenth-century Georgia—and those listings which contain the key words will be printed out for the client.

RESEARCH DESIGNS

Once the review of the literature has been completed, the researcher chooses a suitable research design, which is made up of one or more techniques for collecting appropriate new information or data. Sociologists generally collect data that already exists from a variety of possible sources or, when necessary, create it themselves with surveys, field studies, or experiments.

Sources of Existing Data

There are many sources of already existing quantitative information. Each year, governments and other organizations release large amounts of statistical information of potential use to social scientists. The census of any country is one of the most vital sources of information available to sociologists. In the United States, for example, the Bureau of the Census publishes its census report every ten years which contains information on population sizes, birth and death rates, housing, income, and a range of other subjects. The Bureau of the Census also continually issues supplemental reports and estimates of changes since its last official ten-year report. The *Statistical Abstract of the United States*, which is issued yearly and available in most libraries, is the best single compendium of official statistics. In Canada, Statistics Canada publishes census information every five years with supplemental reports in between. The *Canada Year Book* is the best single compendium of governmental statistics. Statistical information from nongovernmental business and community organizations is also often available and of potential use. Of these, the World Bank's *World Development Report*, issued annually, is of especial use for comparative economic and social data on most of the world's countries. The United Nations and a number of other international organizations also publish useful compendiums of international statistics.

Many research projects rely on the collection of already existing qualitative types of information. A researcher, for example, interested in the conceptual development of a particular school of social theory, such as functionalism, would collect as information quotations, paraphrases, and summaries of ideas taken from works of those writers. There are other projects whose purpose is to reveal types of themes conveyed in newspapers, books, radio, television, movies, songs, and other communications media. Is media coverage of a particularly controversial issue biased? What do the lyrics of popular music reveal about cultural values? The researcher collects examples from the type of media of interest which can then be analyzed.

Interviews and Surveys

There are two basic types of interviews for collecting information that are used in sociological research: interviews of knowledgeable informants and survey interviews. Both involve face-to-face meetings between researchers and people from whom they seek information.

In the first, the sociologist, like a reporter, seeks out knowledge-able informants about the issue at hand and interviews them to gather information. A researcher, for example, who was studying upper-class social life in a particular city might seek an interview with the local newspaper's society editor. This type of interviewing is a basic procedure engaged in at one time or another in almost all research projects. Its purpose is to collect information and insights from people who have direct experience with the issue at hand.

The purpose of survey interviews is somewhat different. It is to determine the distribution of a variable or variables of interest—such as attitudes, party affiliations, or income—among a population of people. Survey interviews involve administering standardized questionnaires to groups of respondents and then tabulating the results.

In surveys (and other research techniques as well), a distinction is made between universes and samples. Universes are the ultimate focus of the research. The sociologist hopes to gather data which indicate, for example, the distribution of income in the United States, her or his universe. Samples are the actual groups from which data is collected. In some cases, such as national censuses or small-scale research, the sample and the universe coincide. But for most research it would be prohibitively expensive and time-consuming to actually survey all members or cases in a universe. In that type of research, the sample must be drawn so that a plausible case can be made that its characteristics are generalizable—the key work in this type of survey research—to the universe of ultimate interest.

Sociologists use the statistical probability technique of randomization to create generalizable samples. Preelection surveys are the best-known examples of this technique. If done well, their results have a high degree of accuracy for predicting actual outcomes. Their use is now a commonplace part of the political landscape. What is remarkable about such polls—and a mystery to many people—is how on the basis of interviews with as few as 1,200 people, they can accurately predict outcomes for elections with over 100 million votes cast. The secret of that success has been the application of mathematical probability theory to social science problems. According to probability theory, if a sample is carefully drawn out of a population or universe, the range and internal variations in its characteristics will closely match that of the larger population. In order for the two to match, members of the sample must be randomly drawn, meaning that each has an equal chance of being selected. If each is randomly selected, then little or no bias will exist to distort the distribution of characteristics within the sample.

Most preelection surveys today use computers to create randomized lists of telephone numbers. Those homes are then called for the survey. This technique works well in the United States, since most voters have telephones. The technique did not work well in earlier periods when substantial numbers of low-income people could not afford telephones. For that reason, numerous preelection surveys in 1948 erroneously predicted that Thomas Dewey, the Republican, would defeat Harry Truman for the presidency. Democratic voters tended to have less income than Republicans and were therefore less likely to have telephones. The sample, drawn from telephone books, therefore was biased by overrepresenting Republican voters. For the same reason, telephone polling would not work for contemporary Third World countries where substantial parts of the population still do not have service. Where telephone polling is inappropriate, mail and in-person surveying must be used.

While election polls are the best-known examples of use of the technique of survey sampling to efficiently learn about the characteristics of a large population, there have been a wide range of other applications of the technique in the social sciences. Sociologists are often interested in finding out distributions of objective characteristics such as income, religion, occupational groups, or health conditions. They can also be interested in finding out the range and correlates of particular attitudes in a population. What types of workers, for example, hold class-conscious attitudes? Who is most likely to consider himself or herself middle class? Are fundamentalists more likely to be from particular occupation groups?

Case Studies

The basic idea of a field or case study is that by examining one example in depth, much can be learned that is generalizable. A thorough examination of one subculture of hard-drug users, for example, might reveal patterns of behavior and interaction that are generalizable to other groups of users. In this particular case, it would be impossible to survey all groups of users or even to come up with a random sample from which to generalize results. In-depth focus on one group has the additional advantage of revealing the subtleties of interaction patterns which are missed by statistical summaries.

In field studies, the researcher immerses himself or herself in the group or organization. This can either take the form of the researcher's simply being an identified outside observer or it can take the form of participant observation in which he or she becomes a member of the group under observation. The researcher takes copious notes on the activities and interactions of interest. The notes then become the data or observations which are analyzed to produce the study's results. Part of the study's write-up is usually a naturalistic description, which gives the reader a feel for the group's typical interaction patterns, especially those that mark it off from other groups. A novelist's eye for details can be usefully employed. Another part is reserved for theoretically interpreting the meaning of the interaction patterns. The results can be compared with those of similar or related studies, and thereby confirm, refine, or challenge those findings.

Experiments

The basic purpose of an experiment is to gather information on how two or more variables (any changeable characteristic) are related under controlled conditions. An experiment, for example, might be designed to study the relationship between exposure to violence on television and violent behavior in children.

Stated technically, social scientists design experiments to test hypotheses of how variables are related. A hypothesis is a statement of a suspected relationship between variables. A variable that causes changes in another is referred to as an independent variable, while a variable that changes as the result of the effects of another is referred to as a dependent variable. Thus, an experiment could be designed to test the hypothesis that exposure to violence on television (independent variable) leads to increases in violent behavior in children (dependent variable).

The classic experimental design is based on comparing two groups, an experimental and a control group. Each is given an initial pretest to measure the dependent variable of interest. Then the experimental group is exposed to the independent variable of interest while the control group is not. If, as hypothesized, the value of the dependent variable for the experimental group changes (as measured in a posttest), while it does not for the control group, then the direction of causation predicted by the hypothesis is validated. An alternative version of the experimental design involves comparing two or more experimental groups rather than an experimental and a control group.

Social scientists have devised a number of experiments involving small groups of people to test primarily social psychological hypotheses. In these types of experiments, people, usually volunteers, are randomly divided into experimental and control groups and then subjected to exposure or nonexposure to the independent variable of interest. Such small-group experiments may take place in specially constructed laboratory conditions. Rooms, for example, may be designed with hidden microphones and one-way mirrors so that the interaction processes among the participants can be documented and studied.

Experimental or quasi-experimental designs may also be developed to study relationships between variables in normal life settings, but under less controllable conditions. Existing classes of elementary school children, for example, can be separately treated as experimental and control groups in order to measure the effectiveness of a new teaching method. The effectiveness of a new type of public program to, say, decrease drunken driving can be similarly studied by comparing its rates of success before and after introduction or with those of areas where it does not exist.

ANALYSIS OF RESULTS

While the information is being collected, it is sorted into relevant categories for analysis. To analyze something means to break it down into its constituent parts and determine how they are interrelated. To analyze a research problem similarly means to break it down into its constituent parts and specify the nature of interrelationships.

The first task of analysis thus is to categorize the different parts of the research problem. Depending on the nature of the problem, its different parts will be conceptualized in different ways. A study of the origins of industrialism might develop an initial analysis in terms of causes and effects. A study of the causes of high school dropout rates might categorize its data in terms of variables such as parental income of students, grade point averages, and types of available school programs.

The next task of analysis is to specify how the internal parts of the problem are interrelated. In the study of industrialism, the researcher would use the information collected to make a plausible argument that particular types of causes were related to particular effects. Such an analysis would be made in essentially qualitative terms.

When the data collected are of a quantitative nature, statistical inference can be a useful tool for analyzing interrelationships. If the data can be validly expressed in a quantitative form (e.g., the percentage of the unemployed who are minorities), internal relationships can be revealingly expressed as statistical relationships. Brenner (1976), for example, in the study cited in Chapter One, found that as rates of unemployment increase, rates of general mortality increase. Unemployed people have less income to spend on health care, and the stressful nature of unemployment stimulates a variety of physical and mental health problems, including alcohol abuse, drug abuse, and suicidal depression. Brenner technically found a *correlation* between unemployment and mortality rates. A correlation exists when changes in one variable (the unemployment rate in this case) are associated with changes in another (the mortality rate).[2]

A word of caution about the limits of social research is in order.

Skillful analysis of information can help to illuminate vaguely understood areas—such as the nature of drug and other subcultures. It can uncover and bring to light hidden interaction patterns, values, and meanings. Hidden realities can be explored. But social research rarely results in definitive causal proofs. It is a positivistic illusion to believe that sociologists can scientifically accumulate full knowledge of social causes and effects. At best, sociologists can use social research to make plausible cases for this or that causal explanation. Their causal conclusions are always tentative possibilities—if x happens, y is likely to happen. If the rate of unemployment increases, rates of family violence are likely to increase. If a certain amount is invested in a social program to create jobs for inner-city youths, drug-related activity is likely to decrease.

ETHICS AND SOCIAL RESEARCH

As social research has developed over the decades, a number of ethical issues have emerged regarding its purposes and the rights of its subjects.

Research for Whom?

Those who control resources that fund large-scale research—government and private foundations generally—have great power to determine the types of questions that are studied. The powerful can determine that the direction of social research be according to their own interests rather than those of open scientific inquiry. In 1965, it was revealed for example that the Pentagon was funding U.S.-based social scientists to conduct research on Latin American lower classes in order to learn how to thwart the development of revolutionary movements (Horowitz, 1967).

On another less blatant but none the less serious level, most social research follows the general tendency of the powerless always being obligated to turn over information about themselves to the powerful, while the powerful are generally not obligated to reciprocate. Landlords demand to know the exact incomes of renters, but are under no obligation to provide the same information about themselves. Welfare clients surrender considerable sensitive information about themselves and their families in order to receive their payments. The balance of social research continues to have as its focus the powerless and lower classes. Only a minority of social research focuses on power structure studies, for which there is little government or private funding available.

Rights of Research Subjects

By its very nature, social research involves human subjects who cannot be treated in the same ways as the nonhuman subjects of research in the physical and natural sciences. The norms of social research thus differ in important respects from those governing the physical and natural sciences. Subjects of researchers have recognized rights, but often those rights are not completely unambiguous.

Well-being   In no cases should subjects of research be intentionally placed in conditions that could result in bodily or psychological harm. A researcher, for example, could not design an experiment to compare the effectiveness of different methods of torture or the effects of different types of frightening experiences. This is probably the most unambiguous ethical norm of social research, though there have been numerous instances of its being violated.

Respect of Privacy   One can imagine any number of types of research that would result in obvious invasions of privacy through wiretapping of telephone conversations, electronic eavesdropping, hidden cameras, and the like. The ethical problems involved in this type of research are clear, and it is not widely practiced by social scientists. But invasions of privacy do occur in many participant observation types of research which are widely practiced. When researchers gain entry into groups in order to study them by posing as full participants, they are in effect able to observe and study people without their consent. In this instance, the distinction between justifiable social research and intrusive invasions of privacy remains ambiguous.

Protection from Deception and Manipulation   Many types of social research have employed deception in order to obtain valid results. If subjects in a survey or experiment knew, for example, that they were being tested on prejudice they might tell the researcher what they thought was the most socially acceptable answer as opposed to their true feelings. Thus the sociologist would probably develop her or his research design in such a way as to hide its true purposes. But the needs for scientific validity in this type of instance interfere with the rights of human subjects to not be manipulated and deceived. Like the right to privacy, the distinction between ethically justifiable subterfuge in order to obtain valid results and unjustifiable deception and manipulation of subjects remains ambiguous and a dilemma in social research.

Confidentiality   Social science researchers are often involved in collecting information from individuals about their personal lives and attitudes. It is a generally accepted ethical norm that they may use that information as a basis for analytical conclusions, but that they may not reveal the personal identities involved. In general, researchers cannot release the names of sources of information if that release would prove harmful to the subject in question and therefore a violation of the confidence with which the information was given. The results of a survey of sexual practices, for example, might prove embarrassing if informants were identified. How far the principle of confidentiality can be extended though is not clear. For example, researchers of most illegal behavior have an ethical responsibility not to become police informants. But the principle of confidentiality cannot be so absolute as to permit a researcher to knowingly allow, for example, life-threatening child abuse to continue. Ethical norms can hence come into conflict with each other, putting the researcher in the often difficult position of having to decide which takes precedence.

SUMMARY

Social research follows several distinguishable steps: definition of a problem, review of the literature, development of a research design and collection of pertinent information, and analysis of results. Theoretical premises are involved in all stages of research. Once the problem has been defined, the researcher reviews already existing research and commentary on the topic that generally exists in or is accessible through libraries. He or she then develops a research design which includes one or more techniques for collecting new information or data. The techniques for collecting new data involve either using existing information contained in such sources as books, official statistics, or communications media, or developing new information through interviews, surveys, case studies, and experiments. Analysis involves breaking down the problem into its component parts, sorting the collected information accordingly, and then determining how those parts are interrelated.

The carrying out of social research poses a number of ethical issues regarding its uses and the rights of its human subjects. The powerful have the resources to fund large-scale research, and they have been more willing to support research on the powerless than on themselves. There is thus a long-standing contradiction between the logic of power and the ethical and scientific responsibilities of social researchers. The subjects of social research are people who have rights. Human subjects cannot be manipulated by social scientists in the same way that physical scientists can manipulate the nonhuman subjects of their research.

They must be treated respectfully in terms of their rights to privacy, to have information about them held in confidence, and to not be deceived or manipulated. However, the ethical norms governing research are not wholly unambiguous. Social research often confronts ethical dilemmas and gray areas.

Key Terms and Concepts
(in order of presentation)

Research design	Variable
Interview	Hypothesis
Survey	Independent variable
Universe	Dependent variable
Sample	Experimental group
Randomization	Control group
Case study	Analysis
Participant observation	Correlation
Experiment	Confidentiality

Endnotes

1. I am indebted to Nick Welchman of Eastern Connecticut State University for advice on this section.
2. Correlations, a foundation of statistical inference, are expressed as coefficients which range from -1.0 to 1.0. A correlation coefficient of 1.0 means that there is a perfect positive correlation between the variables—every time there is an increase in one variable there is a predictable increase in the other. A correlation coefficient of -1.0 would mean that every time there was an increase in one variable there would be a predictable decrease in the other. A correlation coefficient of 0 means that there is no relationship between the two variables—an increase or decrease in one would not be accompanied by any predictable change in the other. The closer a coefficient is to 1.0 or -1.0, the stronger the relationship between variables. The closer the coefficient is to 0, the weaker the relationship. There are now also additional statistical inference techniques for elaborately measuring the interactions of multiple variables.

Glossary

Agriculture: from Latin *ager*, or "field," and *cultura*, or "cultivation"; hence "cultivation of fields." Type of technology and stage of technological development characterized by large-scale cultivation of fields. In agriculture humans use animal energy, such as oxen, to pull plows to cultivate large fields.

Alcoholism: an addictive condition characterized by a deep-seated compulsion to consume alcohol that results in a significant impairment of the ability to function physically or socially.

Alienation: concept that is used in two different ways within sociology. In the first, which follows from the Marxian tradition, it refers to the objective removal of a condition necessary for human fulfillment and development. In Marx's view, humans needed to perform creative labor and have relations of solidarity with each other in order to fully fulfill themselves. The first condition did not exist for increasingly large proportions of labor forces in capitalist societies. The second did not exist in all class societies. In the second use of the concept, alienation refers to primarily subjective feelings of estrangement, detachment, loneliness, and powerlessness of people within societies.

Analysis: scientific procedure of breaking down a unit or problem of interest into its constituent parts and determining how they are interrelated.

Animism: belief system in which all elements of the physical world—humans, animals, rocks, trees, and so on—are thought to have indwelling spirits which give them life. In some cases the spirits are all different with each having its own separate identity. In others, the spirits are all emanations from one source that unites all human and other creations in nature.

Anthropology: academic discipline which studies contemporary and recent past preindustrial peoples. Anthropologists seek out the cultural configurations and uniquenesses of each people, hence "culture" is the basic unit of analysis of anthropology.

Antithesis: see *Thesis-Antithesis-Synthesis*.

Aristocracy: from Greek *aristos*, or "best," and *kratein*, or "rule"; hence "rule of the best." The self-conception of the feudal landlord class that its rule was based upon natural superiority.

Ascription: attainment of a social position on the basis of birthright rather than achievement.

Asiatic Mode of Production: see *State Society*.

Authority: as used by Max Weber, refers to the type of rationale used by rulers to justify the issuance of commands and the expectation of obedience on the part of the ruled; hence rulers claim the authority to rule over the ruled. Among the bases on which rulers can claim authority are legal right and consent of the governed. See also, *Legitimacy*.

Belief System: see *Common Conscience*.

Bourgeoisie: see *Capitalist*.

Bureaucracy: a large-scale organization based upon specialization, hierarchy, and management and/or owner control.

Capital: wealth that is available for investment in profit-seeking activities.

Capitalism: economic type of society characterized by commodity production and private ownership of the means of production.

Capitalist: a person who derives the majority of income from ownership and investments of capital; an owner of means of production and employer of labor in capitalist societies.

Capital Wealth: wealth in the form of investments that return incomes, such as stocks, bonds, whole businesses, and rental properties, as opposed to personal wealth.

Case Study: technique for collecting information based on an in-depth study of one organization, subculture, or other unit of interest, as opposed to being based on a survey of a number of units.

Character Structure: personality, the unique way in which a person integrates self-perception and role behavior.

Charismatic Legitimacy: concept associated with Max Weber which referred to legitimacy in which people follow and obey because they believe that their leader has an extraordinary ability to lead.

Chattel Slave: the most severe form of slavery in which the slave has no more legal status or rights than that of a piece of property.

Clan: a network of interrelated families that functions as a social, political, or economic unit.

Class Consciousness: concept originally introduced by Marx to refer to commonly held ideas and beliefs that are consistent with the objective interests of a class. In Marxian theory, the development of working-class class consciousness is seen as necessarily leading to socialist consciousness.

Commodity: a product that is bought, sold, or traded through a market transaction. Commodity production is considered to be one of the defining characteristics of capitalist societies.

Common Conscience: concept from Durkheim (1893, p. 79), who concluded that "the totality of beliefs and sentiments common to average citizens of the same society forms a determinate system which has its own life." He called these belief systems collective or common consciences. These commonly held beliefs form systems of thinking which are powerful frames of reference through which individuals largely interpret their experiences. As "determinate systems" they follow semi-autonomous logics of their own.

Communal Society: earliest socioeconomic type of society, characterized by equal access to means of production (such as land and tools) and consumption items (such as food).

Communism: (1) future mode of production predicted by Marx which would be characterized by common ownership of the means of production, social equality, and highly developed forces of production and technology; (2) political ideology which advocates in present conditions the development of socialist modes of production characterized by state ownership of major means of production as a transitional stage leading toward the future development of a communist mode of production.

Concept: intellectual abstraction which is used to categorize and illuminate essential meanings of real-world occurrences.

Confidentiality: ethical research norm that information collected about particular persons should be used only in ways in which personal identities are not disclosed.

Conservatism: political ideology characterized by advocacy of laissez-faire capitalism, that is, allowing societal development to be determined by unregulated market forces.

Contract Labor: type of temporary slavery in which the laborer agrees to work for a particular employer for a specified period of time during which he or she is not free to seek other positions.

Contradiction: in dialectical logic, a problem to be resolved. See also, *Dialectics, Thesis-Antithesis-Synthesis.*

Control Group: in most experimental designs, there exists a group that does not receive the independent variable under study. Changes in its dependent variable or variables are then compared with those of the experimental group in order to determine whether the administration of the independent variable had any differential effect. See also, *Experiment, Experimental Group.*

Cooperative: as used in this text, a type of organization characterized by being small-scale and member-controlled.

Correlation: statistical term that expresses the extent to which changes in one or more variables are related to changes in one or more other variables.

Corvée **Labor:** feudal form of rent payment in which peasants were obligated to work a set number of days in the landlord's fields or doing other such tasks.

Crime Rate: number of reported crimes of all types per 100,000 persons in a population unit.

Crude Death Rate: number of deaths in a given year per 1,000 persons in the population.

Culture: the unique way of life of a society as expressed through its own types of material products and nonmaterial values, customs, and language.

Decision-Making Approach: technique in studies of power structures in which key decisions of a government, organization, or other unit of interest are studied in order to determine who has power.

Democratic Centralism: organizational principle of the Leninist political party. The party is organized hierarchically with higher bodies making decisions which are binding on lower bodies. Base members participate democratically by electing delegates who represent them in the election of top leaders.

Demographic Transition: theory based upon the experience of First World countries which successively moved in states from an initial period of low population growth rates because high birth and death rates offset each other, to a period of high population growth rates because death rates declined while birth rates remained high, to a final period in which population growth rates declined as birth rates declined. Third World high population growth rates can be interpreted as being in the middle stage of the demographic transition.

Demography: specialization within sociology that studies population growths and distributions.

Dependency Theory: an explanation of Third World underdevelopment which holds that it has been caused by exploitative relationships with First World countries, including colonialism and the slave trade in the past, and multinational corporate investments, foreign loans, and unequal international trading relationships in the present.

Dependent Variable: see *Independent Variable.*

Dialectics: philosophical approach to knowledge embraced by Marx and others premised on the belief that all reality is interconnected and constantly changing. Dialectical approaches attempt to interpret all aspects of reality in terms of their interconnectedness with other aspects and their changing natures. See also, *Thesis-Antithesis-Synthesis, Contradiction.*

Dictatorship of the Proletariat: concept first introduced by Marx (1875) and inherited and developed by Lenin as the foundation of socialist states. According to Marx and Lenin, socialist governments had to take the form of dictatorships of the proletariat in order to protect working-class interests and the survival of revolutionary socialism. In practice, the concept of the dictatorship of the proletariat led to the establishment of one-party states in which communist parties monopolized political power.

Discrete: the characteristic of being distinct or unique. In social analysis, categories and measurement scales are based upon discrete criteria if they do not overlap and items can be categorized within only one category. The term *discrete* is usually contrasted to *continuous*, which refers to differences of quantitative degree as opposed to qualitative identity.

Distribution of Income: the proportionate share of total national income (wages, salaries, interest, dividends, rents, profits, etc.) received by different groups within a society, usually stated in terms of percentiles, such as the percent of total national income received by the highest 10 percent of income recipients.

Distribution of Wealth: the proportionate share of total national property owned by different groups within a society, usually stated in terms of percentiles, such as the percent of total national wealth owned by the richest 10 percent. See also, *Personal Wealth, Capital Wealth.*

Division of Labor: specialization and stratification of individuals and groups within social structures or organizations.

Economic Class: a category of people classified according to their shared role in a given type of economic structure.

Economic Structure: the institutionalized way in which a society produces its necessities. Economic structures are composed of typical configurations of economic and social roles. Societies can be classified according to their types of economic structures—communal, state, slave, feudal, capitalist, or socialist. Comparable to the concept of mode of production.

Economic Surplus: see *Surplus Product.*

Economics: academic discipline which studies the production and distribution of goods and services within societies.

Effective Demand: economic concept which refers to those desires and needs for commodities that consumers can afford.

Ethnic Group: a socially defined race or nationality within a society that shares common distinguishing and identifying cultural characteristics.

Eugenics: nineteenth- and early twentieth-century movement in the United States that sought to strengthen the genetic characteristics of the country's people through restricting the reproduction and immigration of people with supposedly weaker genetic traits.

Experiment: research design in which relationships between variables are studied under controlled conditions. Experimental designs involve administering or changing an independent variable and then determining if those changes cause changes in one or more dependent variables.

Experimental Group: in an experimental design, a group that receives the independent variable or variables under study. See also, *Control Group.*

Exploitation: in Marx's technical use of the term, the capitalist expropriation of unpaid surplus value from workers. More generally, any expropriation of surplus products from subordinate classes. See also, *Surplus Value, Surplus Product.*

Family: a living unit of people who are related by blood, marriage, or adoption.

Fascism: extreme right-wing authoritarianism in the forms of movements to conquer state power or governments that rely on using highly repressive means to maintain order.

Feudalism: precapitalist economic type of society characterized by landlord control and peasant labor.

Fief: income-producing opportunity, usually a land grant, given to subordinates within the feudal ruling classes in order to secure their loyalty.

Flexible Accumulation: term used to describe a current stage in industrial development in the developed countries where factories engage in small-batch production of different products in order to serve increasingly diversified consumer demands.

Fordism: term used to describe a stage in industrial development where factories engage in large-scale production of standardized products patterned after the assembly line technique pioneered by Henry Ford in the United States. Many analysts argue that Fordism now has been surpassed by flexible accumulation techniques in the developed countries. See *Flexible Accumulation.*

Formal Organization: an organization with an intentionally defined structure and goals.

Formal Rationality: concept associated with Max Weber to refer to a type of rationality characterized by goals that have exactly calculable means to their attainment. Weber believed that bureaucracies were based upon the concept of formal rationality. Weber compared formal rationality to *substantive rationality*. See also, *Substantive Rationality*.

Formal Structure: the intentionally defined division of labor, in terms of specializations and levels of authority and power, that prevails within an organization. See also, *Informal Structure*.

Functionalism: a theoretical approach to the study of societies in which societies are seen as systems and their subparts (institutions, families, etc.) are interpreted in terms of what they contribute to the maintenance and survival of those systems.

Gross Domestic Product: the total value of goods and services produced by residents of a country less that derived from foreign activities.

Gross National Product: the total value of goods and services produced by residents of a country.

Group: any collectivity of two or more persons that occurs for intended or unintended purposes. Groups—such as families, churches, social classes, cities, and societies themselves—are the basic sociological units of analysis.

Hegemony: as used by Antonio Gramsci, an early Italian Communist Party leader and major twentieth-century Marxist theorist, it refers to a class establishing leadership over the intellectual life of society through noncoercive cultural means. Gramsci argued that the capitalist class's hegemony over intellectual life enabled it to rule largely without having to resort to force. In a parallel manner, if the working class were to assume power and govern effectively, it would have to first establish its hegemony over the intellectual life of a society.

Herding: see *Pastoralism*.

Horticulture: from Latin *hortus*, or "garden," and *cultura*, or "cultivation"; hence "garden cultivation." Type of technology and stage of technological development in which societies subsist through cultivation of small plots of land. In horticulture, humans use their own muscles as sources of energy and hand-held hoes as tools to cultivate garden-sized plots of land.

Hunting and Gathering: earliest type of technology and stage of technological development in which societies subsisted by hunting animals and gathering wild fruits and vegetables.

Hydraulic Civilization: label used by some scholars for a form of ancient society in which the state came into being in order to direct the construction of and oversee the maintenance of irrigation and other systems of controlling major rivers.

Hypothesis: a statement of a suspected causal relationship between variables.

"I" and "Me": distinction originated by George Herbert Mead to indicate that one part of the self, the "me," is formed socially through interaction with others, and the other part, the "I," results from the person's own internally generated actions and reactions.

Imperialism: in general use, concept which refers to any empire in which one country dominates others. Lenin (1916, p. 737), in a more restricted use, identified modern imperialism as occurring when monopolies "play a decisive role in the economic life" of powerful countries from which they derive surplus capital which is then invested in weaker, dependent countries.

Indentured Servitude: type of temporary slavery in which the laborer is owned by another for a defined period of time.

Independent Variable: a variable that is thought to cause change in one or more other dependent variables.

Industry: Type of technology and stage of technological development characterized by the use of nonanimal sources of energy, such as electricity, steam, fossil fuels, or nuclear fission, to drive machines in the production process.

Infant Mortality Rate: the number of infants who die before their first birthday per 1,000 live births in a society, city, or other unit.

Informal Structure: regular interaction patterns within organizations that occur outside of those defined and specified by the formal division of specializations and levels of authority and power. See also, *Formal Structure.*

Institution: (1) abstract configuration of positions, roles, and norms oriented to the attainment of a type of social need or goal, for example, the economic institution; (2) any concrete configuration of positions, roles, and norms, for example, Harvard University is an institution.

Institutional Structure: the totality of institutions within a particular area, for example, all of the economic institutions in a country together constitute its economic structure, all of the political institutions, its political structure, and so on.

Intelligentsia: somewhat amorphous concept. In one use it refers to educated people such as writers and artists who produce and explain ideas for the public. **Interview:** a meeting in which a researcher solicits information from a respondent.

Iron Law of Oligarchy: concept associated with Robert Michels which indicated that all large-scale organizations, regardless of democratic intentions, tended to be dominated by their leaders.

Kinship: type of interrelationship based on common ancestry or marriage.

Labor Force: persons engaged in the production of goods or services within a society.

Landlord: feudal class based upon control of landed estates and collection of rent from peasants.

Legal-Rational Legitimacy: concept associated with Max Weber, type of legitimacy in which people obey because they believe that their leaders have been selected through rationally designed constitutional procedures.

Legitimacy: acceptance by the ruled of rulers' claims of authority. See also, *Authority.*

Liberalism: political ideology characterized by advocacy of public regulations and programs to bring about reforms in capitalist societies.

Looking Glass Self: concept originated by Charles Horton Cooley to indicate that judgments and reactions of others largely influence a person's sense of self, self-esteem, and self-worth.

Lumpen Bourgeoisie: economic class term for the lowest levels of Third World small-business owners such as street peddlers and service providers.

Magic: belief system in which supernatural means are used to control natural phenomena. The communal practitioner of magic invokes a chant or uses an object assumed to be invested with supernatural powers to attain a naturalistic end, such as to ensure success in a hunt, to make it rain, or to cure a sick person.

Marginalized Population: Latin American social science term for unemployed and subemployed people who gain incomes outside of the regularly employed labor force.

Marxism-Leninism: approach to Marxism originally developed in the Soviet Union which followed Lenin's views regarding imperialism, the formations of revolutionary organizations and strategies, and the establishment of one-party dictatorships of the proletariat in socialist societies.

Materialism: philosophical approach to knowledge which starts from the principle that directly experienced reality exists and develops according to its own immanent—as opposed to spiritual or metaphysical—causes.

"Me": see *"I" and "Me."*

Means of Production: tools, raw materials, and land used by labor to produce goods.

Mechanical Solidarity: concept associated with Emile Durkheim that refers to the form of social cohesion within past societies with simple divisions of labor. In those societies, according to Durkheim, cohesion and solidarity were produced by a unifying ideological force, which in most cases was a single religion such as the medieval Catholic church. Solidarity was produced mechanically in the sense that it was the result of an external energy source. Durkheim contrasted mechanical and organic solidarity. See also, *Organic Solidarity.*

Membership Association: as used in this text, a type of large-scale organization which is formally controlled by its members.

Middle Class: social class concept that refers to people who identify themselves as being between the upper class on the one hand and the working and lower classes on the other.

Mixed Economy: a contemporary economy which contains both significant private and state ownership of major means of production.

Mode of Production: see *Economic Structure*.

Modernism: see *Postmodernism*.

Modernization: The concept of modernization in sociological theory encompasses the great shifts in social development that occurred by the end of the nineteenth century in the developed countries, including the transition from feudalism to capitalism in Marxian theory, the development of complex divisions of labor (Durkheim), and the development of formal-rational work structures (Weber). In a more restricted meaning, the concept of modernization identifies an approach to Third World development espoused by the International Monetary Fund, the World Bank, and a number of sociologists. According to this approach, premodern values and institutions are the basic obstacles to development in Third World countries. Consequently, development can only occur when Third World countries promote and adopt more modern values and institutions.

Multinational Corporation: a corporation that owns plants or has investments in more than one country. Also known as a transnational corporation.

Nation: a people with a common language and culture that has evolved historically in a commonly occupied territory.

Nationality: group that constitutes a nation or national minority. See *Nation* and *National Minority*.

National Minority: a nationality that exists within a territory where one or more other nationalities make up the majority. There are two types of national minorities. Immigrant national minorities are made up of peoples, such as the overseas Chinese, who have migrated from their home to a new territory where one or more other nationalities predominate. Indigenous national minorities are made up of peoples, such as Native Americans in the Americas or Aborigines in Australia, who have lost majority status within their territories due to large-scale immigrations of other peoples.

Nouveau Riche: French term for first-generation capitalists whose fortunes have been newly acquired. They are often portrayed as lacking the upper-class refined culture of the old rich, that is, of people born into and raised within the upper class.

New Middle Class: economic class made up of employed professionals and middle-level managers.

Nomads: peoples who continually move residence locations in order to hunt, gather, or cultivate new lands.

Norm: rule or value governing the performance of a role.

Nuclear Family: family unit made up exclusively of parents and their children.

Objective Social Life: observable interaction that takes place between people.

Old Middle Class: see *Small-Business Owners Class.*

Organic Analogy: view that societies are like biological organisms, with each being composed of different organs that have specialized functions, for example, the brain, heart, and nervous system in the human body and the economy, family, and state in the social body. See also, *Functionalism.*

Organic Solidarity: concept associated with Emile Durkheim, the type of cohesion between persons that exists in modern societies with complex divisions of labor. Order and cohesion are based upon interdependence of roles. Durkheim contrasted organic solidarity to mechanical solidarity. See also, *Mechanical Solidarity.*

Participant Observation: technique of information collection based on the researcher's becoming an active member of the group under observation and then recording information about it.

Pastoralism: type of technology and stage of technological development characterized by producing food and other necessities from domesticated herds of animals such as goats, cattle, and sheep.

Patriarchy: literally, "rule of the father." Concept used to refer to male domination over females.

Peasant: economic class made up of rural laborers who work and primarily live off cultivation of a small plot of land. In some uses, restricted to rural laborers who produce primarily for their own consumption, as opposed to for a market. Also used as a social class concept for the rural poor who can be made up of subsistence farmers, market farmers, and laborers.

Peonage: system of debt slavery, which is based on creditors claiming the right to control the future labor of debtors as payment.

Personal Wealth: wealth in the form of properties that are used for the consumption needs of the owner, such as a house that is lived in, as opposed to capital wealth. See also, *Capital Wealth.*

Petite or Petty Bourgeoisie: see *Small-Business Owners Class.*

Political Science: academic discipline which studies political processes and how governments function.

Popular Classes: Third World term for members of the social working and lower classes who often make up absolute majorities of populations.

Population Density: demographic concept which indicates the average number of people who live within a square mile or kilometer within a particular country. It is determined by dividing total population by total square miles or kilometers.

Positional Approach: technique used in power structure studies in which the occupants of powerful political, economic, and other types of positions are identified and studied.

Positivism: approach to sociology originated by Auguste Comte which advocates using methods of research developed in the physical and natural sciences.

Postmodernism: Thought movement with manifestations in the social sciences, art, literature, architecture, and other areas. Postmodernists identify rationalization and standardization with modernism which they see as oppressive and destructive of human values. In place of the modernist concepts of progress, standardization, rationalization, and universal truths, they stress the concepts of relativism, diversity, quality, and pluralism.

Primary Research: type of research in which the researcher generates data which had not existed previously, such as by administering a survey or carrying out direct observations.

Progressive Taxation: method of taxation in which higher-income groups are taxed at higher rates than lower-income groups. Progressive taxation is used as a means to redistribute some income from upper to lower levels within societies.

Proletariat: Marxian term for the working class. See *Working Class*.

Push and Pull Factors: the causes of migration away from and toward particular locations. Demographers analyze migration patterns in terms of what causes people to leave particular locations and attracts them toward others.

Quitrent: form of feudal rent payment in which peasants give the landlords proportions or set quantities of their harvests. Also called rent in kind.

Race: concept that has had various meanings in terms of groups identified from the sixteenth century onward. By the nineteenth century, races became increasingly identified as populations with fixed biological characteristics (skin color, type of hair, etc.). But because attempts to develop a scientific taxonomy of different races have failed, race is no longer used as a scientific concept. Nevertheless, the terms *race* and *racial* continue to have important social meanings and references attached to them. Race in this latter sense refers generally to people who share the same range of skin color.

Racism: ideology based on belief in the biological inferiority and superiority of different races.

Randomization: statistical technique for ensuring that the characteristics of a sample are likely to match those of the universe of ultimate interest. A random sample exists when each member of the universe has had an equal chance of being included in the sample. See also, *Universe*.

Redistribution of Wealth and Income: a usually politically designed attempt to alter a given distribution of wealth (such as through land reform) and/or income in a society in order to achieve particular goals, such as social justice or economic development. Redistributions of wealth and income can be designed in the interests of lower, middle, or upper levels of the population.

Religion: belief system in which prayers or other supernatural means are used to attain supernatural ends.

Rentier: French term for a nonworking capitalist who receives an income from the ownership of stocks, bonds, and other investments.

Reputational Approach: technique used in power structure studies in which powerful individuals are identified through surveys of knowledgeable informants and then studied.

Research Design: a plan of how to collect new information for a research project. Research designs involve selecting one or more techniques for collecting new information, such as through use of existing sources (government statistics, books, etc.), interviews, surveys, case studies, and experiments.

Role: the behavior expected of people who occupy particular social positions.

Sample: see *Universe.*

Sanction: social reward to encourage conformity to a norm or punishment to discourage nonconformity.

Scientific Management: school of managerial consultants and studies founded by Frederick Taylor that developed such research techniques as time and motion studies to find ways to increase worker productivity.

Secondary Research: technique of research based on the analysis of preexisting data, such as from government and business statistics.

Self: a person's sense of her or his own being.

Self-esteem: the positive or negative evaluation that one holds of personal worth or self.

Setting: the physical or social location within which social interaction takes place.

Single-Parent Family: family unit composed of a single parent—due to death, divorce, or separation of the other parent—and children.

Slave: a laborer whose labor power is owned by another.

Slave Society: economic type of society based upon the predominant use of unfree or slave labor to produce surplus products.

Small-Business Owners Class: economic class made up of individuals and families who derive their primary incomes from the ownership and operation of businesses which do not have significant numbers of hired employees. The working owner is the primary producer in the business, not a hired labor force.

Social: any interpersonal situation in which a person orients her or his actions to one or more others.

Social Class: groups of people who share common standards of living and perceive themselves as social equals different from classes above or below them.

Social Democracy: political ideology characterized by the advocacy of an evolutionary, gradual development of socialism, mixed economies of both private and state ownership, and political pluralism.

Social Mobility: stratification concept which refers to intergenerational and intragenerational movements of people up and down class hierarchies.

Social Position: the place occupied by a person engaged in social interaction.

Social Structure: the grand total of all institutions within a society.

Social Survey: technique for collecting data in which respondents are asked to answer questions.

Social Theory: a systematic, concept-based explanation of how social life functions and changes.

Social Wage: indirect income received by workers in the form of state-subsidized services, such as free education, health care, and the like. Contrasted to individual wages or the income directly received from employers.

Social Work: profession which renders assistance to individual victims of a variety of social problems such as poverty, homelessness, alcoholism, and domestic violence.

Socialism: (1) economic type of society characterized by state ownership of the major means of production; (2) political ideology, of which there are a number of varieties, which advocates development of socialist types of economies.

Socialization: concept used in three different manners in sociology: (1) the process by which individuals learn and adopt the values, norms, and roles of particular societies; (2) the process by which governments take over ownership of businesses, as in "the socialization of the means of production"; (3) the process by which individuals engaged in production within modern societies become increasingly interdependent as divisions of labor become more specialized, extensive, and global, as in, "the increasing socialization of production relations."

Society: a population that shares a common territory (usually), government, and period of existence.

Socioeconomic Structure: as used in this text, typical fusions of economic and class structures that have occurred in world history, e.g. a feudal economy with landlord and peasant classes, or a capitalist economy with capitalist and working classes.

Sociology: from Latin *socia*, or "society," and Greek *logos*, or "knowledge" or "study"; hence the "study of society"; the scientific study of societies and social life.

State: the politically governing power of a society. As used by Max Weber (1918), "a human community that [successfully] claims the monopoly of the legitimate use of physical force within a given territory."

State Society: early economic type of society in which the state was the major owner or controller of land and other means of production and collected tax or tribute payments from the surplus products of subjects. Comparable to the concepts of the Asiatic and tributary modes of production.

Status: concept used in two different ways in sociology: (1) the prestige attached to a person or his or her social position; (2) any position within a social hierarchy.

Status Inconsistency: sociological concept which refers to situations when a person does not have equal levels of educational achievement, occupational position, and income, as when a person with low educational achievement occupies an occupational position that requires great skill, or when a highly educated person occupying a professional position receives relatively low pay.

Stepfamily: family unit in which there exist children and parents who are not biologically related.

Stratification: specialization within sociology that studies social inequality due to class, gender, nationality, racial, or other types of positions within societies.

Subculture: the unique way of life of a regional, class, nationality, or other type of subgroup within a society as expressed through its own particular types of material products and nonmaterial values, customs, and language.

Subjective Social Life: how people think and feel about themselves, others, and what they do, as it is affected by their interaction in society.

Subsistence Production: production of only basic survival necessities, absence of surplus products.

Substantive Rationality: concept associated with Max Weber which defines rationality in terms of qualitative goals whose attainment may or may not be calculable. Weber compared the substantive concept of rationality to the more limited concept of formal rationality. He believed that the cultural drift of the West favored a shallow formal concept of rationality at the expense of substantive considerations. See also, *Formal Rationality*.

Surplus Product: production in excess of survival necessities. Surplus products are available to be accumulated or traded.

Surplus Value: in Marxian economic theory, the amount of new value that is created by labor in each step of a production process. Surplus value is the remainder after the cost of production is subtracted from the value of the product. Marx maintained that workers produced but did not receive surplus value. Rather, capitalists expropriated the surplus value produced by workers and used it to form new capital and as the source of their own incomes.

Survey: technique for collecting information in which questionnaires soliciting particular types of information (such as attitudes, income, or religious affiliation) are administered to samples of respondents and the responses are tabulated.

Synthesis: see *Thesis-Antithesis-Synthesis*.

Taylorism: pejorative term for attempts to increase productivity by treating workers mechanistically as factors of production without due regard for their specifically human needs. See also, *Scientific Management*.

Technology: from Greek *techne*, or "techniques," and *logos*, or "knowledge"; hence "knowledge of techniques" (especially of production). Social scientists distinguish the following stages of technological development—hunting and gathering, pastoralism, horticulture, agriculture, and industry.

Theory: logically consistent explanation of causes and interrelationships which occur in reality.

Thesis-Antithesis-Synthesis: stages or moments of dialectical development. According to one dialectical approach, all changes in reality proceed through these stages. In the thesis stage something exists as is. A contradiction emerges within it forcing the change of its original condition. It is now in the antithesis stage. The contradiction is resolved in the synthesis stage which is simultaneously the thesis of a new round of triadic development. See also, *Dialectics, Contradiction*.

Traditional Legitimacy: concept identified with Max Weber, type of legitimacy in which people obey a ruler or rulers out of long-standing habit as opposed to reason.

Two-Stage Theory of Revolution: theory originally associated with V.I. Lenin which maintains that revolutions go through two stages. The revolutionary's strategic goal in the first stage, around which broad unity can be developed, is to overthrow an old unpopular regime. The strategic goal of the second stage is to develop a radical new government to take its place. Around this goal less unity is possible. Hence a struggle ensues over the direction that the revolution is to take.

Two-Wage-Earner Family: family unit in which both the principal male and female adults pursue full-time income-producing occupations outside of the home.

Type: a classification of objects which have a distinguishing characteristic or characteristics that unite them as belonging together and different from others.

Typology: a classification scheme in which different types are determined by interrelating two or more variables.

Universe: term used to refer to the ultimate population that a research project is attempting to understand. The term is usually used in conjunction with the concept of a sample, the unit or group from which information is actually collected. Presumably, the distribution of the characteristics of the sample are generalizable, that is, they approximately match those of the universe of ultimate interest.

Urbanization: long-range trend in domestic migration characterized by the movement of people from rural areas to cities.

Vanguard Party: concept originally associated with Lenin. Refers to political parties made up exclusively of leaders who see and agree with the need for revolutionary changes. The concept is based upon the observation that in revolutionary periods populations generally divide into those opposed, those in the middle, and a vanguard in favor of radical changes.

Variable: concept most often used in quantitative research that refers to changeable and measurable characteristics, such as rates of unemployment, sizes of family incomes, or years of education completed. It can also be used to refer to any changeable condition, regardless of whether it can be expressed in exact quantitative terms. Thus something so general as the development of capitalism could be considered as a variable.

Village Communities: Early horticulturally based peasant villages.

Working Class: economic class made up of persons who sell their labor to employers. Also used as a social class concept to refer to people who identify themselves as working people who are above lower-class and below middle-class people.

World-System: the network of economic relationships that exist between the world's societies. Most world-system theorists believe that location within the world-system largely influences the character of a domestic economy.

Appendix

Countries of the World, 1992, Grouped within Current United Nations
Classifications and Listed in Descending Order of Life Expectancies

	Total population (millions)	GNP per capita (US$)	Infant mortality rate (under 1)	Life expectancy at birth (years)
A. Developed Market:				
Japan	124.5	26,930	4	79
Switzerland	6.8	33,610	7	78
Sweden	8.7	25,110	6	78
Norway	4.3	24,220	6	77
Netherlands	15.2	18,780	6	77
Canada	27.4	20,440	7	77
France	57.2	20,380	7	77
Australia	17.6	17,050	7	77
Italy	57.8	18,520	8	77
Spain	39.1	12,450	8	77
Greece	10.2	6,340	8	77
Finland	5.0	23,980	6	76
Denmark	5.2	23,700	7	76
Germany	80.3	23,650	7	76
Austria	7.8	20,140	7	76
United Kingdom	57.7	16,550	7	76
New Zealand	3.5	12,350	8	76
USA	255.2	22,240	9	76
Belgium	10.0	18,950	9	76
Israel	5.1	11,950	9	76

	Total population (millions)	GNP per capita (US$)	Infant mortality rate (under 1)	Life expectancy at birth (years)
Ireland	3.5	11,120	6	75
Portugal	9.9	5,930	11	75
South Africa	39.8	2,560	53	63
B. In Transition:				
Lithuania	3.8	2,710	17	73
Georgia	5.5	1,640	25	73
Albania	3.3	790	28	73
Czech Republic	10.4	..	11	72
Slovakia	5.4	..	12	72
Poland	38.4	1,790	14	72
Bulgaria	9.0	1,840	16	72
Armenia	3.5	2,150	29	72
Estonia	1.6	3,830	20	71
Belarus	10.3	3,110	20	71
Latvia	2.7	3,410	22	71
Azerbaijan	7.3	1,670	37	71
Hungary	10.5	2,720	15	70
Ukraine	51.9	2,340	21	70
Romania	23.3	1,390	23	70
Russian Fed.	148.3	3,220	28	69
Kazakhstan	17.0	2,470	43	69
Tajikistan	5.7	1,050	65	69
Uzbekistan	21.5	1,350	56	69
Moldovia	4.4	2,170	31	68
Kyrgyzstan	4.5	1,550	49	66
Turkmenistan	3.9	1,700	72	66
C. Asian Socialist				
North Korea	22.6	970	25	71
China	1,188.0	370	35	71
Viet Nam	69.5	240	37	64
Mongolia	2.3	780	61	63
D. Developing:				
Hong Kong	5.8	13,430	6	78
Cuba	10.8	1,170	10	76
Costa Rica	3.2	1,850	14	76
Kuwait	2.0	16,150	14	75
Singapore	2.8	14,210	6	74
Jamaica	2.5	1,380	12	73
Panama	2.5	2,130	18	73
Chile	13.6	2,160	15	72
Yugoslavia (former)	23.9	3,060	19	72
Uruguay	3.1	2,840	20	72
South Korea	44.2	6,330	8	71
Malaysia	18.8	2,520	14	71
Sri Lanka	17.7	500	15	71

	Total population (millions)	GNP per capita (US$)	Infant mortality rate (under 1)	Life expectancy at birth (years)
United Arab Emirates	1.7	19,860	18	71
Trinidad and Tobago	1.3	3,670	19	71
Argentina	33.1	2,790	22	71
Venezuela	20.2	2,730	20	70
Mauritius	1.1	2,410	20	70
Mexico	88.2	3,030	28	70
Colombia	33.4	1,260	17	69
Oman	1.6	6,120	24	69
Thailand	56.1	1,570	27	69
Saudi Arabia	15.9	7,820	35	69
Jordan	4.3	1,050	25	68
Tunisia	8.4	1,500	32	68
Lebanon	2.8	2,150	35	68
Paraguay	4.5	1,270	28	67
Syrian Arab Rep.	13.3	1,160	34	67
Dominican Rep.	7.5	940	42	67
Iran	61.6	2,170	44	67
Turkey	58.4	1,780	70	67
Honduras	5.5	580	45	66
El Salvador	5.4	1,080	47	66
Ecuador	11.1	1,000	47	66
Brazil	154.1	2,940	54	66
Nicaragua	4.0	460	54	66
Algeria	26.3	1,980	60	66
Iraq	19.3	1,500	64	66
Philippines	65.2	730	46	65
Peru	22.5	1,070	46	64
Guatemala	9.7	930	55	64
Morocco	26.3	1,030	50	63
Libya	4.9	5,310	70	63
Indonesia	191.2	610	71	62
Egypt	54.8	610	43	61
Bolivia	7.5	650	80	61
India	879.5	330	83	60
Kenya	25.2	340	51	59
Pakistan	124.8	400	95	59
Namibia	1.5	1,460	62	58
Papua New Guinea	4.1	830	54	56
Zimbabwe	10.6	650	60	56
Cameroon	12.2	850	74	56
Ghana	16.0	400	103	56
Gabon	1.2	3,780	95	53
Congo	2.4	1,120	82	52
Côte d'Ivoire	12.9	690	91	52
Nigeria	115.7	340	114	52
Senegal	7.7	720	90	49
Eritrea	3.3	120	123	47
Angola	9.9	610	170	42

252 Appendix

	Total population (millions)	GNP per capita (US$)	Infant mortality rate (under 1)	Life expectancy at birth (years)
E. Least Developed:				
Botswana	1.3	2,530	45	61
Lesotho	1.8	580	108	60
Myanmar	43.7	220	83	57
Haiti	6.8	370	87	56
Togo	3.8	410	86	55
Madagascar	12.8	210	110	55
Liberia	2.8	450	146	55
Nepal	20.6	180	90	53
Bangladesh	119.3	220	97	53
Sudan	26.7	420	100	52
Yemen	12.5	520	107	52
Zaire	39.9	230	121	52
Laos	4.5	220	98	51
Tanzania	27.8	100	111	51
Cambodia	8.8	200	117	51
Burkina Faso	9.5	290	101	48
Burundi	5.8	210	108	48
Mauritania	2.1	510	118	48
Bhutan	1.6	180	131	48
Central African Republic	3.2	390	105	47
Chad	5.8	210	123	47
Ethiopia	53.0	120	123	47
Somalia	9.2	150	125	47
Mozambique	14.9	80	167	47
Benin	4.9	380	88	46
Mali	9.8	280	122	46
Rwanda	7.5	270	131	46
Niger	8.3	300	191	46
Zambia	8.6	420	113	45
Guinea	6.1	460	135	44
Malawi	10.4	230	143	44
Guinea-Bissau	1.0	180	141	43
Sierra Leone	4.4	210	144	43
Afghanistan	19.1	280	165	43
Uganda	18.7	170	111	42

Source: UNICEF (1994, p. 64).

Bibliography

AMIN, SAMIR. 1980. *Class and Nation: Historically and in the Current Crisis* (Susan Kaplow, tr.). New York: Monthly Review Press.

ANDERSON, PERRY. 1974a. *Passages from Antiquity to Feudalism*. London: Verso.

ANDERSON, PERRY. 1974b. *Lineages of the Absolutist State*. London: NLB.

ANDREWES, ANTONY. 1967. *The Greeks*. London: Hutchinson.

BALLANTINE, JEANNE. 1993. *The Sociology of Education: A Systematic Analysis*, 3rd ed. Englewood Cliffs, NJ: Prentice Hall.

BARAN, PAUL. 1957. *The Political Economy of Growth*. New York: Monthly Review Press.

BARCLAY, WILLIAM, JOSEPH ENRIGHT, and REID T. REYNOLDS. 1970. "Population Control in the Third World." *NACLA Newsletter*, Vol. 4, 8 (December); pp. 1–18.

BARKIN, DAVID. 1990. *Distorted Development: Mexico and the World Economy*. Boulder, CO: Westview.

BELL, DANIEL. 1973. *The Coming of Post-Industrial Society*. New York: Basic Books.

BERRY, RALPH E., JR. and JAMES P. BOLAND. 1977. *The Economic Cost of Alcohol Abuse*. New York: Free Press.

BLAIR, JOHN. 1972. *Economic Concentration*. New York: Harcourt Brace Jovanovich.

BLAUNER, ROBERT. 1964. *Alienation and Freedom: The Factory Worker and His Industry*. Chicago: University of Chicago Press.

BLOCH, MARC. 1933. "Feudalism, European." *Encyclopedia of the Social Sciences*. New York: Macmillan.

BLOCH, MARC. 1940. *Feudal Society* (L.A. Manyon, tr.). Chicago: University of Chicago Press, 1961.

BOGGS, JAMES. 1963. *The American Revolution: Pages from a Negro Worker's Notebook*. New York: Monthly Review Press.

BRAVERMAN, HARRY. 1974. *Labor and Monopoly Capital*. New York: Monthly Review Press.

BRENNER, M. HARVEY. 1976. *Estimating the Social Costs of National Economic Policy*. United States Congress: Joint Economic Committee.

BRUNDENIUS, CLAUS. 1981. *Economic Growth, Basic Needs and Income Distribution in Revolutionary Cuba*. Lund, Sweden: Research Policy Institute.

BRUNT, P.A. 1971. *Social Conflicts in the Roman Republic*. New York: Norton.

CARNEGIE TASK FORCE. 1994. *Starting Points: Meeting the Needs of Our Youngest Children*. New York: Carnegie Corporation of New York.

CASTRO MARTIN, TERESA and LARRY L. BUMPASS. 1989. "Recent Trends and Differentials in Marital Disruption." *Demography*, Vol. 26, no. 1, pp. 37–51.

CENTERS, RICHARD. 1949. *The Psychology of Social Classes: A Study of Class Consciousness*. Princeton, NJ: Princeton University Press.

COLLINS, PATRICIA HILL. 1993. "Toward a New Vision: Race, Class, and Gender as Categories of Analysis and Connection." *Race, Sex & Class*, Vol. 1, no. 1 (Fall), pp. 25–46.

COOLEY, CHARLES HORTON. 1902. *Human Nature and the Social Order*. New York: Schocken Books, 1964.

DAHL, GUDRUN. 1979. "Ecology and Equality: The Boran Case." In *Pastoral Production and Society*. Cambridge: Cambridge University Press.

DANIEL, P. 1972. *The Shadow of Slavery: Peonage in the South 1901–1969*. Urbana: University of Illinois Press.

DAVIE, MICHAEL. 1987. *Titanic: The Death and Life of a Legend*. New York: Alfred A. Knopf.

DAVIS, JAMES F. 1991. *Who is Black? One Nation's Definition*. University Park: Pennsylvania State University Press.

DAVIS, KINGSLEY and WILBERT E. MOORE. 1945. "Some Principles of Stratification." *American Sociological Review*, Vol. 10, pp. 242–249.

DAVIS, MIKE. 1986. *Prisoners of the American Dream*. London: Verso.

DAVIS, MIKE. 1990. *City of Quartz: Excavating the Future in Los Angeles*. London: Verso.

DEEVEY, EDWARD S., JR. 1960. "The Human Population." *Scientific American*, Vol. 203, no. 3 (September), pp. 195–204.

DOMHOFF, G. WILLIAM. 1967. *Who Rules America?* Englewood Cliffs, NJ: Prentice Hall.

DOMHOFF, G. WILLIAM. 1983. *Who Rules America Now?* Englewood Cliffs, NJ: Prentice Hall.

DURKHEIM, EMILE. 1893. *The Division of Labor in Society* (George Simpson, tr.). Glencoe, IL: The Free Press, 1964.

DURKHEIM, EMILE. 1897. *Suicide* (J.A. Spaulding and George Simpson, trs.). Glencoe, IL: The Free Press, 1964.

EINBINDER, S.D. 1992. *A Statistical Profile of Children Living in Poverty*. New York: National Center for Children in Poverty (Columbia University School of Public Health), unpublished document.

EISENSTADT, S.N. 1966. *Modernization: Protest and Change.* Englewood Cliffs, NJ: Prentice Hall.

ENGELS, FREDERICK. 1884. *The Origin of the Family, Private Property and the State.* Moscow: Progress Publishers, 1948.

ENGELS, FREDERICK. 1888. Note to the 1888 edition of Karl Marx and Frederick Engels. 1848. "The Communist Manifesto." In Karl Marx and Frederick Engels. 1970. *Selected Works in Three Volumes.* Moscow: Progress Publishers.

FARNSWORTH, CLYDE H. 1988. "Money Loss Grows for Poorer Lands, World Bank Finds." *The New York Times*, December 19, p. 1.

FINLEY, M.I. 1980. *Ancient Slavery and Modern Ideology.* New York: Viking.

FRANK, ANDRE GUNDAR. 1969. *Capitalism and Underdevelopment in Latin America.* New York: Monthly Review Press.

FREUD, SIGMUND. 1930. *Civilization and Its Discontents.* New York: W.W. Norton, 1962.

FREUD, SIGMUND. 1933. *Why War?* Paris: International Institute of Intellectual Cooperation (League of Nations).

FURSTENBERG, FRANK F., JR. and ANDREW J. CHERLIN. 1991. *Divided Families: What Happens to Children When Parents Part.* Cambridge, MA: Harvard University Press.

GELLES, RICHARD J. 1985. "Family Violence: What We Know and Can Do." In Eli H. Newberger and Richard Bourne (eds.), *Unhappy Families: Clinical and Research Perspectives on Family Violence.* Littleton, MA: PSG Publishing Co., Inc.

GERTH, HANS and C. WRIGHT MILLS. 1953. *Character and Social Structure.* New York: Harcourt, Brace and Company.

GILBERT, DENNIS and JOSEPH A. KAHL. 1987. *The American Class Structure*, 3rd ed. Chicago: The Dorsey Press.

GIRARD, CHRIS. 1993. "Age, Gender, and Suicide: A Cross-National Analysis." *American Sociological Review*, Vol. 58, no. 4 (August); pp. 553–574.

GODELIER, MAURICE. 1969. *Sobre el modo de producción asiático.* Barcelona: Ediciones Martínez Roca.

GODELIER, MAURICE. 1978. "The Concept of the Asiatic Mode of Production." In D. Seddon (ed.), *Relations of Production*, London: Frank Cass.

GRAMSCI, ANTONIO. 1985. *Prison Notebooks: Selections.* New York: International Publishers.

GULLIVER, P.H. 1955. *The Family Herds.* London: Routledge & Kegan Paul.

HAGEN, E.E. 1962. *On the Theory of Social Change.* Homewood, IL: Dorsey.

HAMPER, BEN. 1991. *Rivethead: Tales from the Assembly Line.* New York: Warner Books.

HARVEY, DAVID. 1989. *The Condition of Postmodernity.* Oxford, UK: Basil Blackwell.

HAYWARD, JACK. 1980. *Trade Unions and Politics in Western Europe.* London: Frank Cass.

HERRNSTEIN, RICHARD J. and CHARLES MURRAY. 1994. *The Bell Curve: Intelligence and Class Structure in American Life.* New York: The Free Press.

HIGGINBOTHAM, ELIZABETH. 1993. "Sociology and the Multicultural Curriculum." *Race, Sex & Class*, Vol. 1, no. 1 (Fall), pp. 15–24.

HOCHSCHILD, ARLIE with ANNE MACHUNG. 1989. *The Second Shift: Working Parents and the Revolution at Home.* New York: Viking.

HOFFERTH, S., ET AL. 1991. *National Child Care Survey, 1990.* Washington, DC: Urban Institute.

HOROWITZ, IRVING LOUIS. 1966. *Three Worlds of Development.* New York: Oxford University Press.

HOROWITZ, IRVING LOUIS. 1967. *The Rise and Fall of Project Camelot.* Cambridge, MA: MIT Press.

HOWE, CAROLYN. 1992. *Political Ideology and Class Formation: A Study of the Middle Class.* Westport, CT: Praeger.

HUNT, KATHLEEN. 1988. "Subduing the Lion Killers," *The New York Times Magazine*, December 18, p. 42.

HUNTINGFORD, G.W.B. 1953. *The Southern Nilo-Hamites.* London: International African Institute, 1969.

KAGARLITSKY, BORIS. 1988. *The Thinking Reed: Intellectuals and the Soviet State 1917 to the Present* (Brian Pearce, tr.). London: Verso.

KAMMEYER, KENNETH C.W. and HELEN GINN. 1986. *An Introduction to Population.* Chicago: The Dorsey Press.

KLEIN, HERBERT S. 1986. *African Slavery in Latin America and the Caribbean.* New York: Oxford University Press.

KRADER, LAWRENCE. 1975. *The Asiatic Mode of Production.* Assen, The Netherlands: Van Gorcum & Comp, B.V.

LEAR, MARTHA WEINMAN. 1988. "The New Marital Therapy." *The New York Times Magazine*, March 6.

LEMBCKE, JERRY. 1988. *Capitalist Development and Class Capacities.* Westport, CT: Greenwood Press.

LEMBCKE, JERRY. 1993. "Classical Theory, Postmodernism, and the Sociology Liberal Arts Curriculum." *The American Sociologist*, Vol. 24, nos. 3–4 (fall–winter), pp. 55–68.

LENIN, V.I. 1902. *What Is To Be Done?* In V.I. Lenin. 1970. *Selected Works in Three Volumes.* Moscow: Progress Publishers.

LENIN, V.I. 1916. *Imperialism, The Highest Stage of Capitalism.* In V.I. Lenin. 1970. *Selected Works in Three Volumes.* Moscow: Progress Publishers.

LENIN, V.I. 1917. *The State and Revolution.* In V.I. Lenin. 1970. *Selected Works in Three Volumes.* Moscow: Progress Publishers.

LENIN, V.I. 1918. "The Proletarian Revolution and the Renegade Kautsky." In V.I. Lenin. 1970. *Selected Works in Three Volumes.* Moscow: Progress Publishers.

LENSKI, GERHARD and JEAN LENSKI. 1982. *Human Societies*, 4th ed. New York: McGraw-Hill.

LIVI-BACCI, MASSIMO. 1992. *A Concise History of World Population.* (Carl Ipsen, tr.) Cambridge, MA: Blackwell Publishers.

LORD, WALTER. 1955. *A Night to Remember.* Mattituck, NY: Amereon House, 1987.

LUKACS, GEORG. 1923. *History and Class Consciousness.* London: Merlin, 1971.

MADDOX, BRENDA. 1976. *The Half-Parent.* New York: Signet.

MALTHUS, THOMAS ROBERT. 1798. *Essay on the Principle of Population.* New York: Macmillan, 1894.

MANNHEIM, KARL. 1936. *Ideology and Utopia*. New York: Harcourt, Brace.

MARCUSE, HERBERT. 1955. *Eros and Civilization*. Boston: Beacon, 1966.

MARX, KARL. 1844. *Economic and Philosophic Manuscripts of 1844*. Moscow: Progress Publishers, 1959.

MARX, KARL. 1858. *Grundrisse: Foundations of the Critique of Political Economy* (Martin Nicolaus, tr.). Harmondsworth, Middlesex: Penguin, 1973.

MARX, KARL. 1859. *A Contribution to the Critique of Political Economy*. Moscow: Progress Publishers, 1970.

MARX, KARL. 1865, "Wages, Price and Profit." In Karl Marx and Frederick Engels. 1970. *Selected Works in Three Volumes*. Moscow: Progress Publishers.

MARX, KARL. 1867. *Capital*, Vol. I. Moscow: Progress Publishers, n.d.

MARX, KARL. 1875. "Critique of the Gotha Program." In Karl Marx and Frederick Engels. 1970. *Selected Works in Three Volumes*. Moscow: Progress Publishers.

MARX, KARL and FREDERICK ENGELS. 1846. *The German Ideology*. Moscow: Progress Publishers, 1976.

MARX, KARL and FREDERICK ENGELS. 1848. "The Communist Manifesto." In Karl Marx and Frederick Engels. 1970. *Selected Works in Three Volumes*. Moscow: Progress Publishers.

MASS, BONNIE. 1976. *Population Target: The Political Economy of Population Control in Latin America*. Brampton, Ontario, Canada: Charters.

MEAD, GEORGE HERBERT. 1934. *Mind, Self, and Society*. Chicago: University of Chicago Press.

MEYER, MICHAEL C. and WILLIAM L. SHERMAN. 1987. *The Course of Mexican History*. New York: Oxford University Press.

MICHELS, ROBERT. 1911. *Political Parties*. New York: The Free Press, 1967.

MILES, ROBERT. 1989. *Racism*. London: Routledge.

MILIBAND, RALPH. 1973. *The State in Capitalist Society*. London: Quartet.

MILLS, C. WRIGHT. 1953. *White Collar*. New York: Oxford University Press.

MILLS, C. WRIGHT. 1956. *The Power Elite*. New York: Oxford University Press.

MILLS, C. WRIGHT. 1961. *The Sociological Imagination*. New York: Grove Press.

MORGAN, LEWIS HENRY. 1877. *Ancient Society*. New York: World Publishing, 1963.

MOYNIHAN, DANIEL P. 1965. *The Negro Family: The Case for National Action*. Washington, DC: U.S. Department of Labor.

NATIONAL CENTER FOR CHILDREN IN POVERTY. 1990. *A Statistical Profile of Our Poorest Citizens*. New York: NCCP, Columbia University, 154 Haven Avenue.

NATIONAL OPINION RESEARCH CENTER. 1977. *General Social Survey*. Ann Arbor, University of Michigan Press.

NAU, HENRY R. 1990. *The Myth of America's Decline*. New York: Oxford University Press.

NORTON, ARTHUR J. and LOUISA F. MILLER. 1992. *Marriage, Divorce, and Remarriage in the 1990's*, U.S. Bureau of the Census, Current Population Reports, Series P23–180. Washington, DC: U.S. Government Printing Office.

O'CONNER, JAMES. 1973. *The Fiscal Crisis of the State*. New York: St. Martin's Press.

PELTON, LEROY H. 1981. "Child Abuse and Neglect: The Myth of Classlessness." In Leroy H. Pelton (ed.), *The Social Context of Child Abuse and Neglect*. New York: Human Sciences Press.

PETERS, GARY L. and ROBERT P. LARKIN. 1983. *Population Geography*. Dubuque, IA: Kendall/Hunt.

PHILLIPS, PAUL. 1990. "The Debt Crisis and Eastern Europe." *Monthly Review*, Vol. 41, no. 9 (February), pp. 19–27.

POPE, WHITNEY. 1976. *Durkheim's Suicide: A Classic Reanalyzed*. Chicago: University of Chicago Press.

PORTER, JOHN. 1965. *The Vertical Mosaic*. Toronto: University of Toronto Press.

POULANTZAS, NICOS. 1976. *Political Power and Social Classes*. London: New Left Books.

PRONASOL [PROGRAMA NACIONAL DE SOLIDARIDAD]. 1990. *El Combate a La Pobreza*. Mexico City: El Nacional.

REYNOLDS, LARRY T. and LEONARD LIEBERMAN. 1993. "The Rise and Fall of 'Race'." *Race, Sex & Class*, Vol. 1, no. 1 (Fall), pp. 109–127.

RODNEY, WALTER. 1972. *How Europe Underdeveloped Africa*. London: Bogle L'Overture.

ROSENAU, PAULINE MARIE. 1991. *Post-Modernism and the Social Sciences*. Princeton, NJ: Princeton University Press.

ROSTOW, WALT W. 1960. *The Stages of Economic Growth*. Cambridge: Cambridge University Press.

RUSSELL, JAMES W. 1989. *Modes of Production in World History*. London: Routledge.

RUSSELL, JAMES W. 1994. *After the Fifth Sun: Class and Race in North America*. Englewood Cliffs, NJ: Prentice Hall.

RUSSELL, PHILIP L. 1994. *Mexico Under Salinas*. Austin, TX: Mexico Resource Center.

RYAN, MARY P. 1979. *Womanhood in America: From Colonial Times to the Present*, 2nd ed. New York: New Viewpoints.

SAHLINS, MARSHALL. 1972. *Stone Age Economics*. Chicago: Aldine.

SCHUMPETER, JOSEPH A. 1927. *Imperialism and Social Classes*. New York: Augustus M. Kelley, 1951.

SEGAL, MARCIA TEXLER. 1993. "The Academic Confrontation with Patriarchy: Two Decades of Feminist Theory and Practice in Sociology and Related Disciplines." *Race, Sex & Class*, Vol. 1, no. 1 (Fall), pp. 95–108.

SHANNON, THOMAS RICHARD. 1989. *An Introduction to the World-System Perspective*. Boulder, CO: Westview Press.

SIMMEL, GEORG. 1922. *Conflict & The Web of Group Affiliations*. New York: The Free Press, 1964.

SIMPSON, GEORGE EATON and J. MILTON YINGER. 1985. *Racial and Cultural Minorities*, 5th ed. New York: Plenum.

SIMPSON, MILES E. and GEORGE H. CONKLIN. 1989. "Socioeconomic Development, Suicide, and Religion: A Test of Durkheim's Theory of Religion and Suicide." *Social Forces*, Vol. 67, no. 4 (June); pp. 945–964.

SPRUIT, INGEBORG P. 1982. "Unemployment and Health in Macro-Social Analysis." *Social Science and Medicine*, Vol. 16, no. 22, pp. 1903–1907.

STARK, EVAN and A. FLITCRAFT. 1988. "Violence Among Intimates: An Epidemiological Review." in V.B. Van Hasselt, et al. (eds.), *Handbook of Family Violence*, pp. 293–319. New York: Plenum Press.

STARK, RODNEY and WILLIAM S. BAINBRIDGE. 1982. "Toward a Theory of Religious Commitment." *Journal for the Scientific Study of Religion.* Vol. 19, pp. 114–128.

STEFANSSON, CLAES-GÖRAN. 1991. "Long-term Unemployment and Mortality in Sweden, 1980–1986." *Social Science and Medicine*, Vol. 32, no. 4, pp. 419–423.

SWEEZY, PAUL M. 1953. *The Present as History*. New York: Monthly Review Press.

SWEEZY, PAUL M. 1956. "Power Elite or 'Ruling Class'?" (pamphlet). New York: Monthly Review Press.

SWEEZY, PAUL M. 1980. "Post-Revolutionary Society." *Monthly Review*, Vol. 32, no. 6 (November); pp. 1–13.

SWEEZY, PAUL M. and HARRY MAGDOFF. 1990. "Perestroika and the Future of Socialism." *Monthly Review*, Vol. 41, no. 10 (March), no. 11 (April).

SWINGEWOOD, ALAN. 1991. *A Short History of Sociological Thought*, 2nd ed. New York: St. Martin's Press.

SZYMANSKI, ALBERT. 1983. *Class Structure: A Critical Perspective*. New York: Praeger Publishers.

TUMIN, MELVIN. 1953. "Some Principles of Stratification: A Critical Analysis." *American Sociological Review* 18 (August); pp. 387–394.

TURNER, JOHN KENNETH. 1910. *Barbarous Mexico*. Austin: University of Texas Press, 1969.

UNICEF (UNITED NATIONS CHILDREN'S FUND). 1990. *The State of the World's Children 1990*. New York: Oxford University Press.

UNICEF. 1994. *The State of the World's Children 1994*. New York: Oxford University Press.

UNICEF. 1994b. *Crisis in Mortality, Health and Nutrition* (Economies in Transition Studies Regional Monitoring Report, no. 2). Florence, Italy: UNICEF International Child Development Centre.

UNITED NATIONS. 1994. *World Economic and Social Survey 1994*. New York: United Nations publication.

UNITED NATIONS CONFERENCE ON TRADE AND DEVELOPMENT. 1993. *Handbook for International Trade and Development Statistics 1992*. New York: United Nations publication.

UNITED NATIONS DEVELOPMENT PROGRAMME. 1994. *Human Development Report 1994*. New York: Oxford University Press.

U.S. BUREAU OF THE CENSUS. 1984. *Statistical Abstract of the United States*. Washington, DC: U.S. Government Printing Office.

U.S. BUREAU OF THE CENSUS. 1989. *Statistical Abstract of the United States*. Washington, DC: U.S. Government Printing Office.

U.S. BUREAU OF THE CENSUS. 1991. *Child Support and Alimony: 1989*. Current Population Reports, Series P-60, no. 173. Washington, DC: U.S. Government Printing Office.

U.S. BUREAU OF THE CENSUS. 1993. *Poverty in the United States: 1992.* Current Population Reports, Series P60-185. Washington, DC: U.S. Government Printing Office.

U.S. BUREAU OF THE CENSUS. 1993b. *Money Income of Households, Families, and Persons in the United States: 1992.* Washington, DC: U.S. Government Printing Office.

U.S. BUREAU OF THE CENSUS. 1994. *Statistical Abstract of the United States: 1994.* Washington, DC: U.S. Government Printing Office.

U.S. CONGRESSIONAL JOINT ECONOMIC COMMITTEE. 1986. "The Concentration of Wealth in the United States." Washington, DC: U.S. Government Printing Office.

VOGT, JOSEPH. 1975. *Ancient Slavery and the Ideal of Man* (Thomas Widemann, tr.). Cambridge, MA: Harvard University Press.

WALLERSTEIN, IMMANUEL MAURICE. 1974. *The Modern World-System: Capitalist Agriculture and the Origins of the European World-Economy in the Sixteenth Century.* New York: Academic Press.

WALLERSTEIN, IMMANUEL MAURICE. 1984. *The Politics of the World-Economy: the States, the Movements, and the Civilizations.* New York: Cambridge University Press.

WALLERSTEIN, JUDITH and SANDRA BLAKESLEE. 1989. *Second Chances: Men, Women and Children a Decade after Divorce.* New York: Ticknor & Fields.

WARNER, W. LLOYD, M. MEEKER, and K. EELS. 1949. *Social Class in America.* Chicago: Social Research Associates.

WEBER, MAX. 1905. *The Protestant Ethic and the Spirit of Capitalism.* New York: Scribners, 1948.

WEBER, MAX. 1918. "Politics as a Vocation." In Hans H. Gerth and C. Wright Mills (ed. and tr.). 1958. *From Max Weber: Essays in Sociology.* New York: Oxford University Press.

WEBER, MAX. 1918b. "Science as a Vocation." In Hans H. Gerth and C. Wright Mills (ed. and tr.). 1958. *From Max Weber: Essays in Sociology.* New York: Oxford University Press.

WEBER, MAX. 1921. "Structures of Power." In Hans H. Gerth and C. Wright Mills (ed. and tr.). 1958. *From Max Weber: Essays in Sociology.* New York: Oxford University Press.

WEBER, MAX. 1922. *Economy and Society.* New York: Bedminster Press, 1968.

WEBER, MAX. 1923. *General Economic History.* New York: Collier Books, 1961.

WEBSTER, ANDREW. 1984. *Introduction to the Sociology of Development.* London: Macmillan.

WEISSKOFF, RICHARD and ADOLFO FIGUEROA. 1976. "Traversing the Social Pyramid: a Comparative Review of Income Distribution in Latin America." *Latin American Research Review,* Vol. 11, no. 2; pp. 71–112.

WESTERMANN, WILLIAM L. 1955. *The Slave Systems of Greek and Roman Antiquity.* Philadelphia: American Philosophical Society.

WILLIAMS, ERIC. 1944. *Capitalism & Slavery.* New York: Capricorn Books, 1966.

WITTFOGEL, KARL A. 1957. *Oriental Despotism: A Comparative Study of Total Power.* New York: Oxford University Press.

WORLD BANK. 1988. *World Development Report 1988.* New York: Oxford University Press.

WORLD BANK. 1990. *World Development Report 1990*. New York: Oxford University Press.

WORLD BANK. 1994. *World Development Report 1994*. New York: Oxford University Press.

ZEITLIN, MAURICE, KENNETH LUTTERMAN, and JAMES W. RUSSELL. 1973. "Death in Vietnam: Class, Poverty, and the Risks of War." *Politics and Society*, Vol. 3, no. 3 (Spring); pp. 313–328.

Photo Credits

Page 32, photo of cave painting courtesy of American Museum of Natural History; *page 33,* Old German farm print, XVth century from Boccaccio, de Claris Mulieribus by Johann Zainer courtesy of New York Public Library Picture Collection; *page 34,* photo courtesy the U.S. Department of Agriculture; *page 47,* the ruins of Chichén Itzá, Mexico courtesy of Laimute E. Druskis; *page 49,* raffle poster by Sandler courtesy of The New York Historical Society; *page 53,* woodcut "Peasants at Market" by Albrecht Dürer courtesy of Library of Congress; *page 83,* photo by Ken Heyman courtesy Woodfin Camp & Associates; *page 90,* Rwandan refugees by Patrick de Noirmont courtesy REUTER/The Bettmann Archive; *page 133,* "The Outbreak" by Kathe Kollwitz courtesy Library of Congress; *page 135,* riots in South Central Los Angeles by Sam Mircovich courtesy REUTER/The Bettmann Archive; *page 157,* "Splendor and Misery" by Tina Modotti, courtesy of Fototeca del Instituto Nacional de Antropología e Historia, Mexico; *page 185,* Charlie Chaplin in "Modern Times" courtesy of The Museum of Modern Art/Film Stills Archive.

INDEX

A

Aborigines, 41
Africa, underdevelopment and, 52
African-Americans, 17, 149, 162, 167, 195, 213, 216
Agency for International Development, 67, 161
Agribusiness, 210
Agriculture, 35, 37, 83, 156, 208, 215
    definition, 32
    labor force in, 33, 73, 82
Albania, 78, 79
Alcoholics Anonymous, 197
Alcoholism, 6, 7, 191, 196, 197, 203, 222
Algeria, 101, 134, 139, 145
Alienation, 1, 4, 11, 18, 184, 215, 222
    class and, 46, 97
    Marx's theory of, 94
    Durkheim and, 114
    Weber and, 115, 120
    Postmodernism and, 122
Allende, Salvador, 141, 143
Alwin, Patricio, 141
Amin, Samir, 69, 82
Analysis of Results, 227, 228, 230
Anarchism, 142

Anderson, Perry, 47, 51
Andrewes, Antony, 51
Angola, 101
Animism, 43, 44
Anthropology, 9, 11, 25, 46, 222
Apartheid, 140
Argentina, 81, 85, 86
Aristide, Jean-Bertrand, 132, 141
Aristocracy, 58, 138
Armenia, 78
Artisans, 152
Ascription, 54
Asian Socialist Societies, 72, 81
Asiatic Mode of Production, 47
Associations, 80, 186
Austerity Policies, 87
Australia, 9, 73, 214
Authoritarianism, 142
Authority, Weber's Theory of, 135
Azerbaijan, 78
Aztecs, 47, 108

B

Bainbridge, William S., 114
Ballantine, Jeanne, 110
Bangladesh, 210
Baran, Paul, 82, 214

Barclay, William, 212
Barkin, David, 84
Belarus, 65, 78, 80
Belgium, 210
Belief Systems, 108, 109, 114
Bell, Daniel, 74
Berry, Ralph E., Jr., 196
Blakeslee, Sandra, 194
Blaming the Victim, 211
Blauner, Robert, 76
Bloch, Marc, 52
Boggs, James, 76
Boland, James P., 196
Bolshevik Revolution, 61, 99, 104, 127
Borana, 38
Botswana, 41
Brady Plan, 87, 88
Brain Drain, 215
Braverman, Harry, 184
Brazil, 49, 61, 84, 85
Brenner, M. Harvey, 8, 227
Brunt, P.A. 51
Bulgaria, 78–80
Bumpass, Larry L., 192
Bureaucractic Organizations, 180–84
Bush, George, 61, 89, 143, 153, 161

C

Canada, 72, 75, 81, 163–68, 223
    class and race in, 163–68
Capital, 85, 88, 152, 153
    accumulation of, 52, 60, 73, 76, 82,
        117, 165
    concentration of, 165
    definition, 59
    Marx's theory of, 97
    and wealth, 159–61, 174
Capitalism and Capitalist Societies,
    30, 35–39, 55–61
    and Asian Socialist Societies, 81
    competitive, 100
    and Dependency Theory, 82
    and Economic Classes, 152, 155
    and Feudalism, 55, 58
    Marx's Theory of, 4, 96–98
    monopoly, 100
    in North American Development,
        163–68
    and Political Structures, 25
    and Slavery, 51
    and Socialism, 61–66
    and Sociological Theory, 94

and State Theory, 131
    Transition from Socialism to, 78–80
    and Weber's Theory of, 116–18
Carlson, Beverly A., 191
Case Studies, 225, 230
Castro, Fidel, 99, 137
Castro Martin, Teresa, 192
Catholicism, 7, 107–9, 112, 116, 117
Celibacy, 55
Centers, Richard, 154
Central America, 84, 216
Central Planning, 63, 65, 81
Character Structure, 21–23
Charisma, 137
Cherlin, Andrew J., 193, 196
Child Abuse, 197, 201, 230
Child Care, 86, 169, 171, 198, 199,
    201–3
Chile, 140, 143
China, 64, 66–68, 72, 81, 91
    ancient, 36, 47, 136
    population policy in, 213
    revolution in, 62
Clan 43
Class, 35, 60, 114, 148–75, 202
    and capitalism, 91
    capitalist, 62, 97, 105, 131, 152
    conflict, 98, 150
    consciousness, 98, 105
    in developed societies, 152–55
    in developing societies, 155–58
    economic, 42, 47, 90, 150–73
    economic and social, 150
    and gender, 170–72, 174
    landlord, 54
    lower, 22, 113, 154, 156, 166, 173,
        198
    lower middle, 154
    Marx's theory of, 95–98
    middle, 105, 111, 152–56, 161–67,
        170, 173, 225
    mobility 54, 158, 159, 220
    new middle, 105, 152, 155, 162, 165,
        173
    old middle, 152, 165
    origins of, 44
    peasant, 155–58. See also, Peasants
    and political ideology, 142–44
    popular, 158
    in postwar socialist societies,
        158–59
    and race, 162
    and race in North America, 163–68

ruling, 98, 103, 133
slave, 50, 150
small business owners', 152, 166
social, 6, 11, 110, 151, 154–59, 162,
    166
structure, 24, 158, 163–65, 173
and socioeconomic structures, 25,
    28
and the state, 128, 131–34
upper, 111, 154, 173
upper middle, 154
working, 50, 96, 98, 101, 104, 111,
    133, 144, 152, 154, 156, 162, 166,
    173
Clinton, Bill, 138, 153
Cold War, 66, 73, 89, 145, 146
Colombia, 95
Colonialism, 73, 82, 134, 139
Columbus, Christopher, 51
Commensality, 154
Commodity, 51, 59, 97, 123, 155, 156
Common Conscience, 107–9
Communal Societies, 36, 37, 39–47,
    55, 96, 150
Communism, 212
    ideology of, 62, 144
    political parties, 139
    as mode of production, 63, 96
Complex Societies, 19, 44, 114
Comte, August, 3, 4, 105, 121
Concept, 5, 6, 12
Confidentiality, 230
Conklin, George H., 114
Conservatism, 101, 142, 143, 147
Conservative Party (United Kingdom),
    59
Consumerism, 60, 153
Contract Labor, 50
Control Groups, 226
Cooley, Charles Horton, 22, 29
Cooperative Organizations, 177, 180
Cornia, Giovanni Andrea, 80
Corporate Concentration, 75
Corporations, 10, 20, 75, 77, 85, 177,
    180
Correlations, 174, 195, 227, 231
Corvée Labor, 53
Counterinsurgency, 161
Counterrevolution, 104
Creative Labor, 14, 97
Crime, 1, 2, 6, 79, 202
Cuba, 62, 66, 67, 69, 91
Culture, 24–26

and Weber's theory, 117, 119,
    120–23
Czarism, 101, 102
Czech Republic, 78, 79

D

Dahl, Gudrun, 32
Daniel, P., 50
Davie, Michael, 148
Davis, Kingsley, 92,
Davis, F. James, 167
Death Rate, 8, 80
Deevey, Edward S., 205, 208, 209
Dehydration, 192
Democracy, 137–39, 147, 186
Democratic Centralism, 104
Democratic Party (U.S.), 59, 144
Demographic Transition, 208, 209, 217
Demography, 5, 11, 204, 216
Dependency Theory, 82
Depression
    economic, 75, 143
    mental, 227
Dewey, Thomas, 225
Dialectics, 95
Dictatorship of the Proletariat, 63,
    104, 133
Distribution of Income, 60, 61, 160,
    200, 224
Division of Labor, 21
    Durkheim's theory of, 106–12
    and economic classes, 151–53
    formal in organizations, 177
    and gender, 169, 199
    international, 82, 85
    origins in early societies, 44
Divorce, 80, 114, 171, 191–95, 201,
    203, 220
Domestic Violence, 9, 168, 197, 198
Domhoff, G. William, 130
Durkheim, Emile, 7, 60, 94, 95,
    105–16, 120–23, 127, 130, 131,
    146, 179

E

Economic Development, 69–89,
    211–13
Economic Structure, 24, 28, 36, 60, 65,
    131, 163
Economics, 9, 11, 116
Ecuador, 41

Effective Demand, 160, 200
Egypt, 32, 36, 47, 145
Einbinder, S.D., 195
Eisenhower, Dwight David, 60, 182
Eisenstadt, S.N., 82
El Salvador, 143, 161
Elitist Theory, 127
Engels, Frederick, 4, 43, 62, 95–107, 122, 128, 131, 168
England, 5, 8, 26, 35, 50, 52, 58, 62, 74, 78, 131, 143, 144, 164, 215
Environment, 89, 178, 190, 196
Eros, 15
Ethiopia, 134, 136
Ethnocentrism, 25
Eugenics, 212, 217
Experimental Design, 226
Experimental Group, 226

F

Family, 8, 21, 189–203
    and maquiladora labor force, 86
    nuclear, 192
    origins, 42
    planning, 209
    single-parent, 192–96
    step, 192–96
    social policy, 201
    and suicide, 112
    two-wage-earner, 198, 201, 203
Farnsworth, Clyde H., 87
Fascism, 115, 120, 142, 143, 147
Feminism, 168, 169
Feminization of Poverty, 171
Feudalism, 19, 36, 52–55, 58, 108, 117, 164, 173, 176
Fief, 58
Field Studies, 223, 225
Figueroa, Adolfo, 161
Finland, 197, 199
Finley, M.I., 51
First World, 66
Fixed Accumulation, 77
Flexible Accumulation, 76, 77
Flitcraft, A., 197
Forces of Production, 63
Fordism, 76
Foreign Debt, 86
Foreign Domination, 103
Foreign Investment, 85, 87
Formal Structure, 178

France, 5, 24, 58, 59, 62, 100, 110, 134, 135, 144, 145, 164, 199
    revolution, 4, 102, 105
Franco, Francisco, 141
Frank, Andre Gunder, 82
Franklin, Benjamin, 118
Free Trade, 69, 87, 89
Freud, Sigmund, 14, 15, 27, 191
Functionalism, 105, 122, 127, 223
Furstenberg, Frank F., Jr., 193, 196

G

General Agreement on Tariffs and Taxes (GATT), 89
Gelles, Richard J., 197
Gender, 148–51, 168–71, 174, 199
Germany 58, 62, 65, 100, 120, 135, 138, 142, 144
Gerth, Hans H., 23, 43, 130
Gilbert, Dennis, 154
Ginn, Helen, 208
Girard, Chris, 114
Godelier, Maurice, 47
Gramsci, Antonio, 132, 147
Greece, 36, 49–51, 57, 72, 144
Group, 1
Guatemala, 161
Gulliver, P.H., 32
Guyana, 113

H

Haiti, 81, 85, 132, 141
Hamper, Ben, 76
Harvey, David, 75
Hayward, Jack, 78
Health Care, 59, 63, 191, 199–203, 227
Hegel, G.W.F., 95
Hegemony, 55, 58, 131, 133
Hermeneutics, 124
Herrnstein, Richard J., 60
Hitler, Adolf, 137
Ho Chi Minh, 99, 101, 137
Hochschild, Arlie, 171
Hofferth, S., 199
Holland, 68, 164
Homo sapiens sapiens, 12, 13, 55
Horowitz, Irving Louis, 67, 228
Horticulture, 32, 47, 164, 208
Hungary, 65, 78–80, 160
Hunt, Kathleen, 32

Hunting and Gathering, 30, 32, 37, 41, 164
Huntingford, G.W.B., 32
Huxley, Aldous, 208
Hypothesis 42, 105, 168, 205, 216, 226

I

Ideology, 98, 158, 159, 174
  political, 141–46
  racism as, 162, 165
Immigration, 212, 214, 218
Immigration Act of 1921, 214
Imperialism, 99, 100, 105
Impersonality, 120, 122
Incas, 47
Indentured Servitude, 50
India, 36, 68, 85, 100, 116, 134, 210
Indigenous Peoples, 41, 52, 163–65, 168
Individualism, 60, 108, 112, 113, 123
Indochina, 100, 101, 134
Indus Valley, 47
Industrial Revolution, 4, 52, 208
Industrial Societies, 30, 38, 68
Industrialization, 32, 33, 37, 85, 86, 88, 152
Inequality, 2
  and capitalism, 60
  class, 149–51
  and Durkheim's theory, 110
  ethnic, 162
  in formerly socialist societies, 79, 158
  gender, 168
  international, 70
  and political ideology, 143
  racial, 162–68
Infant Mortality Rates, 72, 92
Informal Structure, 178
Infrastructure, 73, 80
Instincts, 15
Institutions, 20–22, 29
Institutional Structures, 17, 24, 25, 28, 68, 82, 130
Intelligence, 110, 124
Intelligentsia, 103
Interest Groups, 127, 130
International Monetary Fund, 67, 86
Interviewing, 224
Ireland, 81, 134
Iron Law of Oligarchy, 186

Israel, 134
Italy, 62, 78, 142, 144

J

James, William, 22
Japan, 59, 67, 68, 73, 85, 100, 113, 136, 210
Jie People, 38
Johnson, Lyndon Baines, 212
Just in Time Production, 76

K

Kafka, Franz, 115, 122
Kagarlitsky, Boris, 47, 62
Kahl, Joseph A., 154
Kammeyer, Kenneth C.W., 208
Kennedy, Jacqueline, 153
Khomeini, Ayatollah, 137
Kinship, 20, 24, 27, 42, 106
Klein, Herbert S., 51
Krader, Lawrence, 47
Kuwait, 72

L

Labor Forces, 59, 77
  and class development in North America, 165
  definition, 93
  and development, 83
  participation of women, 169–71
  postindustrial distribution, 74
  and state employment, 61
Labor Unions, 78, 185
Land Reform, 161
Landlords, 36, 52–56, 58, 102, 104, 131, 150, 164, 228
Larkin, Gary L., 213
Latino Population (U.S.), 171, 175
Latvia, 78
Lear, Martha Weinman, 194
Least Developed Societies, 72
Lebanon, 141
Leftism, 142
Legitimacy, 122, 132, 134–36, 140, 141, 146, 147, 160, 196
Lembcke, Jerry, 125, 186
Lenin, V.I., 62, 99–105, 133, 137, 145
Lenski, Gerhard, 32
Lenski, Jean, 32

Liberalism, 142, 147
Life Chances, 148
Livi-Bacci, Massimo, 209
Looking Glass Self, 22
Lord, Walter, 148
Luther, Martin, 117
Lutterman, Kenneth, 148

M

Maasai, 38
Maddox, Brenda, 196
Madeira, 51
Magdoff, Harry, 65
Magic, 43, 44
Malinowski, Bronislaw, 106
Malnutrition, 34, 191, 210
Malthus, Thomas Robert, 204–9, 216
Mannheim, Karl, 143
Manufacturing, 74, 144
Mao Zedong, 99, 132, 137
Maquiladora Industry, 86
Marcuse, Herbert, 15
Marginalized Population, 156, 158
Marx, Karl, 4, 47, 62, 94–107, 115,
    120–23, 128, 146, 150, 176
Marxism, 62, 99, 130, 139, 144
Marxism-Leninism, 99, 139
Mass, Bonnie, 212, 213
Materialism, 95
Mead, George Herbert, 14, 22, 27, 29,
    124
Meritocracy, 111
Mesopotamia, 32, 36, 47
Mestizos, 167
Metís, 167
Mexico 2, 26, 50, 65, 77, 84–86, 139,
    174, 192, 210
    class and race in, 163–68
Meyer, Michael C., 50
Michels, Robert, 186
Migration, 41, 80, 213–16, 218
    push and pull factors, 214, 218
Miles, Robert, 162
Miller, Louisa F., 192, 195
Mills, C. Wright, 8, 23, 32, 43, 127,
    130, 152, 155
Minorities, 22, 25, 162, 167
Mixed Race Persons, 167
Modes of Production, 35, 47, 51, 62, 99
Modernism, 121
Modernization, 67, 82, 91, 114, 121
Moldovia, 78

Monogamy, 43
Moore, Wilbert E., 92
Mosca, Gaetano, 127
Moynihan, Daniel Patrick, 195
Mozambique, 101
Multinational Corporations, 85
Murray, Charles, 60

N

Nandi, 38
Nations, 134, 162
National Minorities, 162
Native Americans, 163
Nau, Henry R., 73
Nazi Party, 62, 212
Neo-Malthusianism, 217
New England, 35, 164
New Guinea, 41
Nicaragua, 161
Nigeria, 87
Nixon, Richard M., 134
Nobility, 131
Nomadism, 41
Norms, 137, 147, 229, 230
North American Free Trade
    Agreement (NAFTA), 89
North Atlantic Treaty Organization
    (NATO), 62
Northern Ireland, 134
Norton, Arthur J., 192, 195
Nouveau Riche, 154

O

O'Connor, James, 61
Ogata, Sadako, 89
Organic Analogy, 106
Organic Solidarity, 109
Organizations, 176–88
Orwell, George, 2
Overpopulation, 204, 208, 210–12, 217

P

Palestine, 32
Pareto, Vilfredo, 127
Participant Observation, 225, 229
Partido Revolucionario Institucional
    (Mexico), 92
Pastoralism, 32
Patriarchy, 168
Peasants, 19, 22, 107, 164, 165, 216

feudal, 36, 53–56, 58
  in Russian Revolution, 101, 103
  in state societies, 47
  Third World, 143, 155–58
Pelton, Leroy H., 198
Peonage, 50
Persia, 47
Personality, 14, 21, 23
Peters, Gary L., 213
Phenomenological Sociology, 124
Philippines, 87, 100
Phillips, Paul, 65
Pinochet, Augusto, 140, 143
Pluralist Power Structure Theory, 127
Poland, 65, 78–80, 160
Political Sociology, 126, 131, 146
Pope, Whitney, 114
Population, 204–19
  control, 211, 217
  density, 210
Populism, 181
Porter, John, 130
Portugal, 72, 135, 144
Positivism, 3, 105, 122
Postindustrial Societies, 32, 34, 74, 165
Postmodernism, 121
Power Elite, 130
Power Structure Studies, 126, 128, 129, 146, 228
  decision-making, 126, 129
  positional, 129
  reputational, 127
Preelection Surveys, 220, 224, 225
Prehistory, 32, 39
Prejudice, 229
Preliterate Societies, 9, 30, 31, 106
Private Property, 43, 45, 47, 53, 58, 75, 168, 179
Privatization, 65, 81, 89, 145, 159
Progressive Taxation, 160
Prostitution, 43
Protestantism, 7, 116–18, 123, 146, 220
Puerto Rico, 51, 100, 134, 212, 213

Q

Quitrent, 53

R

Race, 60, 138, 148, 162, 171, 174

discrimination, 17, 22, 149, 151, 162, 171, 174, 221
racism, 22, 52, 114, 162, 165, 168, 195, 212, 216, 220
Radcliffe-Brown, A.R., 106
Randomization, 224
Rationality, 117–20, 123
  formal, 119, 120, 123
  substantive, 118, 119
Reagan, Ronald, 2, 61, 143, 145, 161
Redistribution of Income, 161
Refugees, 89, 216
Religion, 109, 121
  and development of capitalism, 116–18
  in early societies, 43
  in state societies, 48
  and suicide, 114
Rentiers, 152
Republican Party (U.S.), 59
Research Design, 222, 229, 230
Review of the Literature, 221, 230
Revolution
  agricultural, 32
  Bolshivik, 62, 127, 144
  and circulation of elites, 127
  and Gramsci, 133
  industrial, 4
  Iranian, 145
  Lenin's theory of, 99–105
  Marx's theory of, 98
  Sandinista, 95
  Third World, 139
Reynolds, Larry T., 162
Reynolds, Reid T., 212
Rightism, 142
Rockefeller Foundation, 211
Rodney, Walter, 52
Role Theory, 16–23
Romania, 78, 79
Rome, 16, 35, 36, 49, 51, 57
Rostow, W.W., 82
Russell, James W., 38, 148
Russell, Philip L., 84
Russia, 62, 65, 79, 101
Ryan, Mary P., 169

S

Sahlins, Marshall, 41
Sanctions, 20, 23, 27, 213
Schumpeter, Joseph, 151, 154
Scientific Management, 182–84

Second World, 62, 66, 67, 72, 88, 90, 95, 99, 104
Self, 21,
Service Employment, 33, 74
Settings, 17
Shannon, Thomas Richard, 68
Sherman, William L., 50
Simmel, Georg, 18
Simpson, Miles E., 114
Simpson, George Eaton, 162
Sino-Soviet Split, 145
Slavery and Slave Societies, 48–52, 164
  ancient, 36
  classes, 150
  new world, 36, 167
  and racism, 162
  state, 131
Slovakia, 78, 79
Small Businesses, 178–80, 187
  decline of, 75, 105
  owners as a class, 152, 166
Social Interaction, 12, 14–17, 19, 22, 27
Social Justice, 95, 104, 111, 122
Social Positions, 17, 18, 20, 22, 27
Social Research, 220–31
Social Structure, 24, 28
Social Wage, 159, 160
Social Work, 9–11
Socialism, 4, 61, 65, 78, 81, 91, 95, 99, 103, 115, 142, 144, 147, 173
Socialist Societies, 57, 61–67, 81, 90, 150, 158, 168
Socialization, 20, 26, 113, 130
Society, defined, 24–28
Socioeconomic Structures, 25, 28, 30, 35–38, 55, 57, 58, 64, 66, 67, 91, 114
Sociological Theory, 94–125
Sociology
  defined, 1
  history, 3
South Africa, 67, 72, 140, 141
Spain, 78, 100, 144, 145, 164
Spanish-American War, 100
Spruit, Ingeborg P., 155
Stark, Evan, 197
Stark, Rodney, 114
State, 10, 21, 58–63, 130–41
  in Durkheim's theory, 108–11
  family social policy, 201

  Marx's theory of, 98
  and political ideology, 141–46
  population policies, 213
  single-party, 104
  terrorism, 143
State Societies, 36, 39, 46–48, 56, 150
Status, 22, 29, 42, 74, 102, 111, 136, 142, 159, 183
Status Inconsistency, 111
Stone Age, 31
Subcultures, 26, 225
Suicide, 7, 8, 11, 80, 110–15, 123
Superego, 191
Surplus Value, 97
Survey Research, 224
Sweden, 8, 59, 61, 73, 78, 199
Sweezy, Paul M., 62, 65, 154
Symbolic Interactionism, 29
Szymanski, Albert, 92

T

Taxes, 20, 45, 47, 61, 89, 110, 150, 161, 176
Taylor, Frederick, 182–84
Taylorism, 184
Technology
  eras, 30–35
  definition, 30
  development, 72–77, 81–88
Thanatos, 15
Theology of Liberation, 124
Third World, 2
  classes, 155–58
  definition, 66
  development, 35, 82–88
  distributions of income, 160
  fascism, 142
  malnutrition, 191
  population conditions, 208–15
  poverty and children, 191
  runaway factories in, 77
  single-party states, 139
  socialism, 65
Titanic, 148
Torres, Camilo, 124
Tracking in Schools, 110, 113
Traditional Legitimacy, 136
Truman, Harry S., 225
Tumin, Melvin, 92
Turkana, 38
Turkmenistan, 78

Turner, John Kenneth, 50
Typology, 140, 178

U

Underdevelopment, 37, 52, 114, 221
Unemployment, 77
  and anomie, 114
  and health care, 200
  and migration, 215
  and mortality, 8, 227
  in socialist societies, 63, 79
  structural origin, 8
United Nations, 66, 69, 70, 72, 78, 79,
  81, 89, 212, 216, 223
United Nations Children's Fund
  (UNICEF), 79, 80, 191, 192
United States, 89
  child care, 198
  Chinese in, 50
  class and race in, 163–68
  distribution of income, 60, 160
  divorce and family reorganization
    in, 192
  domestic violence in, 197
  elections, 138
  family social policy, 201
  Fordism in, 75
  gender inequality, 170–72
  health care, 199
  history of sociology in, 5
  labor force, 61, 74, 77, 169
  labor unions, 78
  national power, 130
  offshore production, 85
  political parties, 143
  poverty in, 192
  racial inequality, 148, 162
  slavery, 49–51
  social class identification in, 154
  subcultures in, 26
  Third World population control poli-
    cies, 211
  as world power, 66, 68, 73
United Way, 129
Urbanization 32, 198, 214, 215, 218
Union of Soviet Socialist Republics
  (USSR), 78
Uzbekistan, 78

V

Vanguard Party 102, 104
Variables, 13, 118, 123, 224, 227
  dependent, 226
  independent, 226
Vietnam 62, 66, 72, 81, 91, 101
  South, 161
  War, 100, 148, 212
Village Communities, 46, 47
Vogt, Joseph, 51
Volkswagen, 85

W

Wallerstein, Immanuel Maurice, 69,
  82
Wallerstein, Judith, 194
Wardlaw, Tessa, 191
Warner, W. Lloyd, 151, 154
Watergate, 134
Wealth
  as capital, 59
  and definition of economic classes,
    150
  distribution of, 159
  and economic surpluses, 46
  and origins of the state, 45
  personal, 159
Weber, Max, 52, 94, 106, 107, 115–23,
  127, 130–36, 140, 146–48, 150,
  154, 176, 184
Weisskoff, Richard, 161
Westermann, William L., 51
Williams, Eric, 51
Wilson, Charles, 60
World Bank, 60, 61, 63, 67, 69, 70, 72,
  83–87, 160, 169, 209, 223
World War I, 101, 103, 115
World War II, 62, 72, 76, 78, 90, 101,
  113, 120, 137, 143, 144, 209
Writing, invention of, 30, 31

Y

Yinger, J. Milton, 162

Z

Zeitlin, Maurice, 148